Ghanaian Popular Fiction

'Thrilling Discoveries in Conjugal Life'
& other tales

Western African Studies

Willing Migrants
Soninke Labor Diasporas, 1848–1960
FRANÇOIS MANCHUELLE

El Dorado in West Africa
The Gold-Mining Frontier, African Labor & Colonial Capitalism
in the Gold Coast, 1875-1900
RAYMOND E. DUMETT

Nkrumah & the Chiefs
The Politics of Chieftaincy in Ghana, 1951–60
RICHARD RATHBONE

Ghanaian Popular Fiction
'Thrilling Discoveries in Conjugal Life'
& Other Tales
STEPHANIE NEWELL

*From Slavery to Free Labour in Rural Ghana**
Labour, Land & Capital
in Asante, 1807-1956
GARETH M. AUSTIN

*Between the Sea & the Lagoon**
An Eco-social History of the Anlo of South-eastern Ghana,
c.1850 to Recent Times
EMMANUEL AKYEAMPONG

*forthcoming

Ghanaian Popular Fiction

'Thrilling Discoveries in Conjugal Life'
& other tales

STEPHANIE NEWELL

Smuts Memorial Research Fellow in African Studies
University of Cambridge

James Currey
OXFORD

Ohio University Press
ATHENS

James Currey
73 Botley Road
Oxford OX2 0BS

Ohio University Press
Scott Quadrangle
Athens, Ohio 45701

British Library Cataloguing in Publication Data
Newell, Stephanie
  Ghanaian popular fiction : Thrilling discoveries in
conjugal life & other tales. – (West African studies)
1. Ghanaian fiction (English) – History and criticism
2. Popular literature – Ghana – History and criticism
I. Title
823'.009'9667
    ISBN 0-85255-556-3 (James Currey paper)
    ISBN 0-85255-557-1 (James Currey cloth)

Library of Congress Cataloging-in-Publication Data
Newell, Stephanie, 1968-
  Ghanaian popular fiction : "thrilling discoveries in conjugal life" & other tales /
Stephanie Newell
    p. cm. – (Western African studies)
  Based on the author's dissertation (Ph.D., University of Birmingham, England)
  Includes bibliographical references and index.
  ISBN 0-8214-1367-8 (alk. paper) – ISBN 0-8214-1368-6 (pbk.: alk. paper)
  1. Ghanaian fiction (English)–History and criticism. 2. Literature and society–Ghana.
3. Authors and readers–Ghana. 4. Popular literature–Ghana–History and criticism. 5.
Decolonization in literature. 6. Imitation in literature. 7. Ghana–in literature. I. Title. II.
Series.
PR9379.N49 2000
823.009'355–dc21   00-044129

    ISBN 0-8214-1368-6 (Ohio University Press paper)
    ISBN 0-8214-1367-8 (Ohio University Press cloth)

Typeset in 10¹/₂/12 pt Monotype Ehrhardt
by Long House Publishing Services, Cumbria, UK
Printed & bound in Great Britain
by Woolnough, Irthlingborough

Contents

List of Illustrations

Acknowledgements

I am indebted to Karin Barber for the inspiring, incisive comments she made when this book first took shape as a PhD thesis at the University of Birmingham. Warm thanks also are due to Richard Priebe of Virginia Commonwealth University for his generosity in lending me the numerous interviews he recorded with Ghanaian novelists in the early 1970s.

Inspiration arrived in the form of Isabel Hofmeyr in 1998: my ideas in Chapter 5 were stimulated by her comments about John Bunyan's *Pilgrim's Progress* in Africa. Jan Newell has been a sensitive and critical reader at all times, and she helped enormously with my archival research in Ghana as well as with the indexing of this book. Thanks also to Nyadia Sulemana Nelson for the enormous role he played in helping to distribute reader questionnaires to students throughout Ghana in 1998.

Akosua Gyamfuaa-Fofie showed great generosity in July 1995 and again in January 1998 when she suspended very busy writing and publishing schedules in order to participate in interviews and deliver me to bookshops and printers around Kumasi. Her commitment to Ghanaian literature and phenomenal productivity undoubtedly will inspire subsequent generations of women writers in the country. I should like to thank the managers and staff at the bookshops and printing presses in Kumasi. Especial thanks are due to Lyn Innes for her helpful suggestions on the book as a whole, and to Terry Barringer and Sarah Irons for their efficiency in locating books, microfilms and reference material. Thanks also to Pietro Deandrea, Paul Nugent and Martin Japtok for reading and commenting on chapters of the book. Friendship and support have come from Helen Harrow, Bethan Benwell, Joanna Lewis, Angela Smith and Anna Kerr.

Research trips to West Africa were made possible by grants from the Carnegie Trust for the Universities of Scotland and Stirling University between 1995 and 1997. A bursary was provided by the Centre of West African Studies at the University of Birmingham in 1997, enabling me to continue with my PhD research against all the odds. Additional chapters were researched and the manuscript was completed with the generous financial assistance of the Smuts Memorial Fund and Robinson College in Cambridge.

Thanks are due to the editors of several journals for their permission to reproduce material published prior to the completion of this book: sections of the introduction and Chapter 1 were published as 'Redefining Mimicry: quoting techniques and the role of readers in locally published Ghanaian fiction', *Research in African Literatures*, Vol. 31, No. 1 (2000); a version of Chapter 2 appeared as 'Making up their own

Acknowledgements

Minds: readers, interpretation and the difference of view in Ghanaian popular narratives', *Africa*, Vol. 67, No. 3 (1997); portions of Chapter 6 were incorporated into an article published as 'Popular Publishing in Nigeria and Ghana: production processes and marketing techniques in the non-textbook sector', *The Book Collector*, Vol. 49, No. 1 (2000); Chapter 8 appeared in its entirety as 'Those Mean and Empty-Headed Men: the shifting representations of wealth in two Ghanaian popular novels', *ARIEL*, Vol. 29, No. 4 (1998).

Introduction

The relevance of postcolonial theories
to the study of West African popular literatures

Migration and mimicry have become key concepts in recent theoretical debates about the global flows of people, ideas and ideologies in the postcolonial world. 'Globalisation' theorists tend to focus upon the effects of Western popular culture as it permeates postcolonial societies. In response to the spread of mass-communications networks from Western cities into far-flung ex-colonial societies, theorists such as Ulf Hannerz (1990, 1992) and Arjun Appadurai (1990, 1991) have sought to assess – in general and transcultural terms – the impact of imported popular genres upon local populations. When metropolitan genres are absorbed and 'mimicked' by consumers for whom they were *not* produced, these theorists ask if we are witnessing another, more invidious form of colonialism, a type of invasion which occupies the very imaginations and fantasies of new audiences (Hannerz, 1992: 236); or perhaps, as Appadurai (1990) suggests, cultural imports from the West are being radically transformed by their perfor-mances in new contexts.

Other postcolonial theorists, including Edward Said (1993) and Homi Bhabha (1994), have focused recently upon cultural flows in the opposite direction. Different in so many other respects, both Said and Bhabha trace the impact of postcolonial migrations upon ideas and ideologies in metropolitan countries. Through the experience of displacement, Bhabha writes, the migrant takes up a position in the zones 'in-between' cultural certainties, introducing doubt into homogeneous concepts such as national identity and national history (Bhabha, 1994: 1). Composed of a 'contrapuntal ensemble' of influences, the migrant is, in Said's words, a 'nomad' who passes to and fro on the thresholds of other people's homelands (Said, 1993: xxix). Migration exemplifies the 'postcolonial' condition, and the migrant's displacement from a community and locality forms the critical channel through which 'newness' enters the world (Bhabha, 1994: 212–35).

1

Introduction

One of the problems with the centrality of migration in current postcolonial theory is that there is a more or less submerged dichotomy between the 'global' and the 'local'. The migrant's subjectivity seems to have been constructed in a different way to that of the person who stays at home. Hannerz in particular constructs the globe-trotting migrant as an ideal subject, setting 'him' over and against local populations: 'there are cosmopolitans, and there are locals', he writes (1990: 237). The former possess 'an intellectual and aesthetic stance of openness toward divergent cultural experiences', while the latter can never match this 'ideal type', for locals are unable to transcend their parochial faith that the practices of their home-cultures are natural and universal (pp. 237–48). Implicitly or explicitly, the local emerges as the migrant's counterpoint in many theories of global cultural flows. Apparently incapable of bringing 'newness' into the world, the local receives images from abroad rather than responding, like the migrant, in a dynamic, creative way to the cross-currents of international culture. Hannerz does not disguise his view of the local as a passive recipient of what he calls 'alien' forms and predicts that:

> Peripheral culture will step by step assimilate more and more of the imported meanings and forms, becoming gradually indistinguishable from the center. At any one time, what is considered local culture is a little more penetrated by transnational forms than what went before it as local culture ... until the end-point is reached. (1992: 236)

Hannerz's gloomy forecast about the erasure of heterogeneity is built around his view that the metropolitan giants at the centre are 'getting the periphery so committed to the imports that soon enough there is no real opportunity for choice', creating a 'dependence' amongst locals upon 'what was initially alien' (*ibid.*).[1]

This book represents a critical response to the way in which many theorists and popular culture critics have employed the concepts of mimicry and migration to generalise about creativity and audience responses in 'postcolonial' countries. Focusing in detail upon instances of inter-cultural and intertextual borrowing within locally published literatures from Ghana and also Nigeria, I set out in Chapter 1 to redefine the concept of mimicry and replace it with the idea that local authors and audiences employ quoting techniques which are far more dynamic and culturally located than allowed for by theorists such as Hannerz. Moments of apparent emulation, when local authors or readers seem to 'adopt' familiar genres such as the romance, need to be culturally contextualised and analysed for the ways in which they transform existing popular templates. What kind of interpretive conventions are in operation, for example, when young Ghanaian readers take up the conjugal models provided within popular narratives

---

[1] Hannerz does comment briefly upon the creative ways in which Nigerian audiences absorb and modify imported forms (1990: 245), but these observations are contradicted by his lengthy analysis of the metropolitanisation of popular culture in Nigeria, a process in which local producers and performers seem to participate most willingly (see 1992: 240–1).

and start to refer to familiar character types in order to prove their opinions about the opposite sex (see Chapter 2)? How are foreign and local forms reconfigured when, as we find in Chapters 2, 9 and 10, local women writers produce novels which seem to endorse the Western mass-produced ideology of romantic love?

It should be apparent already that the term 'local' is not being employed here as a rhetorical device which signifies cultural authenticity and opposes 'global' or 'colonial' culture; nor is it intended to replace the term 'popular' which remains essential to the analysis of literary production in West Africa. Rather, 'local' is used here in a more historically and geographically specific manner: in the first place, it refers to the distinctive modes of popular literary production and dissemination that have developed this century in Ghana. Since the first texts were published in bulk in the 1940s and 1950s, popular literature has tended to be produced in a more artisanal manner than one finds in late-capitalist countries. As in Nigeria, in Ghana authors often respond rapidly to 'hot' issues by producing their own texts, which are distributed within the relatively narrow regional radius determined by the publisher's or author's marketing networks.

In the second place, overlaying and incorporating the first, 'local' refers to a complex, fascinating and much-neglected 'zone of culture' in West Africa which connects Ghana with southern Nigeria, Liberia and Sierra Leone: this Anglophone culture zone dates back at least to the mid-nineteenth century, when migrants between regions exchanged ideas about musical styles, Christian doctrine, publishing technologies, pedagogy and literature (see Waterman, 1990; Collins and Richards, 1982). The national boundaries separating these Anglophone West African states are of course vital to considerations of their cultural differences and development: such distinctions explain the exclusive focus upon Ghanaian literatures in the majority of this book.

As the first chapter will demonstrate, the West African 'zone of culture' cannot be ignored, for it helps to contextualise and explain the themes and character types – particularly in the early texts – to be considered in the Ghana-specific chapters. When theorists such as Hannerz focus on the way that foreign forms are transposed into relatively static local cultures, they overlook the complexity of these regional cultural processes. As Chapter 2 will demonstrate, different constituencies of readers around the world might make diverse, divergent readings of texts, and the same text might be received very differently depending upon the expectations and interpretive conventions of particular readers. Hannerz presents local audiences in postcolonial societies as the passive consumers of a drug-like alien culture, slowly becoming 'committed' to mass-produced Western forms. When this pessimistic appraisal is combined with his distinction between the cosmopolitan (who mediates between cultures) and the local (who simply receives imported forms), one can see how he is failing to account for the multiple, competing meanings – and further texts – that can be generated from an imported form at any one time by its recipients.

Hannerz dwells upon the movement of foreign *forms* to the exclusion of local *audiences*. When he comments upon Nigerian popular culture, he finds that it 'seems fairly permeated with meanings and meaningful forms drawn, or deriving in some other way, from the center' (1990: 240). The centre–periphery model has been brought to the fore here, contrasting the more flexible model of a cultural 'continuum' developed by Hannerz himself in the late 1980s (Hannerz, 1987): as a result, popular culture in Nigeria is presented as imitative rather than innovative. When theorists construct the 'local' in this way, they tend to neglect the complex receptive environments created by authors and audiences, who actively *produce* their own genres and meanings. Perspectives on popular literatures from Africa (and elsewhere) can shift substantially if we contextualise literary creativity in terms of the discursive conventions within which authors and readers operate (see Quayson, 1995).

Since the first local texts were produced in large quantities in Nigeria and the Gold Coast in the 1940s and 1950s, West African authors have been employing distinctive, culturally specific quoting techniques. In much of the literature published locally in Ghana and Nigeria since then, authors have incorporated a variety of 'master' languages from diverse narrative resources. As I explore in Chapter 1 and in several subsequent sections, authors are quite openly displaying their skills in the art of selecting and applying appropriate quotations from other narrative forms, including folktales, sermons, proverbs, plays and religious publications. By skilfully quoting another author's words, they seem to be demonstrating their *own* legitimacy as figures of moral authority in young readers' lives.

It is this West African quoting activity – the *process of quoting* rather than the type of phrase or discourse that is incorporated – which forms the primary motivation for this study of locally-produced literatures in Ghana. Since the earliest days of popular literature in the country, one can find no examples of the simple *reproduction* of foreign templates and no examples of a simple dichotomy separating literary production from the reception of texts. Rather, authors and audiences are continually regenerating popular narratives and character types, creating models from quoted elements and localising the 'foreign' to such an extent that it cannot easily be placed in a separate sphere. As Chapter 2 reveals, audiences' interpretive processes are refractive: they take up and apply textual examples and do not simply reflect or mimic received images. New, non-binary definitions of the relationship between 'local' and 'global' cultures can therefore emerge from contextual studies of African popular literatures.

It would be misleading to regard Hannerz as the sole representative of current globalisation theory. Arjun Appadurai's (1990, 1991) analyses of North–South mass-media flows are more subtle than Hannerz's contrasts between the original and the imitated, the migrant and the local. Appadurai sets out to study the 'cosmopolitan cultural forms of the contemporary world without logically or chronologically presupposing either the authority of the Western experience or the models derived from that experience' (1991: 192). For Appadurai, the challenge is to preserve a sense of local cultural productivity while also recognising hegemonic trends in the export of images and technologies from metropolitan countries. Turning to the figure of the 'local' – in this case, the young, urban Filipino –

4

Appadurai finds that when foreign art forms are mimicked, the performers are often:

> more disturbingly faithful to the ... originals than they are in the United States today. An entire nation seems to have learned to mimic Kenny Rogers and the Lennon sisters like a vast Asian Motown chorus. (1990: 3)

When a young Filipino perfectly mimics American country and western songs, far more is signified than North American hegemony in the field of popular culture. The lyrics of Kenny Rogers' songs evoke nostalgic memories of a past the Filipino youths have never experienced personally. American dreams of a meaningful, lost past are imbued with a new temporality by the young men's mimicry, for they are singing about their *own* aspirations for the future, producing visions of personal comfort and financial security from a sentimentalised version of America's history (pp. 3–4).

By locating the imitated text in its new interpretive context and by analysing the interlocking socioeconomic and political 'scapes' within which locals are situated, Appadurai shows how the locals' performances can transform the meanings previously attaching to the imported form. The imitated form is radically recontextualised by its new performers. Acts of mimicry are therefore more dynamic than a formalist critique would allow, for 'at least as rapidly as forces from various metropolises are brought into new societies they tend to become indigenized' (p. 5). 'If "a" global cultural economy is emerging', he writes, 'it is filled with ironies and resistances, sometimes characterized as passivity and a bottomless appetite ... for things Western' (p. 3). In Appadurai's analysis, 'mimicry' is a creative response to local conditions in a cosmopolitan world. Simply by replicating the foreign form, Filipino youths have localised it and instilled it with meanings that will be relevant to their own lives and futures in an outpost of America's economic empire.

Despite his emphasis on the diverse ways in which global culture is received, Appadurai's example of Filipino 'mimicry' shows popular culture flowing in one direction only, from North to South. The original producer still seems to control the dissemination of popular culture. Non-migratory populations remain relatively passive in both Hannerz's and Appadurai's theories: the migrant might transform the 'warp' of stable cultures by creating a 'woof of human motion' (Appadurai, 1990: 7), but the local simply receives and emulates imported forms, albeit with such perfect skill that the quoted form stands apart from the performer, contrasting his or her socioeconomic realities to such an extent that the 'foreign' element becomes a powerful comment on the performer's own life.

Appadurai's Filipino example illustrates his theory that new social contexts challenge and change the old sets of meanings attaching to a genre. As in Hannerz's work, however, he does not explore any examples of the 'imperfect' mimicry of an imported form. While his argument is persuasive, he does not seem to challenge the assumption that imported forms retain their formal coherence in foreign settings. This is a significant omission from a theory which seeks to explain the function of foreign quotations in local discourses about the self and the future. How would Appadurai or Hannerz approach a performance or text in which the mimicry appears to be 'failing', in which the 'adopted' elements appear to be fragmented, contradictory or insecure?

Perhaps as a result of their global standpoints, both Hannerz and Appadurai neglect locally produced popular art forms. It is here, in the field of local production, that one can find examples of a 'mimicry' which has 'failed' so dramatically that questions have to be asked about the modes of reception brought to texts by readers and the manner in which artists and audiences operationalise their discursive models.

Few detailed historical or comparative studies have been undertaken into locally produced literatures from Anglophone West Africa. Until recently, a large number of the articles that do mention African popular literatures have suggested that when local authors write romances or thrillers, they are simply adopting and mimicking foreign genres (e.g. Kern, 1973; Schild, 1980; Ehling, 1990). Gustav Jahoda's (1959) article on letters written to the problem page of a Ghanaian national newspaper in the 1950s sets the tone for this type of criticism: in an otherwise sympathetic article, Jahoda claims that the confusion of young, educated letter-writers arises from the conflict between established marital codes and their '*adoption* of Western norms, values and criteria of status' (p. 188; emphasis added). Other critics have developed similar 'adoption' models, suggesting that locally published writers are emulating the narrative styles and themes of Western master-texts, participating in what Frantz Fanon might have labelled the first, 'imitative' stage of national literary development (see Ikiddeh, 1971: 108; Fanon, [1963] 1990). As a result of this bias, Anglophone popular literature has tended to be viewed as an art form that is conservative in orientation, limiting readers' room for manoeuvre by confining protagonists – particularly the heroines – to mass-produced, foreign narrative templates (Coulon, 1987; Ehling, 1990).

What is marginalised from this perspective is the entire process to be explored in Chapters 2 and 6 whereby a text reaches the market. In addition, when critics turn to popular publications they tend to neglect reader responses to local publications and also an author's role as the 'reader' of commonly circulating narratives. Local readers are silenced figures in articles offering purely 'literary', textual critiques.[2] In an effort to compensate for this neglected mass of respondents, in the following pages extensive use has been made of reader interviews and questionnaires.

Vast, under-researched archives of locally and privately published novels exist in West Africa. They need to be explored in order to shift the focus away from books commissioned and edited by the multinationals in Africa. In a sense, this domestic production represents the truly 'unofficial' side of popular literature, existing outside the grid of capitalist power relations prevailing over popular art forms in the West and also outside the sometimes heavy-handed intervention of

---

[2] Exceptions include Dodson (1973) on Nigerian market literature and Priebe (1978) on Ghanaian fiction in the 1960s and early 1970s.

editors in material commissioned by multinational publishers. It is necessary to resituate the concept of 'popular' literature in the context of literary production in the region, for if theories of 'mimicry' have to be reassessed in the light of West African narratives, then Western definitions of 'popular' production must be radically overhauled to accommodate publishing processes in West Africa (see Conclusion, below).

Popular narratives produced on the continent continue to be viewed as 'conservative' or 'reactionary' by literary scholars, contrasted with so-called 'serious' African literature. Critics tend to conform to the binary division between 'high' and 'low' literature that still prevails in Western cultural studies. For example, the theorist of postmodernity, Linda Hutcheon (1985), suggests that popular novels in the West are 'insufficiently motivated' (p. 36). Literary models that were dynamic in the past have congealed 'through overuse' into the 'pure convention[s]' of popular genres: popular novels are merely the stale residues of once-vibrant art forms (*ibid.*). When Hutcheon's position is applied to African popular novels, the outcome can be an extreme position, such as that offered by Ulla Schild (1980) in her study of the East African *Afromance* series. Schild argues that *Afromances* are a 'blunt imitation' and an 'exact copy' of European romances (pp. 28–9). The series 'adheres to strictly European conventions' which stem from a European tradition of courtly love which Africans cannot understand (p. 25). 'The Western concept of love', she continues, 'is understandable only if one appreciates its history from King Arthur's round table onwards' (p. 28). If African popular novels are seen to be divorced from history, then not only are they imitating stale conventions, but they are also adopting the stale conventions of a foreign, ex-colonial culture.

In Ghanaian popular publications, as Chapter 1 will show, any distinctions a critic might wish to formulate – between foreign and local elements, or emulated and traditional styles – are of little relevance to the authors and audiences themselves. Ghanaian authors combine quotations from Western texts with a vast array of local narrative resources. Their plots, genres and protagonists are drawn from a jamboree bag in which the 'foreign' cannot be separated from the 'local'. As later chapters will reveal, in a single text protagonists might use quotations from Shakespeare alongside references to folktales to conclude a lengthy argument about the deceptive nature of an African woman's love; the details of a young couple's relationship might be narrated in a language drawn from English romantic novels, while the surrounding text is narrated in a non-romantic register; and the anti-social behaviour of a character might be judged through the quotation of English moral maxims, placed alongside translations of African-language proverbs.

The perfect mimicry of a particular form is irrelevant to this process. Rather, these different types of quotation are being *put to use*, activated by authors and readers: quotations from Western texts and genres are being combined with quotations from other narrative archives, all of which are used as tools to cultivate and refine authors' own didactic projects. 'Cultural entrepreneurs' in West Africa are not necessarily 'gradually master[ing] the alien cultural forms' or manifesting 'metropolitan-oriented sophistication and modernity' in their work, as Hannerz claims for Nigerian popular art forms (1992: 240–1). In the Anglophone publications to be considered and contrasted here, a far more audience-centred enterprise is under way. Authors are selecting quotations from diverse source-texts and operationalising the quotations within narratives in such a way that their *own* messages to local readers will be illuminated.

The argument of this book revolves around the themes of gender and marriage: since the inception of Ghanaian popular literature in the late 1930s, these two themes have formed the focal point of narratives and the fodder for male and female novelists. Indeed, other major preoccupations are absorbed into and expressed through these themes. Alongside a detailed analysis of the distinctive features of Ghanaian popular literature, in all of the chapters broader theoretical issues are raised, deriving from the gender-power relationships which dominate the texts. The apparent differences between men's and women's interpretations of the *same* popular narratives are explored in Chapter 2 and again in the chapters on Ghanaian women's writing; also, the change in male authors' representations of ideal wives and 'good-time girls' is discussed from a historical and socioeconomic perspective in Chapter 8.

Rather than offering anthropological or sociological readings of locally published literatures, throughout the book I emphasise the *textuality* of individual publications. Contextual and historical information is of course essential to one's understanding of local literatures, but none of the texts explored here simply reflects empirically valid 'truths' about the author's or the reader's own society. Instead, authors are employing the written word to express, to mediate and, often, symbolically to resolve commonly held preoccupations about money, religion, marriage, gender and other issues. The texts I have chosen to analyse open up symbolic spaces for the expression of these complex, ideologically mediated attitudes and opinions.

The perspective advanced in this study of Ghanaian popular literature is intended, firstly, to give rise to experimental readings of the texts and, secondly, to introduce an alternative construction of the 'local' into current postcolonial theoretical paradigms, where very often the migrant occupies a privileged subject-position over and against the person who stays at home. Underlying most of the chapters that follow is my conviction that each time familiar narratives are rewritten and published, they are also *re-generated* by authors and readers, endowed with new meanings and a new relevance to the world. Before applying postcolonial theories to specific postcolonial cultures, then, it is necessary first to analyse the distinctive ways in which quotations and familiar narrative templates are activated by the authors and readers of locally produced texts.

1

The Proverbial Space
in Ghanaian Popular Fiction

The good writer is a 'teacher' whose classroom is not limited by any walls
but stretches wherever literate people can be found.
(Udoeyop, 1972)

Local publications in Ghana are complex, hybrid discourses. When Ghana gained full independence from Britain in 1957, followed by Nigeria in 1960, the English language had been spilling for over a century through the cultures outside the colonial administration, permeating the wording of trade deals, maxims and moral tales. Introduced by the first traders, missionaries and administrators – who were themselves immersed in the linguistic and conceptual cross-currents flowing around the coastal West African culture zone – English was employed widely in the colonial civil service, as well as in mission-school classrooms and newspapers.[1] The instant that English-language publications began to roll off indigenous West African printing presses in large numbers in the 1940s and 1950s, it became clear that English had been localised: as dynamic as any language, it had been culturally translated and transformed.

This chapter will discuss the manner in which local writers proclaim the authority of their English-language texts by incorporating a variety of discursive models. For the sake of coherence, I shall focus in detail upon early Ghanaian novels in the first part of the chapter, where I intend to show how, through the quotation of different literary 'master' languages, authors claim legitimacy as writers and also presuppose readers' immersion in a distinctive set of interpretive conventions. The latter part of the chapter speculates about the extent to which the recurrent character types in popular Ghanaian narratives can be seen to fulfil a 'proverbial' function which is recognisable and culturally familiar to readers. In the concluding part of the discussion, the authorial quoting modes discovered in early Ghanaian literature will be extended to Nigeria and tested out upon a recent work of non-fiction by the Nigerian marriage guidance counsellor, Professor M.

[1] A detailed discussion of the debates and disagreements about whether to teach in local or colonial languages can be found in Sanneh (1983).

NEVER TRUST

ALL

THAT LOVE YOU

SIXTH EDITION (ENLARGED)

The World is so Corrupt that it has become difficult to Trust All People

COPIES OBTAINABLE FROM:-

J. C. BROTHERS BOOKSHOP

26 New Market Road, Onitsha.

Copy Right Reserved

1.1 A youthful Nigerian, representing the author Rufus Okonkwo (pseud. J. C. Anorue), posing on the flyleaf of this popular pamphlet.

S. Olayinka (1987). Contemporary non-fiction from Nigeria and Ghana is included at this stage in order to demonstrate the commonality and versatility of the quoting modes to be found in West African publications. This wide range of examples enables me to generalise about the distinctive, culturally specific manner in which Anglophone West African authors operationalise their different types of quotation.

An exemplary instance of the kind of quoting and meaning-making activity to be explored in this chapter can be found in an established oral form – the proverb. When authors quote from 'outside' texts in order to generate further texts of their own, when they cite literary or popular cultural models in order to orientate readers' actions, and when readers actualise texts by citing 'quotable' characters and scenes, then together they are operating in a manner that can be explained through and within the terms of the proverb.

In novels produced locally since the late 1930s, West African authors have drawn upon diverse literary models or prototypes, but they have used the borrowed forms to generate new meanings and create new genres for particular local readerships. In both Nigeria and Ghana, the earliest authors quote from Shakespeare and the Bible, and use the resources of Bertha M. Clay romances and Marie Corelli novels in order to demonstrate their command of 'literary' discourses. Ghanaian authors such as J. Abedi-Boafo and J. Benibengor Blay, who published novels in the 1930s and 1940s, and many of their successors since, seem to be *deliberately* incorporating a wide variety of European literary models into their texts. The strategic and selective nature of their 'mimicry' signifies far more than the effort to emulate imported art forms.

A new kind of authorship and a new kind of authority are emerging in these texts. Locally published fiction is a relatively recent phenomenon in Ghana, as it is in Nigeria. Novels first appeared in large numbers in the 1940s and West African authors often fall into the category known in Ghana as 'youngmen': that is, they are aged between 17 and 35, and have not yet achieved the social and economic status of full adult men. Many pamphlet-writers were recent school leavers in the 1950s and 1960s: in fact, some Nigerian authors had not yet left secondary school (see Plate 1.1). At the time of writing, then, these men probably would have been excluded from the formal status-conferring discourses of their elders.

In a study of 'quoting behavior' in Igbo societies, Joyce Penfield (1983) comments that the prose narrative may serve 'as an alternative linguistic resource to a proverb to convey a similar message when the speakers are restricted by their societal role from using proverbs' (p. 77). This is a persuasive point, considering the status of many popular novelists as 'youngmen'. Aware of the risks and their own subordinate status, Yoruba-speaking youths often preface a proverb with 'permit me to use a proverb', self-consciously seeking permission from the elders who are present. In many areas of West Africa, if a 'youngman' uses proverbs in a clumsy way, he is likely to be criticised severely. In a study of proverbs in Ashanti arbitration cases, Kwesi Yankah (1989) describes how the right to speak publicly in Ghana often is judged through an individual's age, social status and mastery of proverbs: a person can achieve recognition and authority through the eloquent use of proverbs (pp. 202–11). Proverb-speaking is thus presented by both Penfield and Yankah as one of the status-conferring discourses from which the 'youngman' may be excluded.

Penfield suggests that folktales and prose narratives are easily interchangeable with proverbs, 'commonly used in place of proverbs to convey a similar message or stress a point' (1983: 77). Yankah also discovers broad similarities between proverbs and extended narrative forms, commenting that Akan proverbs are sometimes 'truncated in discourse, expanded, embellished, or paraphrased' (1989: 43). The truncated or embellished kinds of proverb may, he says, be termed '"proverbs" in the wider sense' (pp. 89–90). Thus, proverbs are seen by both scholars to be forms of quotation which make up a dynamic cultural archive in West Africa which also contains parables, folktales and prose narratives. In the light of this, young male authors in the region might have found in fiction an alternative platform for the public display of 'proverbial' quotations.

The proverb tends to be offered as what Anietie Akpabio (196?) describes as an expression of 'truths about life': proverbs are based upon 'experience and wisdom. They embody advice, warning, reproach, fate and rules of conduct towards elders, strangers and relations' (p. 1). A young person might attempt to use proverbs, but if the quotations are inappropriate to the situation or ill-formulated, he or she will be derided as a social upstart (Penfield, 1983: 77). Penfield has observed that in Igbo communities, people often intervene with 'unsolicited advice' to an individual: '"Wise" people are expected to be grateful for advice and utilize it to keep them out of danger' (p. 52). Applied cleverly, the quotation demonstrates the user's intellectual prowess yet it appears to be anonymous or the wisdom of another: the proverb-user protects himself or herself from criticism by denying the quotation's openness, making it appear permanently fixed to the situation that is being described (pp. 62–9). When the concerned friends or family of an individual offer criticism on intimate affairs, such as love, marriage and money, interpersonal conflict can be avoided by the quotation of proverbs which guide listeners towards certain decisions.

Yankah's and Penfield's ideas about proverbial discourse can be developed into a paradigm for the *operation* of quotations in locally published West African literatures. Proverbs are 'quotations' that are recognisable and relatively fixed but contain within themselves the potential to be expanded by audiences into clusters of different meanings. The parallel that is being made here relates to the *function* of these various quotations within discourse and the manner in which they are applied by authors and readers to illuminate life-situations. The quotations from foreign and local narrative resources to be found in West African popular texts seem to be authoritative in a similar way to the proverb, containing within themselves a history of common insights, warnings and judgements. Authors activate the quotations when they wish to intervene in and comment upon specific situations; readers familiar with the quoted forms are likely, upon each encounter, to

MODERN ADVICE TO THE PEOPLE

Be a man of your words and think twice before you do anything. Do not be deceived by a woman's beauty because man of straw is worth the woman of gold.

And never allow yourself to be deceived by the sweet tongues and clever movements of some men, when you read, try to understand.

NEVER TRUST ALL THAT LOVE YOU

Never trust all that loves you. Some will love you really but some will love you because of your wealth.

There are some secret enemies who run about in the streets and pretend that they love you, but you know not that they hate you. Some people are very ungrateful, when you do good for them they reward you with bad. Life and love are the happiness of friends but when temptation comes friendship sometimes end in shame. Therefore do not trust all that call you friend. If you take my advice, you will become wise. God help those who help themselves.

LOVE ALL BUT TRUST FEW

When somebody befriends you suddenly and want your love, study the person very carefully in order to find out whether his or her love for you is a true one. It is very dangerous to trust all that love you and call you friend. When you have money, you have many friends but when you are poor, your bad friends will run away. If you think twice and look left and right, you will understand better. When the head is off, the body is useless.

Things are very hard. Temptation always lies on the road to success. If you are not careful you become useless. Not all men who drive along in their cars are gentlemen and not all ladies who put clean and costly dresses are gentle ladies. It is not easy to get a friend whom you will trust.

7

"I was afflicted with a painful sore at heart and mind over the affair to such an extent that I was sometimes fully determined to harm her if ever I met her. But I was always checked by the thought that 'haste is a precept of the devil and leads only to ruin and regret'.

"I also remembered something — a quotation — I learnt during my good old school days and that quickly consoled me before I could have a heart-break.

The quotation runs thus: —

'Fruitless is it to worry constantly about past failures and errors. We have all failed at times. Let us remember those past incidents only as incentives to nobler and loftier achievements in the present and future. Forget about the past, accept it as but the foundation upon which to build and climb toward the sun-kissed summits.'

"I also consoled myself with Lord Hubert Ruthvern's contention that 'there is no ideal woman.' Lord Ruthvern asks 'What makes a woman so charming? — the fact that she is a mass of contradictions, a mixture of virtues and faults; without the faults, she would be simply unendurable.'

Frank continued to tell us that he was completely lifeless those days, always giving the impression that he was not well. He said his feelings worsened, and dense worry hung over his head, when he heard one day that Lucy had been admitted to the Military Hospital . . for what, he did not know.

He however realised that Lucy was suffering over the affair just as he was also suffering; all because of LOVE.

42

Examples of the quoting modes manifested in Nigerian and Ghanaian publications from the 1960s.
1.2 (*above*) Extract from *Never Trust all that Love You* (Okonkwo, 1961: 6–7)
1.3 (*left*) Extract from *When the Heart Decides* (Mickson, 1966: 42)

make a 'formulaic linkage with an entire set of descriptions and reactions [reached] in earlier acts of reading' (Radway, 1987: 196; see Plates 1.2 and 1.3). Compressed into each quotation is a dynamic body of advice, which readers selectively extract and utilise in the process of constructing commentaries about themselves and their futures. As we shall see in the following examples of 'proverbial' discourse, this process differs greatly from the 'local' receptive modes described by postcolonial theorists such as Hannerz and Appadurai.

In J. Abedi-Boafo's novel, *And Only Mothers Know* ([1938] 1946), any preconceptions one might hold about the mimicry of foreign forms have to be sidelined when one sees the manner in which the author uses quotations from foreign texts actively to demonstrate his proficiency in the art of quoting others. After describing the deceitful, promiscuous behaviour of the heroine, who pretends to be a perfect wife while secretly liaising with numerous lovers, Abedi-Boafo employs a distinctive quoting mode:

> Women are the salt of this earthy life; they cheer and encourage us in our struggle for existence; but when we peep through the grey haze of centuries and catch a glimpse of Adam and Eve quitting paradise; see Sampson, the giant, beguiled by Delilah; Job denied sympathy and consolation by his wife ... we, without fear of contradiction, associate ourselves with the reply of Geoffrey Tempest in Marie Corelli's *The Sorrows of Satan*, when Lucio wanted to know why he hated women ... 'It is because they have all the world's possibilities of good in their hands, and the majority of them turn these possibilities to evil. Men are influenced entirely by women, though few of them will own it'.[2] (1946: 20)

The references to Adam and Eve, Samson and Delilah and the marriage of Job take the form of unmarked quotations within half-finished sentences. Before reaching the end of this list of references, Abedi-Boafo's readers probably will be projecting meanings into the gaps and using their knowledge of the biblical character types to generate judgements about what women really are like as wives.

The concluding comment takes the form of a different type of quotation, for the author openly cites a fictional character in *The Sorrows of Satan*. Abedi-Boafo is asserting his authority as an advice-giver on the issue of marriage by staging his moral judgement of Ghanaian women *through* well-known biblical women and, then again, *through* the mouth of a distinctly 'foreign' fictional character. Two layers of quotations separate the author from his judgement. Clearly, neither mimicry nor the author's originality are of concern here, for Abedi-Boafo's *finesse* as a writer stems from the skill with which he applies one type of quotation to the other and thus demonstrates his knowledge of the 'real' problems to be encountered in contemporary marriages (see also Chapter 4).

Abedi-Boafo's explicit use of citations from English-language texts can be contrasted with the quoting mode employed by his contemporary, J. Benibengor

---

[2] Authors' and publishers' original spellings have been respected throughout this book. 'Sic' has not been included beside any apparent typographical errors.

Blay. As I shall go on to demonstrate, despite their *stylistic* differences, these two authors reprocess their quoted material in a similar manner, for in each case readers are invited to extrapolate from the textual examples and apply literary models to their personal lives. In *Emelia's Promise and Fulfilment* (Blay, 1967), which was first published as two separate texts in 1944 and 1945, readers find that after marrying Joe, the heroine Emelia 'had established a hostel in a small apartment of their house where girls of unique honourable character could be taught sewing' (p. 72). Joe and Emelia live in a luxurious house and, in their spare time, 'the lovely couple had taken seriously to literature and for long hours in the night they discussed the great poets and authors' (*ibid.*). They live in a remote part of Ghana but Blay is keen not to dismiss the rural population: 'The neatness of the place and the habit of the people appealed to Emelia who was conversant with the conditions obtaining in other places and the lives of other people' (p. 18).

In one of the few studies of early Ghanaian fiction, Ime Ikiddeh (1971) criticises the way in which Blay imitates an eighteenth-century English literary language and uncritically imposes Victorian moral values upon his protagonists. Emelia's character is 'shallow', he complains, and in narrative style and theme, Blay:

> shows a lack of realism in setting, character and attitude that must shock present-day Ghanaian audiences ... If Canadians and New Zealanders have been stunned by what they now recognise as the colonial slavishness of some of their early writers then Blay perhaps deserves more than pity. (Ikiddeh, 1971: 108)

Ikiddeh's preoccupation with realism combines with an embarrassment at Blay's narrative style and ideological position, creating an image of pitiful 'colonial slavishness'. This position could indeed be supported by the example of Emelia, who is described as 'a figure which Venus might have adored' (Blay, 1967: 11). She is the perfect Christian wife who remains 'always silent' and 'smiling' while her husband visits 'blonde[s] of wide reputation' in the town (p. 105). Described as a 'thoughtful and sympathetic wife', she will 'forgive without arbitration, without pacification, without anything' (p. 115).[3] At the end of the novel, when she is reunited with her repentant husband, she cries, 'Lord of the Heavens full of Wonders, I adore and give thee thanks that I have come to see my love alive and pray that I may have him back to life if 'tis thy will' (p. 127).

When he insists on Blay's 'lack of realism' and blind imitation of European conventions, Ikiddeh is ignoring the possibility that these narratives are not necessarily *meant* to be realistic or original.[4] Certainly, Blay is using rather pompous English prose to position Emelia within a Victorian, Christian model of femininity. Perhaps, in the process, he is also marking his class identification as a member

---

[3] Blay distances his heroine from specifically Ghanaian reconciliation procedures, here. Arbitration and pacification are well-established customary practices aimed at healing rifts between married couples (see McCaskie, 1995).

[4] Ikiddeh's critique also might be reinforced by the example of Blay's poetry, where the poet's romantic yearnings are expressed thus: 'Her winsome features cast a spell/ Upon my nerves and me benumb'd' (Blay, 1961: 96); or, 'Unhappy maid what are you doing here / Vain watching through the passing throng? / Why sit alone so silent, dear – / O will you tell me what is wrong?' (p. 18).

of the educated elite. However, by choosing to use terms like 'conversant', 'conditions obtaining' and 'if 'tis thy will', Blay seems to be removing Emelia from a 'real' social context and emphasising her *writtenness*. Her character has been constructed from an amalgam of quotations from written sources, including Henry Fielding's novel, *Amelia*, published in 1751, as well as the Bible and Christian 'good manners' manuals. Presented as a philanthropic, well-bodiced lady, Emelia is a thoroughly intertextual type. Rather than being 'shallow', as Ikiddeh claims, she is in fact saturated with written maxims about how a good Christian housewife should behave in English middle-class households.

Emelia's legitimacy as a character seems to have been conferred through Blay's use of an English 'literary' style. By contrast, the other characters in the novel are presented in a far less formal manner. Blay's prose style is not therefore simply imitative of English literary conventions. His failure to sustain the 'imitative' mode for characters other than the heroine gives rise to questions about the way in which his references to an English prose style function in the narrative.

Blay's moments of apparent mimicry can be seen as dynamic reapplications of existing literary forms. His narrative *style* needs to be distinguished from the *content* of the novel, for local narrative templates can be discerned immediately in the plot. Emelia's husband Joe is seduced away from his marriage by a beautiful young stranger: as a result, he loses Emelia, who confronts him with the error of his ways before leaving the marriage to set up a dress-making business. After his good wife's departure, Joe loses all of his money to a 'bewildering bevy of good-looking girls' (Blay, 1967: 129); he also loses his job, becomes physically sick and finally learns the lesson that a husband owes his loyalties to his wife and that, as far as women are concerned, 'I shouldn't have cared [so] much about what modern women call love ... extremely decorative, they are inwardly a blood-sucking lot' (p. 128).[5]

The author is engaging with the diverse narrative resources available at the time in Ghana, reworking plots that appear in the novels of his contemporaries and regenerating character types that were circulating in local-language stage shows. To take just one example, Joe's lament against 'what modern women call love' echoes the sentiments of many young men in Ghanaian concert parties. In a performance transcribed by Kwabena Bame (1985: 129–90), a young man sings a story-song containing dire warnings to unfaithful husbands:

Modern women aren't good!
Pardon my bluntness –
Modern women aren't good, they aren't at all good!
They aren't honest to men. (p. 159)

The performer goes on to embellish the 'modern woman' type, singing about the antics of a particularly promiscuous girl.

---

[5] As the discussion of Victor Amarteifio's *Bediako the Adventurer* (1985) in the next chapter will show, the story of Joe, Emelia and the beautiful temptress is a persistent narrative template in locally published Ghanaian fiction.

Blay is not necessarily seeking to proclaim his knowledge of concert party templates, which are themselves influenced by other genres (see Collins, 1994). Rather, through Joe, the author is citing a popular assessment of unmarried women and appealing to a recognisable female character type. Joe's condemnation of 'modern women' occurs at the end of the novel. The preceding narrative is thus repositioned in relation to the local template and Blay can use the popular moral condemnation to authorise his heroine, for Emelia gains legitimacy as a role model for readers by *not* being like the 'modern' type that her husband derides.

In the concert parties of the 1930s and 1940s, Christian parables would be recast in local settings, filled with new characters and with updated versions of familiar folktale types; new lyrics would be sung to the tunes of old Christian hymns, new dances set to the beat of colonial military marches (see Collins, 1994; Bame, 1985). This creative fusion of foreign and local influences cannot be disentangled, nor can 'authentic' African elements be separated from elements which appear to 'imitate' Western art forms. Blay's Emelia and Joe are embedded in a similar cultural context, remaining as heterogeneous as any concert party character. They have been created to explore the theme of marriage in modern Ghana, an issue of great relevance to local readers at the time (see Chapter 4), but Emelia in particular seems to gain her legitimacy as a character through the author's 'quotation' of an English prose style. When one finds an apparent emulation of European master-texts in these novels, then, it is a form of quotation with specific local connotations and not a simple replication of static colonial models.

Perhaps a local reader rather than a scholar should be given the last word on Blay. In the letters column of the *Gold Coast Observer* in 1942, one correspondent from Cape Coast offers a comment on Blay's recent publication, *Short Essays on How to Achieve National Success* (1942?):[6]

'Short Essays' by Benibengor Blay
Hath pleasing message for all men: they say
That Africa in Unity must stand
And face the raging tides from every strand.
This volume bears some simple chapters through
In language flowing sweetly free and true;
His efforts, friends encourage all around:
Shield him when Critics becoming voices sound.
John Benibengor Blay, fight still along
Thy writing battles with an endless song.
Thou tender art, and yet prepared to learn
The accidentals of thy trenchant pen. (Bamfur Filson, 6 Feb 1942: 454)

---

[6] Unfortunately *Short Essays* could not be located in Britain or Ghana, but the title and Bamfur Filson's comments on the content reveal it to be a political rather than a poetic text. Blay's poems were, however, published regularly in the national press and it is likely that Bamfur Filson was familiar with the type of verse cited in the third footnote above and also with what he terms the author's 'language flowing sweetly free and true' (1942: 454).

In offering his reading and review of *Short Essays*, T. Bamfur Filson himself turns out to be an amateur creative writer. This lay-reviewer responds to Blay's publication by publishing his own poem which praises Blay through its manifest content but also through its stylistic quotation of Blay's own poetry. His textual production is thus a form of reception: having consumed Blay's text, this reader is responding by producing his own text.

Numerous examples of a similar writing style can be found in Eastern Nigerian 'market literature', which was produced in bulk by young male school leavers in the 1950s and 1960s. Blay's technique can be compared with that of Miller O. Albert (pseud.) in his short romance, *Rosemary and the Taxi Driver* (1960). Though very different from Blay's grammatically correct, formal prose, Albert's short pamphlet establishes its authority in a similar way to *Emelia's Promise* through the stylistic quotation of a Western 'master' language. Revelling in the art of romance-writing, the narrator introduces his heroine:

> The grim enthusiasm of her ardent lust was bubbling on her romantic face, and her youthful glances of shyness. She had got all the zests of the West and mettled her senses, to bolster up al[a]cr[i]ty, to crack love, romance and joke. (Albert, 1960: 7)

This can be viewed as an example of the effort to emulate the stylistic 'zests of the West', but the seams still show around the edges of Albert's quotation. The author's use of the romance genre is fragmented and unstable.

In a similar manner to Blay, the authors of Nigerian market literature are drawing authority from a shared pool of literary languages, crossing different genres and language registers and, in the process, creating narrative whirlpools that are self-consciously textual. The distinctive 'market literature' style contains English proverbs alongside translations of Igbo maxims; references to Shakespeare plays, B-grade American and Hindi movies and Indian 'mystical' rituals coexist with chunks of purple prose borrowed from the Bertha M. Clay and Marie Corelli novels that were widely available in Nigeria at the time (see Newell, 1996). The elements of this hybrid quoting practice cannot be teased apart, nor can a grid of source references be extracted easily from the texts. Instead, the multiple genres and language registers can be seen to provide maps of the authors' literary experiences, through which authors assert their status as writers and claim the licence to write (see Vail and White, 1991).

Rather than seeing Albert's, Blay's and Abedi-Boafo's different quoting modes as distinct from the rest of the text, their novels should be viewed as totalities. After all, the quotations do not stand in isolation, but function in the context of wider narratives which are produced for local readers. Albert, Blay and Abedi-Boafo are, in their different ways, drawing upon local and foreign narrative conventions, but the act of combination creates models and codes that are impossible to root in fixed sources. Their books bring new worlds and characters into existence for readers and, crucially, their legitimacy as writers seems to depend upon their ability to cite from a range of literary reference points.

The relevance of this 'proverbial' quoting process to West African literature becomes more apparent when one turns to the prefaces, front and back covers of locally published texts. In almost every publication, be it from Ghana or Nigeria, authors use the preface and the cover to set up an 'advice-giving' situation. Readers are told how they will be guided in their own lives through the example of the characters. The values being offered to readers are thus mediated by the protagonists: instead of confronting the addressee directly, advice will remain general and impersonal.

The prefaces and covers of popular novels are explicit in their references to this learn-by-example framework. Often, authors seek to 'entertain and educate', emphasising their didactic role, presenting moral tales that can be applied to young readers' lives. For example, the narrator of E. K. Mickson's *When the Heart Decides* (1966) states, 'I am telling this story ... because I feel it will be a great lesson, in fact, a forewarning to many young men desperately in love, against heartbreaks' (p. 5). At the start of a more recent publication, *The Premature Marriage* by E. K. Kwarteng (1990), the author declares, 'The aim of this book is not only to entertain, delight, and amuse but to educate, instruct and advise' (n.p.). On the back cover of K. A. Bediako's (pseud. Asare Konadu) *Don't Leave me Mercy!!* (1966), readers are alerted to the didactic status of the narrative, for this 'is one of the most starkly moving parables ever written of the forces that shape or mar many marriages of today': through the characters, readers will learn about 'patience, determination, thoughtfulness, quarrels, nagging, relations with in-laws, etc' (n.p.). Introducing a new edition of *Emelia's Promise*, Blay (1967) also draws attention to the moral and social function of his fictional characters: 'In this present world of ours', he writes, 'the part a married woman can play is vital – especially if that part helps her to realise the seriousness of her own responsibilities. Those who would play the role of Emelia will [be] like a beacon light' (p. vi).

Similarly, the authors of Nigerian market literature are unanimous in claiming the mantle of advice-giver. Cyril Aririguzo has written his pamphlet, *The Work of Love* (1963), for reasons that echo most of his contemporaries, 'in order to help many youths to know more of the work of love and how it penetrates' (n.p.). In another pamphlet, *Beware of Women* (1960), readers are told, 'in order to discipline our mongerish African women ... this little but effective booklet has been produced' (Njoku, n.p.). The list of examples is endless.[7] These authors are positioning themselves as authoritative counsellors, utilising an array of explicit quotations and familiar character types to caution young readers, offering them an education in the dangers of urban and married life.

Rather than presenting exceptional stories, plots and characters tend to be repeated across narratives (and many of the forthcoming chapters will return to this point). Through such repetitions, typical relationship problems are portrayed which readers are invited to recognise, identify with and judge for themselves.

---

7. In a questionnaire circulated to 23 young Ghanaian men and women in 1995, over a third of the respondents said that they were influenced in their choice of title by the description on the back cover and the author's comments in the preface.

Local authors call upon a common stock of character types and conventions from folk stories as well as from religious publications, European romances, imported films and local stage-shows. Certain types of character and plot have emerged repeatedly since the 1940s, leading critics to talk in terms of 'stereotypes' (e.g. Ogundipe-Leslie, 1987; Boyce Davies, 1986; Oduyoye, 1995). For example, in Ghanaian fiction one finds repeated representations of tolerant wives who, like Blay's Emelia, await the repentance of their weak-willed husbands; as we shall see in the next chapter, repeatedly the errant heroes have, like Blay's Joe, been tempted into sexual sin and drained financially by promiscuous city women. In contemporary popular fiction one frequently finds 'lip-painted ladies' who deceive honest, unmarried men into parting with their hard-earned savings. Numerous examples of similar plots and character types span the decades, persisting in present-day publications.

It is important to emphasise that these repetitions will *vary* each time they are used; as in Blay's and Abedi-Boafo's citations, authors use existing popular templates to launch a range of different, dynamic attitudes into circulation at a local level. Locally published writers clearly have different personal histories, different educational backgrounds and different writing styles. However, distinct plot templates and character types are repeated in these narratives with a regularity and persistence that demands explanation. Such repetitions do not necessarily provide access to the psychological components of local cultures. While they appear to be fixed, these references to existing narrative models are not static: the person responsible for the act of quotation has the authority to transform the attitudes of readers. The quotations change by their movement across texts, times and locations, and function in an epigrammatic way, appearing as familiar forms which authors can embellish and apply to different situations. Each quotation from another narrative is in fact a reapplication of it, a refraction rather than a reproduction of an established framework.

The proverb functions in a similar way to these intertextual references. The proverb-speaker draws upon a familiar, epigrammatic word-formation and is able, as Yankah says, to 'project or transform attitudes ... under familiar frames laid down by tradition' (1989: 36). Yankah is referring to situated utterances, in this case the use of proverbs in Ashanti arbitration courts. He demonstrates that proverbs do not function merely to describe behaviours in a static way, but to transform attitudes and morally interpret life-situations. Proverbs might be fixed in linguistic terms, but, when applied to specific situations, they offer diverse, dynamic interpretations of the world. Proverbs are applied to situations to make things happen, projecting how things ought to be, and 'new proverbial forms' can be concocted rapidly from a familiar stock of images and phrases (see Bastian, 1993: 149).

In a similar manner, authors might be voicing an entirely new perspective, but they gain authority by re-using character types and citations which circulate already in the archives of their culture: on the one hand, the narrative gains legitimacy as a common reference recurs; on the other hand, even if the references are familiar, each time audiences encounter them, their context, relevance and application will have shifted. While books like *The Sorrows of Satan* and the Bible, or characters like the good-time girl, the errant husband and the ideal Christian wife, might be so familiar as to appear closed to new meanings, authors can fill them with unconventional concerns and creative interpretations. In this way, the author, like the proverb-speaker, licenses what is said by saying it through a recognisable mouthpiece. Simultaneously, authors establish their authority as skilful quoters, earning the reader's confidence by applying the type to an appropriate situation.

The use of different types of quotation to offer advice about sensitive issues is not confined to the earliest publications in Ghana. A similar quoting operation to that undertaken by Abedi-Boafo, Blay and Albert can be found in M. S. Olayinka's non-fictional marriage guidance manual, *Sex Education and Marital Guidance* (1987). 'Dialogue between the client and the marriage counsellor is the instructional strategy' in this Nigerian publication (p. xiv), and in structure and orientation it closely resembles the how-to books that have been published locally in Nigeria since the first days of market literature (see Newell, 1996). In a series of 'case studies' in this book, Olayinka employs dramatic sequences and typical but fictional characters to explore and resolve common relationship dilemmas. Familiar didactic figures such as the unmarried 'youngman', the insubordinate wife, the disobedient daughter and the betrayed wife all visit the counsellor's clinic, taking the form of clients seeking help from the author. The counsellor offers his advice *through* these characters, whose lives he interprets. Through these typical characters he also builds interpretive codes into the text.

Olayinka's cast of clients has been recreated for the benefit of readers, for what he terms 'instructional and illustrative purposes' (1987: xv). Each dramatic dialogue between the counsellor and client is structured in exactly the same way and, by the end of the series of case studies, a pedagogic technique has emerged. Firstly, after listening to each client's predicament, the counsellor narrates a story containing generic characters and a moral dilemma that is comparable to the client's situation. Crucially, these internal stories also contain advice to the character, action taken as a result of the advice, and the effects of the action upon the character's problem. The second stage in the technique is that clients are invited to consider the relevance of the story to their own situation and apply its lesson to their own lives. So when Lade enters the consulting room, desperately seeking 'how to win a girlfriend's love' but unable to say 'nice things' to women, the counsellor narrates an anecdote about a man on a bus who avoids insulting an obese woman by addressing her as his 'well-fed friend' (pp. 51–2). This man is shown to have gained instant popularity amongst the other passengers. Instead of interpreting the story, the counsellor invites his client to 'read' it and learn from its meaning. Only when the client fails to connect with the message does the counsellor intervene to apply its lesson to the young man's life.

Staging his advice indirectly through analogies and the examples of others, the counsellor passes responsibility for meaning-making over to his clients. Having

21

compared 'the game of love' to table-tennis and a boxing match, he asks Lade for interpretations: 'Do you understand what I have been trying to communicate to you?' (Olayinka, 1987: 55). 'I think I do', replies Lade, and explains what he has learnt (*ibid.*). Once Lade has completed his own interpretive process, the counsellor embellishes the young man's conclusions. Relating to 'people' generally rather than to Lade in particular, the counsellor points out that:

> a man who readily accepts defeat will find it extremely difficult to win a fair lady. ... People seem to like men who are dynamic, enthusiastic, diligent, industrious, brave and intelligent. ... Am I explicit enough now? (p. 56)

As with the rest of his advice, these comments remain impersonal, requiring Lade to continue the process of creating, extrapolating and applying meanings.

When it comes to communicating direct advice outside his didactic story-spaces, the counsellor quotes the wisdom of others. He does not stake his claim to authority in the creation of 'original' responses, but, like Abedi-Boafo in *And Only Mothers Know* (1946), by demonstrating his ability to cite others' words. 'I wish to teach you another principle', he tells Lade, 'What is rewarding to one person may not be rewarding to another person. This is clearly implied in an old adage which states, "One man's food may be another man's poison"' (Olayinka, 1987: 57). By the end of their counselling session, Lade has become so proficient in this quoting mode that he is able to narrate a short adventure story and apply it to his own life as a lover, and six weeks after the completion of counselling he returns with two girlfriends in tow having successfully applied his 'newly acquired principles' (pp. 59–60).

When it is the turn of female clients to enter the counselling room, Olayinka's central character adopts a different tone. Most of the Yoruba women he advises have attempted to re-order their emotional lives by taking action: in the process, they have stepped over prescribed gender boundaries. In challenging the status quo, they have all acted disrespectfully in one way or another: one Yoruba wife has slapped her insolent young in-law; another woman has challenged her husband about his extra-marital affair; another woman has intervened in her parents' marriage, insulting her father who is spending the family's scarce housekeeping money on alcohol (pp. 178–85).

The counsellor's guidance becomes prescriptive with these female clients, and he produces proverbs that seal women into rigid social norms. For example, he informs one woman that if she gets divorced, she will:

> be compared with the Yoruba proverbial hen which is taken to the market for sale. If the hen has been all that good at laying eggs and taking proper care of the chicks, the owner would not have taken it to the market for sale. (p. 78)

The implication of this maxim is that, however bad the client's marriage, she should work from within to change it rather than suffering scorn as a divorcee. Popular maxims are quoted repeatedly by the counsellor when he addresses female clients: wives should not be better-educated than their husbands (p. 79);

they should not try to claim 'equality' with men (*ibid.*); 'it is often said that the quickest way to a man's heart is through his stomach' (p. 160); 'the kitchen which a woman proudly regards as her "office" should be kept clean and tidy' (*ibid.*). Blame for social disintegration attaches to female non-conformists. In the case of each female client, it is the wife's assertive attitude rather than the husband's behaviour which has to change, and the counsellor quotes familiar maxims to ensure a corrective rather than a problem-solving approach.

The counsellor's *method* remains the same with his male and female clients, for he invites both groups to extrapolate from didactic stories and apply familiar maxims and character types to themselves. However, the examples he offers to women relate less to the resolution of personal problems than to the enforcement of correct 'feminine' behaviours. Inserting different named characters into the same plot template each time, he depicts the futility of 'self-defeating' behaviour: in eight separate stories aimed at eight female clients, when the main character over-reacts to a clear injustice, that character becomes the one to have committed an offence (Olayinka, 1987: 99, 126–30, 169, 188).

As in the proverbial discourse analysed by Penfield and Yankah, in Olayinka's text the counsellor never confronts an individual directly with his or her short-comings. The story-examples, maxims and analogies are attached to the client's problem in an indirect manner. Interpretations are staged *through* the protagonists of stories and not *upon* the personalities of clients. In each case, these counselling techniques require the client, rather than the counsellor, to unite the example with his or her own interpersonal experiences.

As we can see in Olayinka's application of familiar plot templates and character types in the counselling situation, moral judgements and commentaries are performed through the words of another. The 'clients' interpret the significance of the example and apply it to their own situations. Whether fictional or non-fictional, locally published texts in Ghana and Nigeria seem to share this orienta-tion: they set up 'advice-giving' spaces in which readers are guided indirectly through the example of other characters. Instead of confronting the addressee directly, advice remains general and impersonal. It is precisely this performance of advice *through* the example of another that connects these extended narratives with the 'proverbial' quoting mode described earlier. Authors are calling upon archives of established character types, invoking familiar figures that readers will recognise: these figures are inserted into narrative environments in which the responses they have activated previously in readers may be recalled, complicated, reworked or transformed. In itself, such a repetition or 'quotation' of popular sources is always a reapplication rather than a static replication of an inherited tradition.

One of the most striking pamphlets to support this hypothesis is D. A. Koranteng's *Two Wives or One?* (1987), published by the Presbyterian Church of Ghana. In his Introduction, Koranteng explains that the text contains transcripts of comments made during group discussions and symposia on the issue of polygyny. Attended by trainee teachers, members of the Ghanaian Scripture Union, the Young People's Guild and the Women's Fellowship, 'All these [people's] responses and reactions have been put down in the form of discussions, with several characters taking part' (Koranteng 1987: viii). Koranteng adopts a dramatic format and creates a small cast of characters from his numerous interviewees, condensing the multiplicity of individuals into five distinct, recognisable types: alongside the Pastor who chairs the debates, he includes Adeline Ado, a 'housewife', Papa Kofi, a 'traditionalist' church elder, Issa Alhassan, a male university student and Helena Anku, a married female student (1987: ix).

Koranteng has recreated and limited the communities he encountered in the 'outside world', selecting quintessential characters to form a 'visible community' within the text (see Anderson, 1991). By condensing his respondents into a group composed of familiar character types, Koranteng has contained the 'public' he encountered during his symposia, replacing the unknown and complex masses with familiar figures whose responses exemplify the attitudes that are commonly associated with their types. In a sense, then, he is *protecting* his text by setting up this internal discussion group. This method makes it possible to influence readers' attitudes by attaching certain statements to certain character types; he can also insert stage directions at strategic points in the debate. For example, empathy with Papa Kofi's belief in the value of polygyny is frustrated by the author's representation of him as the familiar blustering, old-fashioned chief: in addition, Papa Kofi's opinions frequently are preceded by derisive stage directions such as, *'feels pleased with himself'*, *'in his usual sentimental outbursts'*, and *'contradicts himself again'* (pp. 4; 24; 27; author's emphasis). Koranteng's reductive method provides his reading public with interpretive pivots, allowing them to reject certain character types and enter the text through the others (see next chapter).

The characters represent distinct viewpoints on the subject of polygyny. Papa Kofi quotes examples from the Old Testament to support his approval of polygyny. The Pastor, on the other hand, reconceptualises polygyny as male infidelity, quoting New Testament injunctions against multiple marriages. As in the proverb-speaking competitions held amongst senior Ashanti men, where a contestant's wisdom is judged by the aptness and fluency of his quotations (Yankah, 1989), Papa Kofi and the Pastor are engaged in a battle of biblical quotations. The Pastor wins each verbal sparring match, demonstrating his proficiency in applying the words of others, and, in the process, proving the superiority of his perspective to the views of 'traditionalists'.

The lay-members of the discussion group also are divided, and they too employ quotations to validate their opinions. As the debate moves beyond theological boundaries and into the field of popular gender debates, Helena and Adeline take up interpretive positions which consistently oppose the attitudes expressed by the men; and in the struggle to blame the other sex, both sides 'quote' from a familiar array of character types, applying them to anecdotal stories about the suffering of friends. The women hold unfaithful husbands responsible for marital tensions: 'most men are the cause', Adeline comments (1987: 47). Insubordinate wives, the men respond, are the root cause of men's infidelities, driving away good husbands with their constant complaints and naggings; in addition, seductive young women go out of their way to tempt husbands into 'sugar-daddy' relationships (pp. 42; 48). Invoking another popular feminine type, Issa and Papa Kofi agree that 'When a woman colours her cheeks and paints her lips, she colours her words and paints her acts' (p. 17). In response, Adeline and Helena agree that, during courtship, 'The men rather deceive the women. Their tongues are full of lies' (p. 17).

This ideological see-saw continues for the duration of the pamphlet. Ideal wives are defined in absentia, as Issa describes how 'some housewives cannot be said to be good companions and helpmates at all. They always grumble' (p. 78). Meanwhile, Adeline defines ideal husbands by their real-life opposites, who 'are difficult. They do not help in the education and welfare of their children' (p. 79). The participants in the discussion seem to be expressing empathy for versions of themselves, projected into their anecdotes as primary points of identification.

Koranteng's familiar characters are themselves quoting from an array of familiar character types. They are taking up interpretive positions which correspond to the social roles implied by their status on Koranteng's cast list: the young women are identifying with the problems of wives; the senior and junior men are projecting themselves into the position of husbands. Two distinct 'reading' constituencies emerge in this pamphlet, and the women's perspectival differences from the men illustrate the manner in which, when readers encounter the same domestic situation, their interpretations of it are gendered at a primary level (see Chapter 2). Although Koranteng has reduced his 'real' interviewees to a narrow range of character types, the interpretive mode they adopt resembles that which prevails among 'real life' readers of popular narratives in West Africa (see Chapter 3). As the next chapter will reveal, however, readers are far more complex than Koranteng's visible community of readers within *Two Wives or One?*

In *Two Wives or One?* the Pastor attempts to mediate between the two sides by weaving biblical examples of monogamous couples into the debate, exercising his authority as a member of the religious hierarchy by summarising what 'Jesus says' about marital fidelity; and he introduces broad Christian precepts that will guide couples through marriage (1987: 18). He treats the argument as a didactic, dialogical space, in which Christian guidance will resolve the disagreements. As the quarrel intensifies, so the Pastor's comments become more abstract and idealistic: 'A man should marry the woman whom he really loves and who loves him in return', he comments, interrupting an argument about the precise reasons for a woman's jealousy of her husband in which Helena cites the views of 'many friends of mine' (1987: 49); 'trust God completely and firmly ... God knows best', he comments in response to Adeline's anecdote about a husband she knew who entertained his girlfriend at the office, only to be discovered by his wife (1987: 57–8).

Ironically, the Pastor's Christian perspective seems to be incapable of accommodating the absolutist and increasingly *non*-dialogical opinions of the gathered group; his interventions and extensive quotations from the Bible are increasingly isolated from the secular debate taking place within his room, and his doctrinal points are rendered superfluous to the on-going, popular disagreement about who is to blame for men's extra-marital affairs. From the outset, Issa, Helena and

Adeline have agreed on the principle of monogamy promoted by the Pastor. Their disagreement concerns marital practices rather than the marital principles he continues to voice, and it is here, in an attitudinal zone untouched by the Pastor, that their differences emerge. At the same time, the Pastor gains strength as an arbiter as the text progresses, intervening with increasing frequency as the two sides polarise. His emergence as a moral force is matched by a brief but significant ideological retreat on the women's part. When Issa asks, 'Who should play second fiddle?' in a marriage, Adeline responds, with Helena's support, 'Naturally the wife … The wife should be submissive out of love and respect' (Koranteng, 1987: 76–7). In the last ten pages of the pamphlet, the Pastor finally surfaces from his biblical exegeses and takes control of the problem: 'Why do the partners put the blame on each other?' he asks, 'There must be something wrong. Men blame the women; the women blame the men' (p. 80). 'The men must be blamed', is Adeline's predictable response (*ibid.*).

The Pastor's final, most targeted intervention occurs in response to Adeline's outburst against men's wastage of household resources on 'outside' wives. He uses the moment to redefine the ideal wife rather than to insist on the necessity of husbands revealing their expenditure or sharing their incomes. Closing down the debate with Christian doctrine, the Pastor returns to the Genesis story to sanction men's status as heads of households. *Two Wives or One?* ends with a catalogue of behavioural imperatives, all of them aimed at wives and all of them familiar to readers of local Christian literature in Ghana. Rather than defining the ideal couple, the Pastor positions himself and his faith within the masculine interpretive community represented by Issa and Papa Kofi. 'As a Pastor, it is my earnest hope and prayer that wives learn to be sober and wise; they must love their husbands and love their children. They must be discreet, chaste and lovers of their homes. They must be good, obedient, friendly and tolerant' (p. 80). His lengthy concluding speech operates according to the same logic that he criticised as being 'wrong' a few pages earlier: by neglecting men's responsibilities and focusing exclusively upon feminine marriage roles, the Pastor is 'blaming the women' for domestic conflicts. In addition, his concluding references to the Genesis story are loaded with a masculine interpretive bias. In a literalist reading of the act of creation, he comments that 'the headship of the husband over the wife has its sanction in the divine act of the building of woman out of man' (p. 81). The Bible has been reinstated as a relevant behavioural guidebook but, in the process of reclaiming authority over the debate, the Pastor has been forced to take a side in the very argument he spent eighty pages attempting to resolve.

These scenes exemplify, in a heightened form, the differences between 'masculine' and 'feminine' positionalities that will be explored in detail in the next chapter. Although they take place between common character types rather than complex social subjects, the gender division of interpretation in Koranteng's pamphlet illustrates the process whereby West African readers actively produce meanings from the narrative or scene before them, extrapolating and judging events from a gender-biased perspective.

The Proverbial Space in Ghanaian Popular Fiction

Ghanaian and Nigerian authors are enlisting quotations from diverse narrative models. Even the earliest authors, writing during the colonial regime, use quotations to create new meanings from their source-texts. They seem to be quite deliberately employing the wisdom and styles of other authors in order to demonstrate their own proficiency as writers. Abedi-Boafo cites the Bible indirectly and Marie Corelli directly; Blay adopts a formal English prose style and also includes indirect quotations from Ghanaian popular narratives; Nigerian pamphlet-writers incorporate the language of racy Western novels and romantic movies; Olayinka and Koranteng invoke a cast-list of familiar West African character types and plots. Each mode of quotation marks a moment in the text when the author uses the discourse of another to generate meanings which are both familiar and dynamic. In none of these instances can the author's quoting activity be set against originality and viewed in derogatory terms.

The provisional alternative framework proposed in this chapter has been inspired by a reapplication of Yankah's idea that some types of extended narrative can be seen as '"proverbs" in the wider sense' (1989: 90). Authors' explicit quotations from foreign texts and also their re-applications of popular character types can be regarded as spilling into the realm of the proverb. As with proverbs, these quotations are epigrammatic forms, loaded with meanings which explode outward when they are cited. Viewed thus, locally published texts in Ghana and Nigeria can be situated in a space which is didactic and non-realist. By allowing both for the quotation of a familiar form and the dynamic reapplication of it in new narratives, it becomes possible to discuss the way these references function within narratives, as well as the way specific reading constituencies respond to familiar types, for as we shall see in the next chapter, different groups of readers often generate different interpretations of the same popular narrative.

2

Making up their Own Minds
Readers, interpretations & the difference of view

Authors write about both moral and immoral acts prevailing in African societies. Those characters that are involved in these immoral acts are severely punished: sometimes they are even sent away from their communities. Whereas those characters who do good or do not practice these immoral acts are awarded prizes.
(Male reader, Tamale, 1998)

In the mid-1960s, the Ghanaian author Asare Konadu adopted the pen-name K. Bediako, and submitted several of his 'light and perhaps a little bit educative' novels to the Presbyterian publishing house in Accra; other manuscripts were sent to local newspapers to be serialised in Sunday supplements (Konadu, 1974). Konadu chose to publish as 'Bediako' because he did not want to jeopardise the international literary reputation conferred on him by the editors at Heinemann, who had rejected all but two of his titles from the *African Writers Series*.[1] He remained convinced, however, of his popular novels' credentials as socially relevant 'problematic stories' which 'pose problems in the relationships' (*ibid.*) and his romances have become bestsellers among young local readers, continuing to be purchased in large numbers throughout Ghana.

Konadu's novels are intended 'to help the youngman in making up his own mind in certain things in his own present society ... [I am] posing to the young-man the problems that he is likely to face if he goes in to get married' (*ibid.*). Konadu's comment conveys the essence of the reader response process that will be explored in this chapter. While he is emphasising the local, contemporary relevance of his fiction, he is not claiming a mantle as an ultimate arbiter of meaning; nor is he instilling his novels with didactic lifestyle instructions for an expectant and gender-neutral readership to discover within the text as they turn the pages; nor is he proclaiming that, as far as interpretation is concerned, the 'birth of the reader must be at the cost of the death of the Author' (Barthes, 1977:

---

[1] Heinemann accepted Konadu's *A Woman in her Prime* and also his novel, *Come Back Dora!*, which was renamed *Ordained by the Oracle*, perhaps to sideline the popular and local appeal of its title (Konadu, 1974; see Conclusion, below). Konadu's other manuscripts were considered unsuitable for an international readership and were returned to the author. He quickly set up his own publishing company, Anowuo Educational Publications, to oversee the printing and distribution of these titles.

148). Rather than asserting or relinquishing control of the meaning-making project, Konadu's brief definition of the popular novelist's role makes a different, culturally specific statement about the interpretive process in Ghana, for he appears to take for granted a mode of reception in which authors and audiences share responsibility for the production of meaning.

Konadu defines his primary reading constituency as a clear-cut social class: 'mainly I have the youth in mind because ... the people who in fact buy [local publications] are the youngmen' (1974). By referring to the 'youngman', he targets the group of men who are, as we saw in Chapter 1, identifiable by their age (17–35), unmarried status, secondary education and relatively low financial position. Facilitating rather than directing the interpretive process, the Ghanaian author helps the 'youngman' to make a self-interested reading of society at large. The young male reader will apply the characters and situations he finds in the text to 'certain things' in 'his own' society, pulling out components for the formation of opinions about contemporary social relations. 'Making up the mind' is thus a moment of readerly participation which parallels authorial creativity. While the narrative itself provides moral leads and emphases, reading is an effectual experience, furnishing young men with relevant characters that can be applied to the off-page world.

As we shall see in this chapter, 'his own' readings might diverge significantly from other readers, who are clustered into different interpretive communities, formed around different identity-pivots to the 'youngman'. In particular, women writers in Ghana tend to inflect or reject the character types circulating in male-authored narratives. Working within a shared set of interpretive and narrative conventions, women are positioned differently in relation to the troupe of familiar characters called into texts by male authors. As the final section of this chapter will demonstrate, women writers offer similar definitions of the function of literature, but, in Akosua Gyamfuaa-Fofie's case at least, a different perspective is presented on the interpretive mode: she seeks explicitly to challenge readers' attitudes by creating alternative role models for young women readers in Ghana. Women writers' 'difference of view' will be related to their positionality as active interpreters, or 'readers', of commonly circulating narratives about gender. Staging recognisable domestic dilemmas, and drawing characters from a common stock of types, Ghanaian women express bias through their reconstructions of familiar figures.[2]

Reading is a situated 'social event', taking place in the context of collective 'assumptions about language and meaning' which precondition an individual's interpretations (Radway, 1987: 7; 189). Before turning the first page of a popular novel, or watching the first scene of a theatrical performance, the 'reader' already occupies a culturally specific receptive position, and each instance of interpretation

---

[2] The word 'feminine' is used in this and subsequent chapters to refer to a woman's social conditioning, to the fluid, dynamic gendering process that takes place in different societies. The term is used to avoid a static, biologically essentialist position based on the assumption that there are intrinsic differences between African men's and women's writing.

is likely to be informed by shared preconceptions about the function of literature (see Rabinowitz, 1987).[3]

The reader survey presented in Chapter 3 indicates that the role of readers is essential to the discussion of printed narratives in West Africa. Indeed, authors acknowledge the readership's participation in the co-creation of novels to such an extent that plots themselves may be transformed or extended. After distributing 50,000 copies of *Emelia's Promise* (1944), which describes the marriage of Emelia and Joe, the Ghanaian author J. Benibengor Blay received a flow of letters. In an interview (1974), he said:

> My readers were asking me in letters and everything, what happened after their marriage? So I put on *After the Wedding* (1945), and we had about 20,000 [copies printed] of that. Then they still said there was a little bit of anti-climax too. Then they said, But what happened after?

Blay's comments are intriguing for the way publications are described as being 'put on' for the readership, presupposing a dynamic relationship as if texts were staged performances. Rejecting the plot structures of English romances, in which courtships generally end with marriage and narrators guarantee that 'they all lived happily ever after', Blay's readers want to know 'what happened *after* the marriage?' Their demands were met with follow-up texts in which there was betrayal, seduction, conflict and reconciliation between Emelia and Joe. The expectations and projections of the readership thus generated additional scenarios.

Blay's readers challenge the notion of the generic 'reader', a formless figure in literary criticism, often summoned into essays to validate interpretations that do not move beyond the text. In order to gauge the popular impact of locally produced narratives in West Africa, both 'the reader' and 'the text' must be refastened to reading communities which are socially positioned and gendered. When asked why he was purchasing a copy of E. Opong-Ofori's *The Wounds of Love* (1988), one young man queuing in the Methodist Bookshop, Accra, replied, 'It is a woman's duty to care for and support her husband because his life is so hard' (personal communication, July 1995). The back cover of *The Wounds of Love* declares this to be the story of 'a Cassanova who gets his fingers burnt on the hot pot of female flesh, with dire consequences for himself and the people around him' (Opong-Ofori, 1988: n.p.). The young customer said that he liked to read novels about intelligent young heroes, who learn from their encounters with 'loose' women and find happiness with their marriage partners in the end. This reader firmly located himself within the text, projecting meanings into the novel he was buying which would be relevant to his range of experiences.

---

[3] 'Reader' is used here to refer to interpreters generally, and theatre audiences are included in the definition alongside readers of popular fiction; similarly, 'narrative' describes the content of both novels and stage shows. While it is important to preserve the generic differences between Ghanaian concert parties and locally published novels, the main focus of this chapter is upon the shared interpretive strategies of audiences and readers.

Authors, readers and fictional characters express a shared set of assumptions that the fictional situation will reveal truths, helping people to form opinions about the most intimate areas of their lives. 'Well, all good fiction must have some relation to real life', says the hero of Blay's *Love in a Clinic* (1957). Refusing to suspend disbelief and 'escape' into a fantasy romance, Blay's character defies, in the process, a cohort of critics who regard African popular genres as escapist (Ehling, 1990; Coulon, 1987; Schild, 1980). Echoing Blay's hero, Ghanaian readers are explicit and unanimous in their assessments of the function of literature and the author's role as a commentator on reality: authors 'are the main agents who teach moral[s]', states one female undergraduate, for 'they normally write about our daily existence, I mean things that happen around us daily' (fL4, 1998);[4] the novelist's role is 'to educate, to conscientise, to inform, to entertain', writes a male student from Accra (mL16, 1998); another young man, a teacher trainee from Tamale, states that, through the deployment of didactic plots and character types, authors teach readers that 'people who make a luxurious living by dubious means suffer after all. Also, people who are hard-working and committed succeed at the end' (mT, 1998). This kind of collaboration between author, character and addressee is presumed *a priori* within diverse popular art forms in West Africa, revealing the underlying aesthetic which informs the reading process (see Barber, 1986; Adeleye-Fayemi, 1995; Asante-Darko and van der Geest, 1983).

Different groups of readers may make up their minds differently about the same locally-produced narrative: their interpretations are acts of 'world construction' which may resist or contest readings by other social groups (Radway, 1987: 187). For example, concert party performances in Ghana are replete with regular crisis points, when audiences divide into distinct reading constituencies. These points represent moments of heightened participation built into the show, when the performance of domestic dilemmas is suspended by the spectators' noisy interpolation of moral judgements. 'The crowd really gets into the story and joins in by singing, clapping, and commenting loudly', one performer, Mr Bampoe, tells John Collins in an interview (1994: 24; see also Cole, 1997). Tending to occur during scenes of marital debate or conflict, the audience's interpretive discord about the events can be regarded as ideological commentaries on their own social lives (see Radway, 1987: 7); and, crucially, a gender divide can be found at the core of their interpretive processes.

In his study of Ghanaian concert parties, Kwabena Bame (1985) notices that the actors:

occasionally arouse competitive feeling[s] between men in the audience on one side, and women on the other. A female impersonator may sing a song full of imputations about the character of Ghanaian men. This will induce women in the audience to offer 'her' money. In reply a comedian, representing men, will

---

[4] The following referencing system has been used to differentiate between respondents: m – male; f – female; L – University of Ghana, Legon; C – University of Cape Coast; A – Accra Polytechnic; T – Bagabaga Training College, Tamale.

sing a song full of even more dangerous imputations against the character of modern Ghanaian women. (p. 67)[5]

A sexual division of interpretation carves the performative space into two spheres: women are reading for feminine models of behaviour, while men are entering the narrative through a masculine point of identification. The audience's money-gifts to selected performers are affective responses to the situation, expressing agreement, pity or approval towards the characters that are portrayed. Clearly divided in their loyalties, the audience is extracting a moral order from their chosen characters and intervening in the plot, advising characters and seeking to transform the outcome of the tale. These responses reveal how marital codes are contested along gender lines, and such a division is highly significant if fictional character types are used by spectators to 'make up their own minds' about situations in their daily lives.

This complex reception process is illustrated by the review of a concert party, *Twere Nyame*, published in February 1942 in the *Gold Coast Observer*. The reviewer declares himself to be 'A Concert Enthusiast', while the author of the play is described as 'a modest Sunday School teacher' who has been influenced by the 'widely read and famous book, *The Basket of Flowers*' (p. 475). The reviewer finds that 'the marriage scene' of the play 'was true to life. The less said about this the better. The insubordination of a certain class of the fair sex was here portrayed by a girl', whilst the husband deserved 'sympathy' (p. 477). 'There must be Police Control in the body of the Hall', the reviewer continues, 'as it is likely that the discipline would be greatly disturbed at the MARRIAGE SCENE' (*ibid.*; author's emphasis). By taking sides with the character type whose social position most closely resembles their own, readers select specific figures *through whom* they can apportion praise and blame, *through whom* they can confirm their own opinions about men's and women's roles.

This reception process contrasts with the model of alienated subjectivity underpinning much reader response theory in the West (Fish, 1989; Iser, 1993). Wolfgang Iser (1989: 214) defines the literary experience as an 'overstepping' of the reader's subjectivity and attitudinal limits. Convinced that the novel must be *novel* in order to qualify as literature, he celebrates the unique capacity of fiction to cross the reefs of mental solitude which separate readers from one another. 'Imposed' habits and perspectives, he claims, are transformed by the reading experience: novels challenge cultural conditioning and, 'relieved of the pragmatic dimension so essential to real life situations', the reading subject is enabled 'to see through the attitudes offered to us, if not imposed on us by our everyday world ... exposing that which constitutes our outlook' (1989: 216; 226). 'Relieved' of these real-life 'entanglements' by the novel, reflection and self-consciousness are made possible (p. 228). Rather than making up their own minds through the text, readers gain a glimpse of how their minds are made up.

---

[5] Bame mentions the female impersonator because there were hardly any actresses in concert parties until recently: among other reasons, it was considered to be a disgraceful profession for women. Collins (1994: 162–70) contains a fascinating interview with a concert party actress.

By contrast, readers in West Africa seem to read for the very 'pragmatic dimension' that Iser cuts loose from the novel, actively seeking an entanglement with familiar situations and constructing their opinions around the range of social subjects created by authors. Readers adopt interpretive positions that depend upon the relevance of fictional types to their storehouse of opinions about marriage partners, 'good-time girls', mothers-in-law, 'sugar-daddies', criminals and prostitutes.

It would be over-reductive to suggest that West African readers are experiencing fictional character types in personal, one-to-one encounters, suspending both the textuality and the fictionality of the narrative in a moment of unmediated identification with their chosen protagonist.[6] Readers' comments reveal a different orientation. After reading about the antics of good-time girls in 'Bediako's' locally published fiction, one archivist (aged 28) in Kumasi commented that 'modern' Ghanaian women have been corrupted by 'Western lifestyles' (personal communication, July 1995). Supported by their materialistic mothers, he said, educated young women use their sexual power to woo managers in urban workplaces and they ignore eligible, 'hard-working bachelors' like himself. This reader's favourite Ghanaian authors, 'Bediako' and E. K. Mickson, showed how such women would be punished in the end.

This 'youngman' is not projecting a biographical experience into the novels: he is making a generalised statement about his social type, the 'hard-working bachelor', and positioning himself within a specific reading community composed of complex economic, age, gender and status differentials. His response conveys a type-to-type encounter: 'Bediako' and Mickson's fictional women *are* regarded as literal figures, but are *applied* using a mode in which the good-time girl is held up as a warning to young men as a social group. The general principle about women, formulated through the text, may then be applied to particular experiences. The fictional good-time girl is thus perceived, not as a closed stereotype with fixed properties, but as a flexible 'proverbial' figure which can be related to different situations in Ghanaian social life.

A vivid example of the divisions that might occur between readers can be found at the end of E. K. Mickson's pamphlet, *Who Killed Lucy?* (1967). In a chapter entitled 'Who Are To Blame, Men or Women?', Mickson sets up an informal discussion group to interpret the failed relationship of his protagonists, Frank and Lucy (pp. 85–102). Frank and Lucy have disappeared from this final section of the novel. Their stormy romance is finished, and the interpretive process is handed over to a fictional 'society' of onlookers, who have just witnessed the violent climax of the relationship.

Mickson's chapter is fascinating for the way it creates an audience *within* the text, setting out reading strategies for what has gone before. During their discussion of the conflict between Frank and Lucy, Mickson's internal commentators

---

[6] Against such presuppositions about readerly immersion in plots and characters one might set the reader responses to a questionnaire I circulated in 1998 (see next chapter), where many Ghanaian readers express clear appreciation of the narrative devices, language and stylistic features of novels.

divide down gender lines. As in Koranteng's *Two Wives or One?*, discussed in the previous chapter, in Mickson's pamphlet, 'The men blamed it on the women and vice versa' (p. 85). No bridge links the binary division of moral blame: having set up a gendered front-line, the onlookers fire volleys of accusations against the opponent. 'It is you the men who are the cause of all this ... You have no morals', one woman says in support of Lucy, who has just beaten up her husband's girl-friend in a public display of jealousy (p. 86); this woman is seconded by 'another woman [who] also argued that men were to blame' (*ibid.*). 'There are some of you women who are never satisfied with anything' (p. 87), a man then says in support of Frank, who has been drinking heavily in hotels and liaising with women; this man is seconded by 'another man [who] also spoke of how some girls deceive men to squeeze money from them' (*ibid.*). In much the same manner as Koranteng's character types, while there is a precise balance between these separate interpre-tive spheres, a resolution does not occur. The narrator comments, 'This discus-sion went on, the men accusing the women and the women blaming the men till they left the hotel' (p. 89).

Mickson's chapter plays out an interpretive process in which Frank's and Lucy's character types are *applied* by the onlookers in a way that reinforces their pre-existing opinions about the other sex. These 'readers' extrapolate truths from the story, and they cite specific incidents in Frank's and Lucy's relationship in order to verify their own interpretive positions. Mickson's commentators are select-ing specific figures and *quoting them* in order to apportion praise and blame, *quoting them* to confirm their own opinions about men's and women's domestic roles.

Finding their attitudes consolidated by the narrative, the readers I interviewed in Ghana tended to regard the good-time girl as a realistic portrayal of urban fem-ininity. Such a concurrence between text and reader signals the moment at which a dynamic mass of opinions and moral assessments infiltrate the readers' lived experiences, becoming given, eternal 'truths' (see Eagleton, 1989). Young men's aesthetic evaluations of texts depend upon their shared assumptions about 'correct' feminine behaviour, and they are taking up interpretive positions which speculate about the potential event of their ever meeting such women personally. By essentialising and universalising popular constructions of femininity, male readers are taking up positions within what Terry Eagleton identifies as the 'moral-ideological imperatives' of the time (p. 77), their perceptions vindicated by the repetition of common character types.

Ghanaian and Nigerian readers are unanimous in their refusal of the differ-ences between men's and women's writing. Without exception, the Nigerian respondents to a preliminary questionnaire circulated to 20 men and women in 1995 stated that the author's gender 'made no difference' to their selection of a title. A smaller majority of the 23 Ghanaian respondents selected 'made no differ-ence' (50.4 per cent) above 'novels by men' (33.6 per cent) and 'novels by women' (16 per cent). When the same question was asked of Ghanaian readers in January 1998, all of the 23 women and 73.6 per cent of the 60 men answered 'made no difference'. If the gender of authors bears little bias, and if the text is regarded as equally accessible to men and women, readers themselves adopt clear gender positions during the reading process, finding interpretive anchors within the narrative for the expression of opinions about relationships, money and marriage.

The readers' letters printed in Kwabena Antwi-Boasiako's novel, *The Hidden Agenda* (1995), demonstrate the persistence of this West African reading mode. One reader, Philip Oti Agyen, accepts the narrative as a moral intervention in the 'realities' of everyday life, declaring, 'Yes! Issues raised in this moving novel cannot be ignored. They depict in no small way the realities of life' (Antwi-Boasiako, 1995: ii). Another letter is from a male reader concerned with urban gender roles: 'The author has spoken convincingly to all over-ambitious women who are preoccupied with self-glorification – a situation which often lands them into trouble' (*ibid.*). Antwi-Boasiako's novel portrays the downfall of an over-ambitious woman, Kate, who abandons her wifely duties in order to seek election as a Queen Mother in Ghana. Having been an 'ideal wife', domesticated and submissive, she becomes a political and sexual tyrant in the process of seeking political office. Until she is tamed by her husband, she is presented as being possessed by Satan, going so far as to use *juju* to further her ambitions.

Antwi-Boasiako's readers are recognising situations *through* this text. Through the figure of Kate, 'masculine' concerns about marital life are interpreted and resolved, though the resolution is achieved not with practical advice to couples about relationships and money, but with the symbolic reformation of the errant wife. The plot is laden with relationship dilemmas which, the letters demonstrate, activate interpretive agreement among male readers about correct feminine positions in relation to men.[7] The readers are employing the reading process to affirm themselves as gendered subjects, entering and reconfiguring the text, rather than being entered and changed by the text.

It is important to preserve an emphasis upon the distinct textuality of popular narratives, which are, after all, selected on their own merits, consumed and enjoyed by large numbers of readers. Locally published authors in West Africa 'read' their worlds in a similar manner to the readerships, taking up ideological positions on contemporary issues, licensing their sympathies and biases through their choice of protagonists and plots. Situated within the same network of power-structures as their readers – though perhaps occupying different positions in social, educational and economic hierarchies – authors respond to current debates by rewriting popular narratives; and their texts set parameters around the interpretive process. Tensions, 'misreadings' and ambiguities may of course arise when interpretations overstep the limits of the character types, for texts are 'open structures demanding productive understanding' (Jauss, 1990: 55), but, by limiting the range of alternatives within texts, authors limit the potential 'misreadings' and restrict the evaluative space in which readers operate.

Within any one narrative, the range of characters through whom readers make

---

[7] There is, of course, a possibility that Antwi-Boasiako composed the letters himself, printing them as publicity material to enhance sales of his novel. If such is the case, one can read the letters as a projection of his hoped-for impact and a definition-by-proxy of the author's role.

their interpretations may be limited. Women in particular may find themselves confined by the feminine character types which predominate in popular narratives. Frequently, during the presentation of men's marital infidelities in Ghanaian novels, *two* female types will be juxtaposed. There is an implicit, didactic structure in these narratives. In Victor Amarteifio's *Bediako the Adventurer* (1985), for example, a ghostly double cleaves to the sexually independent good-time girl: readers witness the bad woman making a monster of the good husband, while his wife lingers in the background as a shadowy, brutalised figure, functioning as a moral reference point for women readers and inhibiting their over-identification with the unattached female character (see also Gyawuh, 1988?; Nyaku, 1984; Opong-Ofori, 1988).

In the Preface, Amarteifio comments that *Bediako the Adventurer* was written originally in Twi and was intended to replace the Eurocentric teaching materials used by missionaries in the 1960s in Ghanaian classrooms. It is 'a story closely related to their [local readers'] own everyday lives', he states, and it is narrated in a 'simple and straightforward style which I hope the average reader in Ghana … can read and clearly understand' (1985: n.p.). Carrying this promise of relevance, readers enter a plot in which Bediako's fall into destitution is activated by his loss of sexual self-control to Feli, the seductive stranger.

This pattern of masculine disempowerment has persisted in Ghanaian popular fiction since the earliest pamphlets were published in the 1930s.[8] An antecedent of *Bediako the Adventurer* can be found in *After the Wedding*, the sequel to *Emelia's Promise* by J. Benibengor Blay (1945): here, financial ruin strikes the husband as if from nowhere after he has struggled with his extra-marital desire for 'a stranger whose real character he did not know' (p. 11). Likewise, in Amarteifio's novel, when Bediako's wife is away from the household giving birth to their second child, 'loneliness threw me into the arms of a trollop, filled my head with straw, and brought about, in my happy and prosperous life, a change quite startling in its suddenness' (1985: 52). 'Enchanted' by such women, chaos enters these husbands' lives: their desires spill over social boundaries, destroying their sense of responsibility to their wives and extended families.

The assertive 'trollop' fills the void left by Bediako's wife, cooking for him, cleaning, 'dusting and rearranging nicely all the furniture in my room' (p. 54). Feli's mimicry of the good wife's domesticity is so precise at this point that without Bediako's repeated, retrospective condemnations of her, the label 'trollop' would sit uneasily on her body. However, once she has displaced the first wife, Feli manifests her true nature as a 'peacock woman', purchasing expensive lace, holding lavish parties and emasculating Bediako by insisting that he obey her every whim (pp. 28; 64–5). Meanwhile, Fosua, the ousted wife, waits patiently for her husband's reformation: 'Whatever his mistakes are', she says, 'he is my husband and I still love him' (p. 63).

---

[8] Kwabena Bame (1985: 90, 103–190) summarises a concert party performance with this plot structure (E. K. Nyame's Band, *Man is Ungrateful*) and includes transcripts of two performances with a similar configuration of characters (*The Jealous Rival* and *The Ungrateful Husband*).

Within the space of two pages, two contrasting 'wife' figures have been juxtaposed, providing readers with an example of how a husband can have his masculinity usurped and undermined by beautiful but unruly 'other women'. When women in concert party audiences are faced with the two female types, they often shout out in protest against female characters who reject marriage roles and children in favour of 'good-time' lifestyles (Bame, 1985: 70). Recognising one element and rejecting the other, their interpretations are limited by the text, their judgement of behaviours performed through the two characters made available on stage.

Each repetition of a familiar female type will be a reformulation of it, rather than a simple replication of her previous incarnations. However, by repeatedly invoking the figure of the infinitely patient wife as a counterpart to the good-time girl, authors are plotting against alternative identifications for women readers. Any other, more assertive female characteristics are contained *within* the wife, who is by no means a simple character: in the span of Amarteifio's novel, Fosua oscillates dramatically between forceful declarations that she wants to earn her own income in the market, and submission to her husband's decision to evict her from the house; throughout the novel, Fosua's toleration of abuse coexists with her financial independence and power in the market-place. By channelling women's autonomous activities into the figure of the wife, *Bediako the Adventurer* contains women readers' protests and desires (see Radway, 1987: 213). When women readers applaud the marital reconciliation and reject the good-time girl, they take up the only other feminine position offered within the text, identifying with a tolerant wife who is embedded within its masculine ideological framework.

In contrast to the two feminine character types which split women's interpretations, there is often only *one* figure for masculine identification in Ghanaian popular novels: it is the husband, who is as fragmented as the wife in his oscillations between power and destitution. The husband's primacy as the pivot for male readers is achieved through the figure of the first-person narrator in *Bediako the Adventurer*. Bediako's life-story is offered as an overtly didactic tale to an immediate audience of three unmarried men, who interrupt with moral comments about his cruelty to Fosua and foolishness for succumbing to Feli. Bediako's wife and daughters are excluded from his story-telling session, making it a gender-specific event targeted at a particular constituency of readers. The mature, financially secure hero recreates his life in the form of 'story-advice' to his juniors. Wealthy and wise, Bediako assumes a paternal attitude towards the story of his youth, standing his young self before his young audience, drawing lessons from it and using it to warn his listeners about their future love choices. Interpretive strategies for the young male reader are embedded in the text in the form of this internal audience, which 'reads' the relationship through the figure of the husband. Similarly, during concert party performances about errant husbands, men will shout advice and warnings to stage-husbands, calling them fools for not taking note of the good-time girl's moral deviancy (Bame, 1985: 71).

37

How have women writers responded to the boundaries that these narratives set around women readers? Feminist critics of African literature frequently emphasise the ways in which male authors have 'stereotyped' women's fluid and multiple social experiences (e.g. Oduyoye, 1995; Boehmer, 1991; Boyce Davies, 1986; Ogundipe-Leslie, 1987). By contrasting men's writing with women's writing, or by presuming that women are excluded from dominant ideological positions, these scholars often perpetuate a basic binary opposition between men's and women's creativity. Women's writing tends to be idealised as a consequence: it occupies a separate gender sphere, outside man's world, where women re-script stereotypes of wifely obedience or sexual promiscuity.

Oppositions of this kind often do not account for the currents of complicity, conformity, reaction and radicalism that can be found in locally published literatures by West African women. Women's writing is intricately intertwined with the plots and genres employed by locally published male authors: as Chapters 9 and 10 will show in more detail, they share men's creative spaces and work with the same palette of character types.

In describing women's 'difference of view', one must not lose a sense of the dynamic nature of reading processes in West Africa, where fictional 'stereotypes' are applied in a way that makes them more fluid than the types on the page at first imply. Women writers are actively 'reading' popular narratives about gender, positioning themselves differently in relation to commonly circulating narratives and taking sides in much the same way that concert party audiences divide. This feminine positionality affects the narrator's presentation of bad marriages, female deviancy and romantic love. Rather than openly challenging or subverting 'masculinist' narratives, or writing from marginal, socially outcast perspectives, women writers are positioned *within*, taking up commonly acknowledged interpretive positions and exploring the flip-side of male-authored narratives.

Any 'difference of view' concerns women's interpretive bias: the radical aspect of this bias, perhaps, is that women are articulating their interpretations in writing, publishing popular novels locally – albeit in small quantities and limited editions – which expand upon the current range of character types and alter the definitions of ideal marriages promoted in locally published fiction by men. Authors like Awura-Ekuwa Badoe (pseud. Kate Abbam), writing in Ghana in the 1970s, have embellished the types, making them palatable. More recently, women writers like Akosua Gyamfuaa-Fofie have emerged, who contest and redefine feminine types (see Chapter 10). These women are using fiction to respond to the male-dominated production process: theirs is a risk-taking art form in that it transcribes women's comments, moving the oral responses of audiences and readers into published narratives and expressing shared, but previously unwritten, interpretations of domestic affairs.

In her study of the attitudes towards marriage of single white-collar women in Accra, Carmel Dinan (1983) finds that her interviewees:

> were ideologically committed to the idea of romantic love as being the basis for
> a successful marital union. ... The woman's ideal of the marital relationship ...

was that it should be of an egalitarian, intimate, companionable nature, involving trust, affection and shared intimacies. (pp. 349–50)

The ideal of intimate, companionable marriages contains an assertion of gender-equality which reinterprets the ideal marriages depicted in locally produced narratives by men, in which the good wife is a creature with an infinite capacity for self-sacrifice and forgiveness.

Ghanaian women's narratives are permeated by this egalitarian conception of romantic love.[9] As the comments of Dinan's interviewees reveal, romantic love is a concept allowing women to assert sexual equality and individual choice, to insist upon emotional unity and mutual respect. Rather than pacifying readers with images of male heroism and female submission, as critics of Western romances claim for their own varieties of the genre, West African romances authorise an extensive critique of the sexual status quo. In the light of this, it becomes easier to see why so many women writers have turned to the romantic novel, a nascent genre in West Africa with the capacity to convey sentiments that have been expressed by women in concert party audiences, but suppressed in popular narratives themselves. Dinan observed the impact of these romantic expectations upon her interviewees, who expressed a 'deep disillusionment and cynicism about the whole institution of marriage' (p. 352). Unable to reconcile the reality of their current sexual partners with their opinions about romantic love, these women rejected marriage itself, unable to tolerate deviations from the ideal. '"Marriage in Ghana?" one woman commented, "Oh it's terrible. It's just absolutely terrible"' (p. 349).

A novelette by Awura-Ekuwa Badoe (pseud. Kate Abbam), *Beloved Twin* (1973), serialised in *Ideal Woman (Obaa Sima)* in 1971–2, illustrates the differences between Ghanaian men's and women's readings of relationship dilemmas, and also the way in which women writers respond by inflecting the characters in popular narratives about marriage. The young first-person narrator of *Beloved Twin*, Ayerley, is set apart from familiar social structures from the outset: the novel opens with a 'migration of the subject' (Boyce Davies, 1994: 1) as Ayerley leaves her family in Accra to take up a librarianship in the far-northern town of Bolgatanga. By crossing cultural boundaries into an alien environment, Ayerley's social roles are stripped away, leaving her without orientation. This opening migration scene immediately removes the protagonist from the pool of feminine character types that predominate in popular narratives, which depend for their impact upon the reader locating individuals within recognisable social relationships. Relating only to herself, neither a wife, a mother, a good-time girl nor a daughter, Ayerley exists as an isolated individual with no role models to draw upon.

---

[9] Since its inception in August 1971 the consciousness-raising project of *Obaa Sima (Ideal Woman)* has been inextricable from the concept of romantic love. The editor, Kate Abbam, defined the magazine as 'a medium for educating the women of Ghana and also ... a mouthpiece for them' (editorial, vol. 10, 1981: 9). Most of the problem pages, features and short stories concern pre-marital female desire: they overflow with 'romantic' sentiments, in which the woman's right to choose her marriage partner is stressed (see Chapter 9). Equality is paramount: rarely do the romances written by women include statements about women's 'natural' differences from men.

Heterosexual romantic love is a primary concern from the outset of *Beloved Twin*. Characters experiencing love fuse together, 'panting with joy and wonder – this is LOVE – LOVE about which the poets have written so much!' (Badoe, 1973: 52; author's emphasis). To feminist readers familiar with mass-marketed romantic genres, this may appear problematical, given that 'romantic love' is an ideology aimed at women in the West, which even the most sympathetic critics consider to have defined 'mature female subjectivity' in relation to 'conservative' ideals of wifely submission to initially disdainful, proactive males (Radway, 1987: 15–16, 186).

Contrasting the swift, singular fixing-up process that occurs in Western romances, where the heroine's life-partner is introduced in the opening chapter, Ayerley meets three different potential partners within the first sixteen pages of *Beloved Twin*, each of whom is described in a romantic language register. By expressing a polyandrous version of romantic desire, Ayerley is differentiated from her feminine counterparts in European and North American romances (see Griswold and Bastian, 1987). She cannot be passive, awaiting the transformation of her love-object. Rather, she is forced to make a rational choice between the several men she meets. The first man, Issaka Mohammadu, appears only once at the start of the novel, signalling the heroine's availability, drawing attention to her single status; he is replaced by the 'beloved twins', Alhassan and Fusseini, who represent contrasting types of ideal man. Both brothers love the heroine: one offers love plus material possessions and a 'western' lifestyle; the other offers love plus frugality and Islam. Ayerley is placed in a position of power, from which she has to choose between them. A subtle interpretive act is required on her part, for the challenge is to discriminate between true love and sexual desire. Yet both men's passion has been narrated in the very language that would usually serve to discriminate between romantic and non-romantic desire: if her 'heart gave a pull' for Alhassan, she was 'drunk with joy' at Fusseini's declaration of love (pp. 14, 33).

It is here that Badoe engages directly with the range of character types circulating in popular narratives of the 1970s, rewriting relationship plots from a feminine perspective. Fusseini is discredited as a potential romantic partner through the invocation of a recognisable popular type. Badoe writes a scene where the wealthy Fusseini gives a lift to his past partner, Abiba, driving her away in his sports car. His 'westernised' lifestyle, which seems superficially to be so compatible with Ayerley's, masks the makings of a sugar-daddy, who uses his material possessions and wealth to attract young women.

If they are acquainted with narratives in which a wealthy man competes for a woman's hand against the earnest offer of love from a poor 'youngman',[10] Badoe's readers will be primed for Ayerley's final choice. Readers familiar with these

---

[10] These contrasting types are most common in the locally published Nigerian pamphlets of the 1950s and 1960s. Romantic love was a key concept in the pamphlets, providing the young male authors with a battery of arguments against fathers who wished to impose old, polygynous marriage partners on their eligible young daughters (see Obiechina, 1973; Newell, 1996).

stories are likely, upon encountering the type, to make a 'formulaic linkage with an entire set of descriptions and reactions in earlier acts of reading' (Radway, 1987: 196): thus, Badoe's opposition between two types of man contains the seeds of its own resolution.

It is interesting to note the way in which Badoe has inherited the triadic structure of Ghanaian popular narratives about marriage, in which the protagonist (the husband or, in this case, the single young woman) is placed alone at the apex, choosing between two contrasting types of potential sexual partner. If the heroine's 'migratory subjectivity' has removed her from the stock of feminine types that informs locally published narratives, the two northern heroes embody distinct and common types of masculinity, primed for an application to young women readers' lives.

Fusseini and Alhassan are variations on a theme, made relevant to unmarried readers in Ghana. On the one hand, there is Alhassan, figuring as the honest 'youngman' who quietly but truly loves the heroine; on the other hand, there is the moneyed, flamboyant sugar-daddy, who tempts the heroine with sweet words and promises of material goods (see also Gyamfuaa-Fofie, 1989). Although Fusseini is not married, his promiscuity parallels the sugar-daddy's behaviour: when his 'old flame' arrives in 'a shimmering dress' (Badoe, 1973: 41), Ayerley is ousted by the good-time girl, discarded by her potential husband who drives the woman home and stays away the next day.

Badoe has transformed the two male character types by re-casting them as twins, making them as young as each other, and unmarried, and embedding them both in the romantic narrative of *Beloved Twin*. The sugar-daddy and 'youngman' are altered by these factors, rendered equal in the heroine's eyes. (Needless to say, in Ayerley there is no trace of the good-time girl choosing pragmatically between money and love.) By focusing on the heroine's ability to discern 'true love' and choose according to her inner responses, Badoe renders the ideal wife and good-time girl irrelevant, but retains a masculine typological framework. Her reasons for rewriting these types clearly echo Konadu's aims: in an interview, Abbam (1974) commented, 'I'm trying to influence people to make up their minds'.

A prolific contemporary woman writer in Ghana, Akosua Gyamfuaa-Fofie, also uses fiction to expand upon the limited cast of female characters through whom readers' opinions are formed. Whereas Konadu's orientation was towards his readers' 'own present society', Gyamfuaa-Fofie defines her authorial aims with reference to a future society where men and women will be equal. To this end, as a writer she works for the attitudinal transformation of Ghanaian readers, seeking to change readers' responses by creating new female character types (Gyamfuaa-Fofie, 1995). As the heroine of *Because she was a Woman* says, 'it is our wrong thinking, wrong believing, and wrong talking that defeats us because what is registered in our minds eventually takes control of our lives' (1990b: 84). Gyamfuaa-Fofie is locating fiction in an aesthetic space where value-judgements, concretised in masculine power-structures, can be reinterpreted and reordered: polemical rather than mimetic, her fiction provides a platform where opinions about gender can be reinterpreted from a feminine perspective.

Gyamfuaa-Fofie is one of the few locally published women writers in West Africa to have written an overtly feminist utopian novel. In doing so, she has radically shifted the boundaries within which readers operate. *Because she was a Woman* (1990b) is dedicated to 'all women who are fighting for a true and just course – women who have been able to break through the fields which hitherto belonged to men' (n.p.). The novel depicts the rise to political power of Aberia Afriyie, who forms the Victorian-sounding 'All Ladies Movement', wins a general election and becomes the first woman president of Ghana. In a fictional format, the novel plays out the sentiments expressed in an issue of *Obaa Sima* which appeared in 1995, illustrating the diffusion of current gender-debates through locally published texts. Kate Abbam's editorial stresses 'the importance of bringing out into the open, women who have assumed leadership roles in the society' and the necessity to recognise them 'as NATIONAL SYMBOLS or ROLE MODELS' (editorial, vol. 22, 1995: 3; author's emphasis). Gyamfuaa-Fofie's novel (which was reprinted in 1996) has incarnated the editor's ideal, performing the discussion in a fictional format which allows the new 'national symbol' to succeed unimpeded.[11]

The story of Afriyie's phenomenal rise to power represents an outright rejection of the feminine character types that have been filtering through Ghanaian popular narratives since the mid-1940s. Retrogressive and sexist characters are shown applying familiar characterisations to Afriyie in their attempts to disempower her: in the course of the novel, she shrugs off accusations that she is a whore, an infertile wife, a 'manly' woman, a witch and a good-time girl. Instead, she is depicted from the outset as an ideal woman, a natural leader and role-model for female readers. The heroine's femininity is neither complex nor realistic. Through this character, one can see how Gyamfuaa-Fofie is employing creative writing to intercede in the formation of opinions about women, working from within to create a heroine that repels 'masculinist' texts. Perhaps a residual character type persists in that she is not single, but engaged to a tolerant, sympathetic man called Kusi. As a fiancée, Afriyie cannot be a good-time girl. Kusi tours the country with her campaign team, attracting the label of 'woman' from critics and struggling to persuade husbands that they must exercise 'patience, tolerance, forbearing, courteousness, consideration and understanding' towards their wives (1990b: 26).

Popular opinions about female submission, persuasive as they may be to readers, are abandoned in the novel by the very characters that voice them. Kusi's critics realise their attitudinal error and finally express support for Afriyie's campaign (p. 44); secretly, in droves, the Ghanaian population vote for the female presidential candidate. The novel offers a deeply optimistic perspective about the

---

[11] Perhaps, in the light of this active debate about women in politics, we can see the politically ambitious, misguided Queen Mother of Antwi-Boasiako's *The Hidden Agenda* (1995) as both a re-reading of Afriyie and a 'masculine' re-orientation of *Obaa Sima*'s perspective.

fluidity of opinions and the possibilities for social change; the narrator comments, 'Isn't it amazing how human attitudes change with circumstances?' (p. 77), and the heroine halts the progress of the plot repeatedly to inspire just such attitudinal changes in the readers.

Just as male authors called upon female types to contain women readers' identifications, Gyamfuaa-Fofie shifts the limits around male readers' identifications and confines them to Kusi by presenting male authority figures – representatives of the status quo – in their most conservative configurations. Afriyie's father, for example, is an extreme masculine type, represented as an ignorant, wealthy polygynist who opposes female education and casts out the heroine and her mother for their disobedience. Cut loose from their social positions as wife and daughter, the women define themselves, like Badoe's heroine, in a sphere outside conventional roles, becoming 'a friend to many women but a threat to the man's world' (p. 21).

Gyamfuaa-Fofie seems to be celebrating in advance the attitudinal transformation of ordinary Ghanaians, who ensure Afriyie's landslide victory. The novel focuses on socio-psychological rather than political changes. In consequence, men are constantly urged by the heroine to participate in housework and childcare duties, to change their views about what constitute feminine and masculine roles; similarly, women are taught to recognise their internalised inferiority, 'to think and do things for themselves without necessarily relying on men to do all the thinking' (p. 24). Afriyie's achievements in office – free education, an 'abundance' of 'cheap food' (p. 86), loans to small land-holders and economic transformation – mark the material benefits of the attitudinal transformation promoted in the narrative, holding out the promise of a land of plenty to sceptical readers who may doubt the capacity of a woman to lead the country.

Gyamfuaa-Fofie's heroine is similar to Badoe's, and significantly different from most of the heroines produced by her locally published male counterparts. By writing about women's social and emotional experiences with men, neither Gyamfuaa-Fofie nor Badoe has reason to utilise, without reinterpreting, the popular figures that support masculine assertions of power: while reformed husbands and passive wives do feature in Gyamfuaa-Fofie's novels, promiscuous single women have little relevance to these women's conceptualisations of female fulfilment in work and marriage. Narrated from a 'feminine' standpoint, young women's social roles are redefined. Separated by time, theme and temperament, Badoe and Gyamfuaa-Fofie nevertheless do seem to share a certain positionality, where a gender division separates men from women in their readings and judgements of texts.

Popular narratives in Ghana circulate within a space containing an understanding between narrators and readers about the mode of reception. Locally published authors stage domestic dilemmas which readers can weigh up and apply to their own life situations; readers participate actively in the construction of an aesthetic which, as Kate Abbam says, 'must be about ourselves, you see' (1974).

A reader-centred perspective is vital to complement the 'straight' literary analysis of popular narratives. Readers cannot be homogenised into a single species: during the reception process, distinct, preconstituted reading communities rise up, identifying 'themselves' in the narrative as gendered social subjects and extrapolating opinions from the text. In this receptive environment, popular narratives take on the appearance of rafts rather than shipwrecks, conveying and buoying up readers' active, self-interested reconstructions of themselves.

3

*Ghanaian Readers' Comments on
the Role of Authors & the Function
of Literature*

In January 1998 reader questionnaires were completed by 83 undergraduates at Accra Polytechnic, the University of Ghana in Legon and the University of Cape Coast, as well as by trainee teachers from Bagabaga Training College (BATCO) in Tamale. The ratio of male to female responses was 60:23, approximately three to one, which accurately reflects the national weighting of male and female students in Ghana's tertiary sector (Adepoju, 1994).[1]

Respondents were asked to give their opinions on subjects such as the role of writers in society, the social effects and functions of literature, their reasons for reading the Bible or the Koran and the qualities that make an ideal marriage partner. The following pages contain an assessment of those sections of the questionnaire which asked for people's opinions about the role of writers and their reasons for reading: other sections of the questionnaire are referred to in subsequent chapters.

Undergraduates represent an elite social class in Ghana and their reading preferences may well contrast with those of other literate groups. When undergraduates' comments are compared with the responses of trainee teachers from Tamale – most of whom are secondary school-leavers with aspirations to attend university one day – no significant contrasts emerge in readers' expectations of literature, nor in their definitions of the writer's moral role. Other school-leavers might, however, diverge in their interpretations and expectations of literature.

Naturally, opinions are diverse in the survey, but some intriguing shared views have emerged about the moral role of writers and the function of literature. When I collected the completed questionnaires, several people mentioned that they had filled in the form in the same dormitory and at the same time as

---

[1] There is a great deal of potential for the expansion of this survey into a large-scale study of reading habits in Ghana.

their friends. The sections on the function of literature and the ideal marriage partner had provoked lively discussions. Student accommodation is divided into men's and women's blocks in Ghanaian colleges, so it would be fair to assume that most of these discussions would have taken place between friends and room-mates of the same sex. A consensus has emerged from several of these debates, for certain views are similarly worded on different forms: such repetitions reveal the active process whereby groups of young, mostly unmarried students have discussed and agreed upon dominant opinions about the uses of literacy and literary meaning.

The majority of respondents were aged between 20 and 30. Of the 60 men who completed the questionnaire, 54 (86.4 per cent) were unmarried, four (6.4 per cent) were married and two (3.2 per cent) did not reveal their marital status. Among the 23 women respondents, 21 (90.3 per cent) were single, one (4.3 per cent) was married and one (4.3 per cent) did not specify her marital status. Among the men, 35 declared their religion to be Christianity, fourteen were Muslim, eight were probably Muslim and three declared themselves to have no religious affiliation. All except two of the women named a Christian institution as their place of worship.[2]

When asked which type of literature they preferred to read, men's first choice was 'novels by African writers' (43.2 per cent), followed by the Bible (22.4 per cent), 'novels by European/American writers' (16 per cent), newspapers (11.2 per cent) and the Koran (3.2 per cent). The leading choice in this section was influenced dramatically by the results from Bagabaga Training College (BATCO) in Tamale, for none of the male BATCO students selected the Bible (or the Koran) as their preferred reading matter. Rather, thirteen out of the eighteen male trainee teachers selected 'novels by African writers' as their first choice, a result which altered the overall position of the Bible from shared first place to second place. By the time the BATCO questionnaires were distributed, the Koran and mosque, omitted from previous versions, had been included on the form. This makes it possible to discover whether or not Muslim students in Tamale were selecting 'novels by African writers' above religious literature. Only half of the BATCO students were Muslim, however: the other half declared themselves to be Roman Catholic. Islam cannot therefore be regarded as *the* factor affecting men's preference for African novels.

Asked to explain their first choice, several male students offered political and Africa-centred reasons for choosing novels by African writers. For example:

---

[2] One of the problems with the questionnaire that arose early on concerned its Christian bias. Until a second draft of the form was distributed, questions about an individual's faith referred only to the Bible and to church, without mentioning the Koran or mosque. People's opinions about religious literature may be disproportionately focused upon Christianity as a result of this omission, although thankfully several male students changed the wording on their questionnaire to include references to Islam. Unfortunately, while several of the women who received the first batch of questionnaires were known to be Muslim, none of their completed forms mentioned the Koran or attendance at mosque. It is probable that, upon seeing the Christian bias of the form, Islamic women simply chose not to complete it.

- 'Most of their novels have some African flavour, and I think it prudent to know much more about myself as an African before trying to explore the rest of the world' (mL11);[3]
- 'They relate more to the African tradition, norms, values and beliefs and are thus thought-provoking' (mL15);
- 'The African writers make us feel proud as Blacks. They also talk about African culture' (mL17);
- 'African novels bring to the fore our ways of doing things, perceptions and our culture. Many of such novels ... project a good image of Africans' (mL21).

Alongside this issue of cultural relevance, many men also praised stylistic, textual features in African novels, such as a novelist's use of familiar proverbs and 'simple' language that is easy to comprehend and learn from. These stylistic elements often were cited as part of broader comments about the educational value of African fiction:

- 'In the books of African writers I always feel at home when I read them. Their characters and choice of words, expressions such as the proverbs and such are sometimes familiar' (mT11);
- 'Normally these stories are related or based on the African way of life and as such you can easily relate ideas of the author to your own environment. This enhances easy understanding of their stories' (mT12);
- 'The language used by most African writers is a test to acquiring a mastery in the English language. The proverbs, the syntax structure are just wonderful' (mL12);
- 'I am more at home with African writers in their treatment of theme, subject matter and diction. Culturally, I understand them more than writers outside the continent' (mL16);
- 'The setting is always in our context. They describe scenes which I can easily picture. Native names are used' (mT3);
- 'There are expressions and proverbs. They also relate their stories to real life situations. They also encourage bravery in people' (mT4).

Men who preferred the Bible emphasised that this book contains the Word of God and as such it both precedes and transcends all fictional texts, carrying a truth-value and moral power which outweighs ordinary literature. One male student from Cape Coast wrote, 'the choice one is the source of all things in the world. It supersedes all other literatures. It guides and teaches life' (mC7). 'I prefer to read the Bible to other books', commented another man from Cape Coast:

> because I believe it is the greatest literature book in the world. Not only that; more importantly it guides me in my daily activities. It shapes me to be able to fit into the society and above all it prepares me for the future. (mC2)

---

[3] m – male; f – female; L – University of Ghana, Legon; C – University of Cape Coast; A – Accra Polytechnic; T – Bagabaga Training College, Tamale.

Other people emphasised the 'inspirational' power and truth-value of the Bible. In addition to its status as a text which guides people's behaviour and contains essential truths, the Bible was recognised by many respondents as a practical, advice-giving text, helping them to manage or 'withstand' anxieties and pressures in their daily lives. A male undergraduate at the University of Cape Coast wrote, 'It has the solutions to all aspect[s] of life pertaining to the situation I might be facing, unlike the other religious books/novels. I just enjoy reading it' (mC3). His room-mate wrote:

> The Bible gives me inspiration and courage. I feel closer to God each time I read the Bible and base[d] on this I feel protected and confident to read the other choices [from the list of preferred types of literature]. It is only when one is at peace that he has time for leisure and the Bible gives this peace of mind for other readings. (mC5)

A student from Legon commented, 'The Bible is an inspirational book which gives me courage and confidence in my whole life to do other things such as reading novels, writing, etc' (mL2).

As for the third most popular type of literature, 'novels by European/ American writers', male respondents repeatedly emphasised the 'suspense', 'action', 'drama', 'sensation' and 'thrill' present in such literature; some also commented on the lessons about 'other cultures' they could learn from foreign fiction. They enjoyed the racy language and plots of foreign novels, naming, amongst others, Sidney Sheldon, Fredrick Forsyth and James Hadley Chase as favourite writers. African authors were hailed as political and social critics with the power to transform society through their work; however, suspense was specified as an essential feature of European and American novels, ranking equally alongside edification in male readers' lists of reasons for choosing particular titles.

Women preferred the Bible above all other types of literature. The Bible was chosen by 64.5 per cent of women: it by far outweighed 'novels by European/ American writers' (21.5 per cent) and 'novels by African writers' (8.6 per cent). This result was not affected by responses from any particular region of Ghana. Unlike their male counterparts, women throughout the country, including Tamale, selected the Bible as their favourite text, explaining their choice as follows:

- 'It is a lamp to my feet and a light to my path ... With the study from the Bible, I will be able to compare what I read from the other novels and other books and also see why people behave the way they do' (fC3);
- 'It is the best book to read, since our dos and don'ts are in it' (fC5);
- 'It provides Spiritual guidance and helps me live a good life' (fC7);
- 'As a Christian, the Bible is my constitution and I've all my rules and regulations in it; also, the Bible is always true and shall never pass away' (fL2)
- 'I get so much inspiration from it' (fL5).

Several women referred to the Bible as the text which gives them comfort during times of distress, helping them to achieve a more 'positive' attitude towards life: the Bible 'lifts up your spirit in a special way', wrote one Cape Coast undergraduate, and it 'leads you on in a more positive way of life' (fC8). Given the large quantity of low-cost, locally published religious pamphlets available in the university bookshops and given the great number of women who admitted to reading religious literature, it was surprising that only one person selected 'religious books by African authors' in the first section of the questionnaire.

When explaining their reasons for preferring particular writers, several readers said that they would apply stories to their own lives. Three women named Akosua Gyamfuaa-Fofie as their favourite author, explaining their preference by referring to the educational value of her fiction:

- 'Her books talk about morality and as a child of God, I prefer reading books that teach good morals' (fL4);
- 'Her stories can be applied in real life situations' (fT1);
- She 'writes books which after reading teaches other ladies lessons on how to live in society and go about their dealings' (fT4).

In a similar manner to these female respondents, the men also described how, when reading their favourite novels, they would seek lessons and character types that could be applied to their own life situations. For instance, despite the emphasis upon suspense in foreign fiction, men's insistence upon relevance did not depend upon an author being African: in addition to the many African novelists named by male students, numerous foreign authors were praised for the lessons to be learnt from their fiction. One male student from Tamale commented that, in addition to suspense, Sidney Sheldon's 'lessons are very practical. Sometimes in his stories I find myself in the same situation' (mT11); another Sheldon fan from Tamale wrote, 'almost all his novels are interesting and as such, a true reflection of real life situation' (mT16). A John Grisham reader from Legon wrote, 'Though Grisham's books are fiction, they are very near to real life situations, i.e., his books are not too abstract' (mL5).

Most people identified personally with the scenes portrayed in novels, saying that through literature they learnt about how moral dilemmas in their own lives could be resolved. In a sense, these readers are taking control of their lives through the text. Whether it is authored by an African or a Westerner, readers are projecting their own experiences into books and then waiting, often in a state of suspense, to discover whether the plot or character they have identified with will end in success or failure:

- In novels one learns 'how to go about things if one encounters similar problems [to those relayed] in the story' (mT17);
- Novelists 'teach a lot of lessons to other Africans and they also reveal how others enjoy at the beginning and suffer at the end through their own making' (fT4);
- 'The lesson I normally learn is that there is the possibility of people being

found in the situation of the writer. This sometimes coincides with an experience I had before and so I see how others take it and get over it' (mT3);

- Writers 'educate the society about the consequences of being either good or bad' (fA2);
- 'Most people in my society are able to come out of their immoral behaviours when they read about the disastrous effects of immorality' (mC2);
- Authors 'play a major role in the promotion of morality in that they always victimise people with bad characters and criminals are always caught and dealt with' (mA3);
- 'I've learnt not to love at first sight' (fL7);
- 'Literature is a microcosm of life. It must be able [to] picture life and let me know my weaknesses and be able to change them' (fL4);
- 'I always learn about the downfalls of some heroes and so I take caution from that' (mT5).

Other people learnt 'issues relating to man–woman relationships' from fiction (mC2) and 'self-control in marital problems' (mL1), as well as more abstract moral lessons against 'social vices', including warnings against 'lying, cheating, fornication ... while respect for the elderly, telling the truth, being chaste and all forms of social virtue are encouraged or inculcated' (mL21).

There was a noticeable contrast between men and women in the sections asking individuals to select their preferred type of literature, to name their favourite author and explain the reasons why that author's publications were enjoyed. The majority of women readers listed female popular novelists from Britain and the United States in these sections, while most male undergraduates listed male African novelists published internationally in Heinemann's *African Writers Series*. Chinua Achebe was by far the most popular African novelist named by male readers in Ghana, particularly amongst the teacher training students from Tamale. When it came to describing the moral role of the writer, however, there was no noticeable difference between the attitudes of male and female respondents. Ghanaian students declared unanimously that writers have a vital moral role to play, as readers' 'guides', 'educators', 'advisers', 'moralists' and 'counsellors'.

Again and again, respondents used the same type of language to describe the edifying role of authors. Implied in many of their comments is the notion that the burden of responsibility for moral change rests with the literate class in Ghana, for readers are regarded as active social subjects with the capacity to learn from books and consequently to change their worlds for the better. Among the women's responses are the following representative opinions about authors:

- 'They write about positive things. ... Sometimes pieces of advice can be written through novel or story books. Therefore they play the role of advisors in the society' (fL6);
- 'Writers can influence the society by writing stories which are morally educative' (fL3);

- 'The role of the writer is to write educative books or novels to enlighten us about social values, cultural values and criticise against the social vices without timidity' (fC3);
- 'They can help shape society. They can correct the wrongs of people' (fC1);
- 'At a time like this when the moral values of the youth especially is drastically being reduced, I think the writers should join forces and write more about what a good moral life is worth instead of writing stories about things that don't really exist in life' (fA2).

A similar set of expectations can be found among male students:

- 'Their writings should be able to teach moral lessons' (mL18);
- 'When you read some books, especially those by most African writers, you get to know that it is not good to practice pre-marital sex [and] a lot of social vices' (mT12);
- 'Yes! They write out messages which help to educate all those who are able to read and write' (mT13);
- 'Educating [the] masses on morality' (mL19);
- 'It is through reading that [we] change the immoral aspect of every individual' (mC6);
- 'Their moral roles ... include: the young must or should always respect the elderly, cheating and lying is prohibited, no sex before marriage and the overall educational development of the African child to become aware and appreciate his culture and to inculcate the above social virtues at a very early age so that the youth would become useful to his society' (mL21);
- 'There are some people who are not lucky to be brought up morally. And such people can learn from books. For instance, how you relate yourself with people' (mT11);
- 'They can use their novels as a medium of education on such issues as prosti-tution, theft, obedience etc. They can use their novels to inform the readers of the dangers associated with such habits' (mL1);
- 'I think they should be watch-dogs over moral decadence. They should teach society about good morals, the values of appreciating what we are and above all the literature and history of our society' (mC11).

All respondents agreed that writers are moral educators and nobody subscribed to a belief in experimental writing or 'art for art's sake'. In every questionnaire respondents stated unambiguously that the central requirement of the creative writer is that he or she must be involved in the positive moral transformation of society, to such an extent that one person suggested that writers give lecture tours and speak at symposia and seminars 'on the importance of morals in the society' (mT16). Writers were expected to create realistic, recognisable scenes through which readers could gain wisdom about behavioural standards and become aware of the rewards for virtue and vice in society. In addition, as previous sections of the questionnaire have demonstrated, many people believed that fiction should be orientated towards a *familiar* reality. Whether foreign or local, writers should be able to assess and resolve the problems experienced locally by Ghanaian readers, and writers should use the story form to advise readers on practical issues affecting their lives.

This Ghana-centredness in definitions of the writer's role is intriguing given the number of American and British popular novelists whose names appear, particularly on women's lists of 'favourite' authors. While choosing Danielle Steel as her favourite author, for example, one undergraduate cited a familiar belief in her comments about the role of writers, arguing that 'since so many people read their pieces, they can educate, admonish and advise society on so many issues' (fC9). Another Danielle Steel reader preferred to read these books because of their realism and the warnings they offer against marrying the wrong type of partner (fA2). Whereas male readers of foreign popular fiction chose thrillers and detective stories and emphasised suspense alongside edification, these women seem actively to have *localised* imported romantic fiction by writers such as Barbara Cartland and Danielle Steel. In choosing to read romances rather than thrillers they have selected titles which are relevant to their own situations as unmarried young women at colleges in Ghana.

Despite male respondents' resounding vote that the gender of an author made 'no difference' to their selection of a title (73.6 per cent), only two women writers were selected by male readers: Barbara Taylor Bradford and Aminata Sow Fall. As I argued in the last chapter, such differences in taste and orientation signify deeper interpretive divisions amongst West African readers, for individuals take up self-centred positions in relation to their favourite texts.

4

'Pen-Pictures' of Readers
The Early Days of Ghanaian Popular Fiction

There is a gap in the opening chapter of Ghana's literary history. Contrasting the current, growing interest in reader responses and African popular literatures, information on the earliest readers and authors is sparse and fragmented. Newspapers from the 1920s and 1930s reveal that a large number of 'literary' clubs and debating societies had been formed in the Gold Coast by newly-literate teachers, clerks, factory workers, school-leavers and civil servants. The programmes of events published by these literary clubs testify to the fact that educated members of the workforce would have been discussing the 'thrilling discoveries in conjugal life' published by, amongst others, J. Abedi-Boafo, R. E. Obeng, Kobina Nortey and J. Benibengor Blay; they would also have been debating the controversial marriage ordinances passed by the colonial government, discussing philosophical and moral issues, and reading the tracts and pamphlets circulated by leading political figures. Amongst various programmes of club activities during 1929, for example, the 'general news' page of *The Gold Coast Times* contained the following item:

Sekondi Literary and Social Club (motto: *Absit Invidia*)
Syllabus of Work for term ending December, 1929.
Sept 2: Discussion on 'The proposition that to be wise is better than to be
    rich'.
Sept 9: Address on Noteworthy Friendship.
Sept 21: Dramatisation of the Scene of Agincourt.
Sept 28: Debate – 'Who was more important in the village, the parson or the
    schoolteacher?'
Nov 4: General and social meeting.
Nov 11: Lecture – 'Christian Marriage'.

Nov 18: Short quotations from the best English Authors with vivid explanations.
Nov 25: Discussion on 'Who would you rather be: Martin Chuzzlewit the Master, or Mark Tapley the Servant?'
Dec 2: General and social meeting.
Dec 9: Essay – A Description of the way in which the snake 'grows young again'.
Dec 16: Lecture: 'Man and his Works – Now and then'.
Dec 23: Election of officers.
Dec 30: General Meeting. (21 September 1929: 4)

Despite the existence of numerous other equally fascinating reports, as yet there are no substantial accounts of the lectures attended by these groups nor the literature they read, and no major studies exist of club members' expectations or responses to the pamphlets they discussed (see Hagan, 1968; Owusu, 1970; Holmes, 1972). It is therefore difficult to discover how the first novels were received by readers in the 1930s and 1940s. Additionally, in contrast to the plethora of articles written about the earliest Nigerian popular literature, few detailed critical studies of the first Ghanaian authors have been published. Several articles have been written on popular literature since the mid-1960s, but theoretical frameworks have yet to be developed for fiction written in the first half of the century (see Angmor, 1996).

This short chapter cannot aim to fill all of these gaps. A book-length historical study is urgently required, covering the first pamphleteers, their readers, their publishing enterprises, marketing strategies and outlets. Research is also required into the kinds of interpretations generated by literary clubs and societies in the 1920s and 1930s, the texts that were set on mission school syllabi, the influence of the Bible on readers' interpretations of literary texts and the impact of missionary teaching techniques on readers' expectations of 'secular' pamphlets. Until the gaps in the country's literary history are filled with full-length studies of Ghanaian popular literature and its readers, it is possible only to speculate about the significance of the earliest authors to the attitudinal and social transformations that characterised the first half of the twentieth century.

What can be described at this stage is the broad cultural and socioeconomic context in which the first authors worked; a sense of the predominant themes and a preliminary theoretical framework can be developed through close textual read-ings of the earliest novels; a sense of readers' expectations and responses to texts can be gleaned from author interviews, where available, and from the references made to readers in prefaces, on back covers and in the novels themselves. The way authors present themselves to their reading public and the way 'virtual readers' are constructed within texts give some sense of the social and interpretive contexts into which books were launched. However, such material is sporadic and untrust-worthy: for example, an 'autobiographical novel' such as J. Benibengor Blay's *Coconut Boy* (1970) is an embellished, fictionalised account of the past, written many years after the author gained popularity; but, despite its problematical generic status, it provides fascinating clues about the creative process and the writer's perception of his readers' requirements in the 1940s.

The 'youngmen' who initiated literary clubs and societies in the 1920s and 1930s were, as the popular label for their class suggests, men who were neither chiefs nor members of the established coastal elites. Defining themselves as the 'intelligentsia', club members promised to live *Absit Invidia* (without envy) (*Gold Coast Times*, 21 September 1929: 4) and 'to help one another intellectually and morally' (*Gold Coast Times*, 21 December 1929: 6). In club manifestos, founders inscribed their desire to 'strive to arouse interest in education and to create an understanding of its true meaning and purpose' (*Gold Coast Times*, 29 March 1930: 4). The 'aims and objectives' of the New Tafo Literary and Social Club, established on 1st September 1941, characterise members' ambitions:

> to foster an intelligent interest in the community in all literary and social activities, to inculcate upon its members the advantages derivable from literary and social pursuits, and to educate public minds on all current affairs by means of public debates, lectures, talks and so forth. ... Thanks to the generosity of Mrs Ella Greenwood and Mr A. F. Posnette, [the Club] has a handsome circulating library of over sixty volumes. Above all, this Club designs to build a Club house, tennis courts, a lending library and to acquire a wireless radio receiving set and a Cinema Pathe Projector, to keep its members and the general public in touch with current world affairs. (*Gold Coast Observer*, 22 May 1942: 41–2)

Members of clubs were 'small boys' with high hopes, experiencing the economic effects of Ghana's entry into a global cash-crop economy and witnessing the expansion of money-making opportunities for cocoa farmers, transport workers, traders, teachers and civil servants (see Nugent, 1995). Between 1891 and 1911, Ghana had become one of Britain's most lucrative colonies, emerging as the largest cocoa exporter in the world. Despite global slumps in cash-crop prices and local agricultural crises, by the 1930s a 'Gold Coast revolution' was under way (Rimmer, 1992: 23), fuelled by the availability of a mission school education and new forms of wealth even to the 'smallest' of 'boys'. For the first time, Africans could 'sit at the same table with a white boss and write with a white man's pen in a book previously used only by the white bosses' (Blay, 1970: 15). Having their sights set on the new employment opportunities provided by the colonial regime, these literate youths were frustrated by the racial discrimination they experienced at work. The derisory label 'scholar' was given to secondary-educated Ghanaian employees in the civil service and their promotion opportunities were restricted on purely racial grounds (Boahen, 1975: 136–7). At the core of many club activities was the desire to build up the self-confidence of this literate class.

In a report on the progress of the Abbontiakoon Literary and Social Club, the founder Mr G. de Wilson emphasised that:

> It is of great importance, I think, to run the Club in a way that we can study the higher problems with the aid of good books; in so doing every member would be able to speak in public without fear or hindrance. ... Let us help

ourselves by studying good things more and more, and in so doing we shall be equipping ourselves for the future. Yes, if we study hard to know the real meaning of every matter, we will soon find that, it has opened to us a new world, and its atmosphere has given us greater ideals. ... I will endeavour to keep the flag of the club flying until we get to the goal. (29 March 1930: 4)

Political tracts, newspapers and novels circulated in these literary clubs, feeding the members' ambitions for increased status and helping them to consolidate their identities as an emergent social class possessing the potential to earn relatively high salaries.

Set in the late 1930s, J. Benibengor Blay's autobiographical novel, *Coconut Boy*, describes the influence of one such literary club at Obosa (i.e. Aboso) mines. Seeking an alternative to the 'drinking, dancing and love-making' he witnesses among mine-workers, the hero, Abuo, borrows books from his white boss and has the light of political awareness 'kindled' by the literary club he joins: 'their debates centred around African intellectuals such as Dr Aggrey, Mensah Sarbah, Ato Ahumah, and J. R. Wood' (1970: 24). Inspired by the discussions, Abuo publishes articles in African-owned newspapers and writes a political pamphlet criticising the gruelling conditions, long hours, low pay and poor quality accommodation suffered by employees in the white-owned mines (pp. 54–84).

Literary clubs were ideal fora for political and moral debates of this kind: they spawned reformist political organisations, such as the Gold Coast Youth Congress and radical political movements, such as the West African Youth League (see Boahen, 1975). Club members absorbed and disseminated the ideas of these organisations. They staged lively discussions of social, political and religious issues, printing schedules of events in national newspapers and reports about recent lectures they had hosted. For example, on 22 May 1942 *The Gold Coast Observer* contained an article entitled 'Report of the Debate on "Which is the more beneficial: Reading or Observation?"' (p. 44). This 'interesting and edifying debate' was held by the Cape Coast Literary and Social Club, founded in 1914 with two houses, the Addisonians and the Shakespearians, which were subsequently renamed after two Africans, Dr F. A. Osam Pinanko (AME Zion Mission) and W. Ward Brew (Cape Coast Bar). The 'observation' camp won the day in this particular debate.

Club members also participated in trade union activities including strikes and boycotts of foreign-owned businesses (Akyeampong, 1993: 243). An article in the British *Times* (24 May 1949), written in the aftermath of the economic riots of 1948, manifests the hostility felt by the British towards the class of men which made up the membership of clubs:

In Accra there are a number of hooligans, of the unemployed literate class, who make a practice of insulting European men and women, scratching slogans on unattended automobiles and intimidating law-abiding Africans. ... Responsible Africans would welcome their suppression, but are afraid to speak out, seeing the tone of the nationalist press, which cheerfully promises to hang or shoot all Africans who co-operate with the British, when the latter go. (cited in Jahoda, 1961: 11)

Labelled hooligans, young men of the 'literate class' arouse a revealing set of anxieties among their colonial caretakers. 'Nationalist' newspapers – such as *The Gold Coast Times*, perhaps – are seen to be particularly threatening. The colonialists are witnessing the important role played by print media in fomenting anti-colonial sentiments, for local printing presses are mass-producing the ideas of a frustrated class of 'scholars'.

When the first authors started to disseminate their pamphlets in the late 1930s, a new generation of readers had emerged, defined not by seniority or birth, but by the social status earned from their educational qualifications. These newly-educated commoners, classed as 'hooligans', 'scholars' and 'small boys' by existing power elites, formed an emergent power-seeking class, competing directly for authority with the older local elites who were themselves negotiating for power with the colonial administration (see Nugent, 1995; Rimmer, 1992).

The names of literary clubs and societies reveal a lot about these readers' ambitions as a new social class. Pamphlets were discussed at venues such as the Optimism Club, the Eureka Club, the Cosmos Literary Club, St. Augustine's Theological College Students' Self-Help Club, the Anum Improvement Society and the Kumasi Gentlemen's Club (see Boahen, 1975; Akyeampong, 1993).[1] Politicians, academics and social reformers lectured at the clubs. In the 1940s the lawyer J. B. Danquah joined intellectuals from Achimota College to tour the country giving talks at club meetings, harnessing the nationalist sentiments of urban 'youngmen' who had ambitions for themselves but restricted opportunities within a racist colonial system. In this climate of frustrated personal ambition, one can appreciate the impact of Danquah's call for self-government in his address to the Youth Conference in 1943: 'Liberty is power. Freedom is power. Education is power. Not power in a vacuum but power in an organised community where your capacity, your attainments, your resources can be put to beneficial use' (Danquah, 1943: 14).

The masculine terminology used to describe this emergent class clearly demonstrates the degree to which men benefitted from the new employment opportunities and from the colonialists' blindness to women's farming and trading activities (see Robertson, 1984a; Clark, 1994). Women were not excluded from these socioeconomic transformations, however, despite the titles (and contents) of history books such as *Big Men, Small Boys* (Nugent, 1995).[2] If women were

---

[1] The Kumasi Gentlemen's Club was rather different from the other societies mentioned here: it was established in the late nineteenth century for the 'new social elite, the *akonkofo* ("rich men", "gentlemen") subscribing to British social influence' (Akyeampong, 1993: 112). Its members were considered so challenging to the chiefly order that it was disbanded by Asantehene Prempeh II as soon as he returned from exile (*ibid.*).

[2] Nugent explains his male-orientated project in the introduction to his book: 'men have generally had access to more arenas in which to exhibit worldly success than their female counterparts' and, as a result, the 'bigness' he focuses upon 'is imbued with gender specificity' (1995: 4).

marginalised from the expanding colonial administration, they were not confined to a static separate sphere where their productive and reproductive activities continued without alteration.

In her study of Kumasi market women, Gracia Clark (1994) explores the after-effects of the colonial bias towards Ghanaian men, describing how women filled the gaps left by male traders at the turn of the century, when the British finally destroyed the Asante chiefs' resistance to colonialism and entered Kumasi as the dominant political power. Clark's study is valuable for the way these 'fundamental reorientations' in trading activities are connected with the emergence and stabilisation, on an ideological plane, of 'gender assigned … trading roles' (p. 316). When men left the markets in search of more profitable work, popular attitudes also changed towards market trading. Clark shows how commodity trading was gendered as 'feminine' between 1910 and 1930, considered by men to be 'low prestige' work, providing 'enough for women but not for self-respecting men' (p. 285). Swiftly replacing men as market traders, Asante women benefitted from these attitudinal shifts and were able to reinforce their newly separate 'feminine' sphere by forming trading organisations and electing Market Queens to regulate commodity prices (pp. 316–18).

The highly educated men entering politics, journalism and law in the 1930s and 1940s were the men who produced the first pamphlets for local Ghanaian readerships. As the next chapter will discuss in more detail, one or two elite women also were publishing fiction at this time. In the early 1930s, Mabel Dove (later Dove-Danquah) started to publish stories in the 'Ladies Corner' of *The Times of West Africa* and her short story, 'Torn Veil', was published alongside a novella by Phebean Itayemi in 1947 (see Chapter 5, below). Isaac Ephson's academic credentials typify the profile of many of these early writers, who were separated by birth and education from the majority of the population. Like other members of the intelligentsia, Ephson was born in the early twentieth century into a wealthy coastal family. He was educated abroad, studying at Trinity College in Dublin, at UCL in London, at the *Ecole Université Internationale* in Switzerland and at Lincoln's Inn in London; he entered the Ministry of Trade and Labour in the late 1950s, became a barrister at the Supreme Court of Ghana in the late 1960s, campaigned against Nkrumah on human rights issues and, unlike his peers, only turned to creative writing at the end of his career.

Most of this information appears on the back cover of *Legends of the Lawless Lord*, published locally in 1981. Ephson seems to be emphasising his intellectual differences from the average reader. Writing 'serious-minded' novels for 'the working class', he aims at 'arousing the interests of the layman in the legal process' and deflecting their interests from 'beer, dances, [and the] frivolous life' (1974). As with the westernised protagonists of their novels, many of the earliest Ghanaian authors were descended from 'long line[s] of literary gents' (Sam, 195?: 1), belonging to wealthy families who had for generations been in contact with traders and missionaries from Europe and West Africa. Born between 1900 and 1923, most of these writers were, or rapidly became, members of the professional

Gold Coast elite: they all travelled to Britain to complete their educations, qualifying as journalists or lawyers before returning to the Gold Coast to work and participate in politics.[3]

The class position of early Ghanaian authors and their protagonists contrasts in every way with the authors and protagonists of Nigerian 'market literature' (see Newell, 1996). Unlike the unmarried, minimally educated youths featuring in the first Nigerian pamphlets, the married couples in Ghanaian fiction play the piano, read the 'great poets and authors' and sit conversing quietly in the drawing-rooms of their mansions (Blay, 1967: 72). Heroes have obtained professional qualifications abroad and their stories are narrated in grammatically perfect English prose. These characters seem to be a class apart from 'the workers' for whom the novels were written (Blay, 1974).

Most members of literary clubs and societies in the 1930s and 1940s would have finished their schooling at a secondary level and, in the absence of higher education opportunities, would have been keen to continue reading and developing their skills. There are, however, important links between elite authors and the new generation of readers. Educated in local Christian schools, both groups would have been familiar with the Christian emphasis on monogamous marriage and would have been aware that by opting for a monogamous union, they could assert their status as a class.

Emergent marriage ideologies

Ghanaian marriage roles were being actively renegotiated and codified during the first half of the twentieth century. Mission school-teachers and British colonialists introduced alternative constructions of masculinity and femininity into existing gender ideologies, where marriage often was considered to be a 'loose' institution, of far less importance to men and women than the matrilineage (Abu, 1983: 161). The marriage ordinances issued by the colonial administration were concerted efforts to find workable definitions of 'legitimate' marriages, upon which adultery, divorce and inheritance laws could be based (Vellenga, 1983). National political discussions thus permeated the most intimate areas of local people's lives.

As in Nigeria in the early twentieth century, a monogamous, nuclear family model emerged as the legally 'correct' form of marriage during this period. 'Much colonial legislation on the family', Dorothy Dee Vellenga notes, 'was aimed at clearly defining and strengthening the marital bond in opposition to the lineage bond' (1983: 145). In seeking to clarify the diverse and fluid varieties of heterosexual relationship in Ghana, the colonial government stimulated much acrimony about what constituted a legitimate marriage and, consequently, legal inheritance. Vellenga describes the popular outcry against the Marriage Ordinance of 1884, which recognised the legitimacy of monogamous rather than polygynous marriages; furthermore, the Ordinance ignored established matrilineal inheritance

---

[3] Much of this biographical information was obtained from Richard Priebe's recorded interviews with Kobina Nortey, J. Benibengor Blay and Isaac Ephson, conducted in 1973 and 1974.

practices and sought to institutionalise the patrilineage, declaring that a husband's property and assets were to be inherited by his widow and children to the exclusion of his matriclan (p. 146). Editorials, newspaper articles, discussion papers, personal diaries, pamphlets, letters pages and High Court records testify to the tensions generated locally by the new definitions of marriage (see Miescher, 1997). The debates continued for more than twenty years until the Ordinance was modified in 1909, allowing one third of a man's estate to be passed to his matrilineage (*ibid.*).

Marriage payments were of particular importance to the chiefs who sat on the Ashanti Confederacy Council (ACC), established in 1935 in an effort to regulate the ways in which newly-rich commoners distributed their wealth (see Arhin, 1995). The chiefs were witnessing the new elite seeking to legitimise its status through excessive bridewealth (and also funeral) payments (*ibid.*: 104). Concerned that 'the use of money would destroy the customary status distinctions' (*ibid.*), members of the ACC also were concerned that changes to existing political hierarchies would be accompanied by an increase in anti-social behaviours such as prostitution: marriage and female sexuality therefore formed moral reference points through which the Asante rulers expressed their loss of power.

Such concerns about the links between social change and moral chaos were not confined to Asante chiefs, anxious to preserve a status quo that had already passed. Many of the letters reprinted in Gustav Jahoda's (1959) study of problem pages in Ghanaian newspapers contain a similar preoccupation with the impact of migration and urbanisation upon female sexuality: 'I cannot make my choice at all', one young man writes, for he 'cannot distinguish between a good and a bad girl' (cited in Jahoda, 1959: 183). Other correspondents ask, 'Please, how can I know that she has fallen for me', 'Is she a true lover?', 'Is this love really from heaven?' (*ibid.*).

Confrontations between widows and the husband's matrilineage were regularly brought before the High Court and debates about the definition of a 'legal' spouse surfaced frequently in the decade prior to Independence (Vellenga, 1983). Whenever marriage and inheritance bills were set before the government in the 1940s and 1950s, teachers, pastors and other professionals would release pamphlets discussing the legislation. Also, the national newspapers would be filled with articles and letters discussing polygyny, bride price, marriage and prostitution (see e.g. 'Our Readers' Forum', *African Morning Post*, 1954). Investing wholeheartedly in the nuclear, patrilineal family model, editorials in the *African Morning Post* throughout 1954 decry the matrilineal inheritance system in Akan areas and ask, 'Why should children in a changing world not be allowed to inherit their own father's property acquired perhaps in many instances with the help of the children?' (*African Morning Post*, 4 October 1954: 2).

Christian churches and the colonial government might have transformed the lifestyles of a minority of elite Ghanaians, but the majority of the population would have been influenced in far more subtle ways by the marriage debates taking place in their communities. Weighing up the personal gains and losses of

Christian monogamy, many couples would get married according to the Ordinance but have their unions ratified by a customary ceremony and continue to live according to established codes. In Asante areas at least, husbands and wives would reside in separate houses, earn separate incomes and invest money in their own matrilineages; divorces and separations remained relatively easy to obtain, and in cases of adultery, penalties and arbitration procedures could be sought in the customary courts (see Abu, 1983; Clark, 1993). Although churches pressurised couples to marry under the Ordinance, the Victorian middle-class ideal of the financially dependent 'housewife' caring for her 'nuclear family' remained largely unworkable in Ghana as in Britain. This domestic model might be present as an *ideological possibility* for Christians, but it bears little relevance to ordinary people's lives.

In taking the opportunity to enter into schools, churches, civil service posts and Christian marriage contracts, the educated generation of Ghanaians would have been entering into dialogue with the 'ideological state apparatuses' brought to Ghana from Europe (see Althusser, 1971). Often, urban employees would undertake a civil marriage in order to qualify for married quarters (Price, 1954: 20). For other Christians, an Ordinance marriage would be followed by customary ceremonies; or a man might marry monogamously in church and then marry a second wife according to customary law; or a person's monogamous marriage might be spliced with one of the twenty-four different forms of recognised heterosexual union existing in Ghana (Vellenga, 1983: 145).

The first locally produced novels in Ghana fed into a society where 'competing models of social reference' were being hotly debated (Akyeampong, 1993: 109). Authors seem to be conscious of their status as generators of narratives that will help to stabilise and codify a 'modern' marriage ideology. They offer 'interesting and educative' stories about relationships (Sam, 195?: n.p.); their pamphlets contain 'practical examples [which cannot...] fail to educate' young women and men (Blay, [1947] 1971: 27). In the preface to *Dr Bengia wants a Wife*, first published in 1953, readers are informed that:

> if one reads it one discovers that there is far more to be gained from it than mere entertainment. The author touches on some important aspects of life, and scores full marks with these words which he puts on the lips of one of the characters: 'The more girls played at promiscuity the more men there would be who would not prefer to shoulder the responsibility of marriage, or would take these responsibilities lightly'. (Blay, 1972: n.p.)

Similarly, the preface to Gilbert A. Sam's novel, *Who Killed Inspector Kwasi Minta? (or for the sake of a woman)* (1950?), declares it to be a story 'of the highly interesting type [which] tells how powerless most men are when face to face with Helen's [i.e. Helen of Troy's] Beauty' (Sam, 1950?: n.p.). Clearly, the moral messages about marriage that an author 'puts on the lips' of a character take priority over 'mere entertainment' in these texts.

Novels can be seen to contribute to an ongoing process, helping educated

Christian men and women in their efforts to navigate the ideological cross-currents surrounding marriage in Ghana. The tensions between competing ideologies would have been experienced at a personal level by many authors and readers, for a young couple's choice of marriage ceremony would send out clear signals about their social status and economic aspirations. Circulating in this social context, pamphlets are both fictional and discursive, written to inspire debate amongst 'students of mankind's foremost social problem – MARRIAGE' (Nortey, 1964: n.p.; author's emphasis).

The relationships depicted in novels are formulated very often within the parameters of a Christian marital ideology: rarely is polygyny endorsed or explored as an issue. 'Good wives' are submissive unto their husbands, tolerating and forgiving infidelities, while 'bad wives' commit adultery, prioritise money over love, or fight their rivals openly in the streets; couples co-reside in the same nuclear household, without the presence of extended family members. As in the Christian how-to pamphlets circulating in West Africa, the earliest novelists seem to be preoccupied with classifying different types of potential wife, defining the ideal woman through her behaviour within marriage: 'Women have distinctions in their various classes', Blay writes in 1945, and the 'good wife' exhibits *Christian* moral qualities which distinguish her from other types of women (Blay, [1945] 1967: 115). Locally produced novels cannot therefore be separated from the discussions generated by the British administration as it attempted to codify marriage through legislation covering adultery, divorce, parental responsibilities, remarriage and a widow's inheritance rights.

In a fascinating account of one 'youngman's' emergence as an author in *Coconut Boy*, Blay describes the role of the writer in these marriage debates. The hero, Abuo, creates a formula that will sell his first novel to a 1940s readership. In the process of defining his authorial intentions, he reveals his reasons for writing and anticipates the kind of expectations that readers will project into the text. After publishing a political pamphlet:

> He wanted to write yet another book, something very stimulating – something about the women who spent all their time at the nightclubs. ... That would sell in thousands. The world of men was always interested in anything about women. ... He would write his book with her [Adjo, his fiancée] in mind so that girls could look up to her and copy her; a woman who would be an example of the woman who could inspire broken-hearted men, and build a home with her chastity. ... [Women readers] needed one of their own sex with the touch of salvation – the touch of modesty and chastity and simplicity. (1970: 87)

Abuo's creativity is inextricable from the moral impact he hopes to have upon male and female readers, for this is 'the type of story the modern girl should read – a story with a moral' (p. 90). In the act of fictionalising his fiancée (who is herself an exemplary, fictional character in *Coconut Boy*) Abuo wishes to alter women readers' behaviour and 'inspire' male readers with faith in the opposite sex. The generic 'nightclub' woman and the 'ideal' wife will be versions of the 'real' women encountered by the hero, extracted from society and set down upon the page: on the one hand, Abuo aims to 'create a pen-picture' of readers and hold a mirror up to their lives (*ibid.*); on the other hand, as he creates different classes of women during the writing process, he intends to inscribe 'real' women with moral meanings, hoping to guide young readers towards fulfilling marriages.

Coconut Boy allows Blay to describe the entire process of a popular novel's conception, production, distribution and reception in the 1940s. He even includes a newspaper review of Abuo's novel, which celebrates the realism of the narrative, 'for the people in the story emerge so clearly that readers might well feel they are real people' (p. 93). Beyond realism, however, is the selling-point of the novel, for the reviewer says, 'it is a story with a moral and dedicated to all true and faithful girls' (*ibid.*). Readers' letters 'pour in' to Abuo, who is 'so happy that the message was getting through' (p. 90). Endorsing or criticising the veracity of the characters, Abuo's readers and reviewers share a common assumption about the function of locally produced literature: all of them identify with the characters by projecting themselves into the text, and all of them seek 'a story with a moral' which will guide them in their selection of a marriage partner.[4]

Blay has described the emergence of a popular genre in which the author exercises moral leadership on the issue of sexual promiscuity, aiming to influence the attitudes of a specific, local reading constituency. Abuo's novel contains a plot and protagonists very similar to those in Blay's own bestseller, *Emelia's Promise* (1944) and its sequel, *After the Wedding* (1945). Modest, chaste, charming and simple, Emelia is like the generic 'good woman' imagined by Abuo (Blay, 1970: 88). Having selected her own marriage partner in opposition to her father, Emelia is presented as an exemplary Christian, labelled 'the faithful wife' and set against her husband's flirtatious, money-minded mistresses (Blay, 1967: 121).

Blay seems to be transposing his own life into *Coconut Boy* in the same way that the hero is transposing his fiancée's life into his novel within the novel. Blay is fictionalising himself, offering himself to readers in the form of Abuo as a role model worthy of emulation. Taking the 'real' and making it exemplary, he is positioning his narrative in a space where readers will simultaneously recognise themselves in the characters and also participate in the production of meanings that can be used to transform their own lives for the better. Introducing a new compilation of his two bestselling novels, entitled *Emelia's Promise and Fulfilment* (1967), Blay draws attention to the social function of his fictional characters: 'In

---

[4] Such a view of the edifying function of literature can be contrasted with the prevailing view of the moral impact of the violent, crime-ridden movies arriving in Ghana from the West. In a reprint of an article first featured in *The British Sentinel* in 1929, the *Gold Coast Times* reported that imported movies are:

> a cause of youthful delinquency ... What can be expected morally of a public school boy or girl who has attended the pictures from childhood and seen all sorts of things pictured – murders, robberies, love scenes, and a multitude of other things we need not mention ... is it to be wondered that they imitate what the hero and the heroine of the scene do? (Lawrence, 1929: 7)

Blay's heroes and heroines can be seen in this context as corrective figures, demonstrating the pitfalls of vice and the rewards of virtuous behaviour.

this present world of ours', he writes, 'the part a married woman can play is vital – especially if that part helps her to realise the seriousness of her own responsibilities. Those who would play the role of Emelia will [be] like a beacon light' (p. vi).

Blay's description relates to his expectations for literature in the 1940s and 1950s. Modes of reading and receptive environments will of course shift over time, yet it is surprising to find that contemporary locally published writers in Ghana express similar assumptions about their advisory role in readers' lives. Interviewed in 1997, the feminist author Akosua Gyamfuaa-Fofie says, 'I view creative writing as a vehicle for social change because I think problems must be faced squarely and the appropriate solution sought for and applied'. Echoing Blay's definition of the author and Konadu's emphasis on 'helping' young readers, she continues:

> As a writer, I think my duty is to educate and entertain my readers. I try to create strong female role models in some of my books. As people want to associate themselves with those who have succeeded, they would choose to try and be like the one who has succeeded in a novel. I think in trying to educate people, you have to give them choice and this is what I try to do. (Interview)

Blay's novelettes were in circulation between 1944 and the mid-1970s; Konadu's novels were first published in 1966 and continue to be reprinted today; and Gyamfuaa-Fofie's novels first appeared in Ghanaian bookshops in the late 1980s. However, these authors' comments about the role of the writer are remarkably similar. Since the mid-1940s, popular fiction in Ghana seems to have involved a clear understanding between authors and readers, a kind of extra-textual contract promising that the space opened up by the text will contain practical advice and opinions about contemporary issues.

In the majority of Ghanaian novels published in the 1930s and 1940s, exemplary and errant newly-weds are placed into a shared domestic space. The custom of duo-local residence, whereby spouses live in separate homes, does not feature in the texts. Rather, husbands and wives are shown co-habiting, suffering the tensions and conflicts generated by this marriage model. There is very little character development in the stories. As in the creative process described in *Coconut Boy*, authors seem to be creating *didactic* character types, using them as bases for explicit moral comments about certain kinds of behaviour. Rather than functioning as realistic figures with complex internal desires, named characters are loaded with moral baggage, embodying the Christian moral concepts of 'fidelity', 'obedience', 'temptation' or 'adultery'.[5]

Authors such as Blay do not, however, simply accept and reflect Christian marital ideals in their novels. If they operate within a Christian moral framework, they also voice suspicions about monogamy, conjugal co-residence, paternity and inheritance through the patrilineage. In one of the earliest novels to be published

---

[5] More research needs to be undertaken into the influence upon local fiction of Empire Day celebrations, which often included morality plays and dramatised parables from the Bible (see Collins, 1994).

in Ghana, *And Only Mothers Know* by J. Abedi-Boafo ([1938] 1946), serious doubts are raised about the Christian belief that a wife will remain faithful to her husband in a life-long marriage.[6] Repeatedly, the narrator of *And Only Mothers Know* questions the presuppositions about women upon which the Christian marriage model is built. If a man is to forsake his matrilineage in favour of patrilineal inheritance laws, the narrator asks, how can he ensure that his wife will remain loyal?

The novel opens with an image of pre-lapsarian, pre-colonial Ghana. The valley of Domiabra is described as an idyllic pastoral location unspoilt by cash-cropping, marital conflict or material greed: cottages 'nestled in the lap of a luxuriant forest' and, after each day of subsistence farming, villagers sing and narrate folktales to the children (Abedi-Boafo, 1946: 1). Within a page this ideal is shattered, for 'the advent of cocoa in the Gold Coast mercilessly robbed Domiabra of her rural pleasures' (*ibid.*). Cash-cropping is seen to introduce sexual sin and greed into the self-sufficient village, transforming it into a place corrupted by 'red-haired' strangers who tempt the women and disrupt harmonious marriages (*ibid.*).

Abedi-Boafo represents Ghana's new economic relationships through a Christian mythological framework. Christianity is not presented as a form of mental colonisation designed to deprive Africans of their rural traditions, as later generations of African novelists have implied in their work. Instead, Abedi-Boafo applies the 'Fall from Eden' template to Domiabra, utilising the fundamental Christian myth to symbolise changing gender relations in Ghana. The story of the Fall provides Abedi-Boafo with a relevant, ready-made parable: through it, he can express the sense of moral chaos that frequently accompanied debates about marriage in Ghana during the first years of the twentieth century. Just as Eve succumbs to temptation when Adam's back is turned, the loss of the 'old order' in Adiambra is epitomised by Ama Kuma, who waits for her husband to travel out of the village before having sex with a stranger (1946: 5). Having gained sexual knowledge, Ama commits adultery with several strange men and becomes pregnant. Referred to repeatedly as a 'serpentine' woman, she deceives her husband into the belief that he is the child's father.

From the title onwards, Abedi-Boafo's primary theme is the conflict between a husband's socially sanctioned authority over his wife and his lack of knowledge about the paternity of her children. On the surface, Ama conforms perfectly to the Christian image of the 'good wife': she smiles innocently when her husband, Owusu, returns from his travels and 'performed her domestic duties with exemplary diligence' (p. 6). Masculine power appears to reign supreme when Owusu beats her up for disobeying his orders, thus 'demonstrat[ing] his full control over his wife' (p. 12). The husband's authority is, however, challenged immediately by Ama's revelation that her daughter was fathered by another man.

[6] R. E. Obeng is said to have written the first Ghanaian novel, but, as Anita Kern (1973) points out, Kobina Nortey claims to have published pamphlets 'for local readers' in the early 1930s. Nortey makes a similar claim in an interview conducted by Richard Priebe (1974).

This revelation emasculates Owusu and undermines the gender ideology within which he has operated. His physical superiority withers under the strength of the wife's secret knowledge.

And Only Mothers Know was written at a time when matrilineal family values were being challenged by the ideal of a patrilineal monogamous household, which the colonial government was attempting to institutionalise. The concept of paternity shifts substantially when patrilineal inheritance is emphasised: in the European Christian model of the family, the father replaces the mother as the source of a child's 'blood'.[7] Abedi-Boafo's novel dramatises the problems surrounding this 'modern' concept of the family. Through the figures of Owusu and Ama, the narrator airs insecurities about paternity and problematises the Christian ideal of monogamy. The loss of authority suffered by the hero demonstrates how, for his lineage to be continued in a patrilineal system, a man needs to be certain of his children's legitimacy. Female adultery and a child's legitimacy have become non-negotiable issues in the novel. Both of these, of course, depend upon the capacity of a woman – outside the control of her husband – to live a life of sexual fidelity. *And Only Mothers Know* thus exposes a loophole in the Christian ideology of masculine authority, for an act of faith is required on the part of men: the 'daughters of Eve' must be *trusted* not to deceive their husbands.

The degree of difference between these competing value systems can be illustrated by the ways in which cases of adultery have been dealt with in Ghana's different court systems. Long before colonial courts were established in Ghana, married couples could prosecute adulterous partners in customary courts, which arbitrated and imposed fines. A large number of cases brought before Nana Sir Ofori Atta in J. B. Danquah's *Cases in Akan Law* (1928) concern adulterous behaviour, and, significantly, most of the decisions are aimed at appeasement, through fines and reconciliation, rather than divorce. By contrast, the colonial High Court considered adultery by men and women to be ample ground for divorce (Vellenga, 1983).

Patrilineal cultures tend to regard female adultery in absolute terms: a wife's infidelity undermines the patrilineage to such an extent that it provides grounds for divorce. In inheritance systems where paternity is central, an unfaithful wife holds the power to destroy her husband's name. Faced with the realisation that a woman can be insincere, controlling and disguising the uses of her fertility, the appearance of chastity is no longer enough. Beneath her actions, she must *be* morally pure, like Blay's Emelia.

It is in the market-place *outside* the patriarchal household that Ama Kuma exercises her sexual freedom and liaises with her lover. The market is represented as a centre of female knowledge that cannot be controlled or known by the 'omniscient' narrator. Contrasting the detailed description of Domiabra village and the vivid, direct account of Owusu's physical assault on his wife, the market is a feminine space containing a chattering, entrepreneurial class of women from

---

[7] M. A. Oduyoye (1995: 115) points out that blood is a 'theological' substance in Akan cultures, symbolising not just membership of the family, but an unbreakable connection with the ancient matrilineage.

which the narrator and his male readers are excluded on gender grounds:

> The whole atmosphere was charged with noise owing to the chattering and giggling and prancing of the girls, interspersed with the rendering of the latest High Life pieces, while the women, in groups of two, three and four, gossiped and narrated, by turns, thrilling episodes of their married life. (1946: 13)

The immediacy of the preceding section has given way, not to reported speech, but to a peripheral commentary on female 'noise'. The women's gossip and 'thrilling' stories remain untranscribed. Their words, it seems, cannot be renarrated and yet, as the narrator emphasises, whatever these women are saying about their marriages is characterised by subversive laughter.

The market women's shared stories imply a knowledge of secrets that escape any physical containment their husbands might attempt to impose. However, Owusu has no resources other than his physical strength. Having observed the market scene from the margins, he reacts to the sound of Ama's 'coquettish laugh' by physically assaulting her once again (p. 14). Commenting on this second thrashing, the narrator invites readers to put on Owusu's shoes and morally evaluate the situation: in apparent exasperation, he asks, 'And what would you have done, dear reader, were you in Owusu's shoes?' (*ibid.*). The rhetorical question implies that, for husbands, there are few alternatives to physical force: and yet a man's fists have been shown already to be inadequate for the control of wives.

The gender theorist, R. W. Connell (1987), has argued that in patriarchal cultures, when one encounters repeated references to certain female types, one also finds where the 'dominant masculine ideology' is most insecure (p. 183). Nervously patrolling the boundaries of their social constructs, men attempt to reinforce their power by endlessly repeating static, transparent images of women. Women can then be contained through the range of familiar figures circulating in popular culture (*ibid.*). Defenders of the gender hierarchy return compulsively to these types, reinforcing and repeating their constructions in an effort to control the movements of real women in the world beyond their representations.

Ama Kuma is a perfect example of this 'anxious masculinity'. As we have seen, at first sight she seems to embody the ideal wife, a familiar didactic type in Ghanaian popular narratives. Her spiritual cleanliness seems to be in perfect harmony with her physical appearance. The narrator comments that Ama Kuma:

> proved herself an invaluable asset to the family. ... She did her work with patience. ... She was a perfect model of beauty and the mild sweetness of expression that animated her features made her seem the very embodiment of love. In short, she had all the finer qualities. (Abedi-Boafo, 1946: 4)

The single word 'seem' undermines the narrator's effort to encase Ama in the body of the ideal wife and before this 'perfect model' has settled, the narrator adds, 'but some women will be women as we shall learn later' (*ibid.*). Warnings are introduced into the type embodied by Emelia in Blay's bestsellers, for Ama is a masked woman, concealing a power that 'only our mothers know'. Through the word 'seem', the character splits her own type and escapes from it: as a result, she remains absolutely other, untouchable and impossible to contain. Incapable of replicating the ideal, she threatens the narrator's efforts to place and control her.

In the interpretive section at the end of the story, the narrator attempts to make sense of Ama's duplicity, appearing as a first-person presence in the text and trying to stabilise the marital ideology his heroine has subverted so successfully. The effort fails, however, for the narrator cannot know the 'cogent and tangible reasons for every shade' of women's behaviour (p. 17). 'Indeed', he concedes, 'woman is the hardest and most difficult problem for a man to solve; she looks like the innocent flower, but is the snake under it' (*ibid.*). Abedi-Boafo has failed to settle his narrative down with the simple, sweet-natured wife evoked in the opening pages. Ama Kuma's secret knowledge has destabilised the Christian model she embodied momentarily in the opening pages, and both monogamy and patrilineal descent are shown to be foundering in the face of her promiscuity.

This type of wife exposes the flaws in Christian and colonial definitions of 'legitimate' marriage, but Abedi-Boafo can offer no ideological alternative to Ama Kuma. Closing the novel with an extended commentary which includes cross-references to the Bible and quotations from European novelists and dramatists, the narrator suggests that Ama's failure to be a good Christian wife is, finally, beyond comprehension:

> The supreme idea behind the thrilling story of Owusu Ansah and Ama Kuma is not to vilify the status of woman in human society but to point out ... [t]he futility of man's attempt to penetrate into the secrets of woman, his fitting counterpart. (Abedi-Boafo, 1946: 19)

By accepting the impossibility of 'penetrating' women, the narrator does nothing to resolve the doubts his story has raised about Christian constructions of femininity. Men's efforts to fix wives into appropriate character types, to construct templates and draw lessons from them, are shown to be 'futile'. 'In fact', the narrator concludes, 'woman is an enigma; she is the most difficult and baffling problem confronting the sages of the world' (p. 20).

Unable to resolve the contradictions raised by its central character, *And Only Mothers Know* ends with an anti-climax. Reiterating his anxiety about paternity in contemporary Ghana, the narrator asks, 'Who but mothers know how many innocent men have been held responsible for children that are the offspring of some ragged, dirty fellows!' (p. 21). Unlike the conventional closures of folktales, where narrators can resolve characters' moral ambiguities and tie up the loose threads of plots, the closing pages of Abedi-Boafo's novel exhibit an ongoing inability to find, within a Christian moral framework, a workable solution to the 'enigma' of women. The Eve figure gets off 'scot-free' after her 'inglorious acts' (p. 22), escaping without the death or punishment that attaches to errant women in folktales (see Oduyoye, 1995); the Adam figure fails to regain his domestic authority, unable to retrieve the status quo described in the opening pages.

Unlike Blay's Emelia, Abedi-Boafo's didactic character types have not fulfilled their moral function in the tale and, as a result, the Christian marriage model remains saturated with doubt at the end. The tragic lesson seems to be that however innocent a wife appears, ultimately a man must accept that in a patrilineal system, 'he grows alone, he sickens and suffers alone, and he dies alone for how we come into this world we love ONLY OUR MOTHERS KNOW' (Abedi-Boafo, 1946: 22; author's emphasis). If he adheres to the principle of patrilineal descent, a Ghanaian man might find that he is a stranger to himself, utterly dependent upon the way his mother has exercised her sexuality.

In *And Only Mothers Know*, the story of Ama's infidelity forms a backdrop for the narrator's interpretations of Ghanaian marriage roles. As in Blay's novels, the narrator's world-view is explicit and centralised, expressed through quotations from European master-texts. Through the characters of Ama Kuma and Emelia, Abedi-Boafo and Blay explore and attempt to resolve the tensions that surface in Christian marriage ideals. Unlike *Emelia's Promise* and *After the Wedding*, however, where Emelia is hailed by the narrator as the 'prototype of true womanhood' (Blay, 1967: 130), Abedi-Boafo's novel fails to construct an exemplary Christian wife.

Readers are invited by both authors to participate in the judgement of characters: addressed directly as 'you' and 'dear reader', they are asked to assess whether or not a protagonist's response is morally appropriate. By creating good and bad wives and encouraging readers to comment upon their behaviour, Blay and Abedi-Boafo are actively generating marital codes for the new generation of readers. Working within a Christian model – problematising some elements, adapting and absorbing others – these authors are engaging with the marriage debates taking place in the 1930s and 1940s. Their novels set themes in place for subsequent generations of Ghanaian popular novelists, whose attention, to date, has remained focused almost exclusively upon the problem of finding a trustworthy partner for the journey into marriage.

5

An Incident of Colonial Intertextuality
The Adventures of the Black Girl
in her Search for Mr Shaw

On 11 January 1932, a sprightly 75 year-old Irishman disembarked in Cape Town with his wife at the start of a mission to persuade the white community to abandon race and class as markers of social difference and adopt in their place a revolutionary mode of thinking. He echoed and updated the image of the European missionary, except, in the case of this evangelist, his Book was *The Communist Manifesto* and his target group for conversion was not the African community but English-speaking whites. Armed thus, George Bernard Shaw set about his task without further delay, giving interviews and speeches filled with witty but subversive comments, the full meaning of which often dawned upon listeners long after the author had recommenced praising their country (see Holroyd, 1997: 640–1).

Shaw offended many whites with his revolutionary pronouncements, but he also charmed South Africans with his verbal and physical antics during his stay in the Cape, springing through the rocks in 'amazing display[s] of agility' and 'striding about, with his beard blowing in the breeze' (*CT*, 14 Jan 1932: 7).[1] Levels of concern were therefore intense when, at the end of the couple's five-week stay, as they travelled east to Knysna, Shaw crashed their car in the veld: whilst he cleared 'a ditch; a hedge; a fence; a formidable bunker; and several minor cross-country obstacles', he left his wife with serious injuries which delayed their departure by five weeks (*CT*, 22 Feb 1932: 9).

It was during Charlotte's recovery period that Shaw commenced and completed the satirical short story which forms the starting point for this chapter. *The Adventures of the Black Girl in her Search for God* (1932) is modelled on John

70

Bunyan's *Pilgrim's Progress* (1684) and also on Voltaire's *Candide* (1759), both of which are embedded in the text as points of reference and departure. Shaw's European models, one devotional and the other satirical, are both 'spiritual quest' narratives, men-with-a-mission stories, containing protagonists who engage with the problems of Christian salvation and move through symbolic landscapes filled with emblematic characters. Additionally, both the *Pilgrim's Progress* and *Candide* are notably non-realistic and didactic, and they would for that reason have appealed to an ideologue seeking to replace the status quo with a vision of future perfection.

Shaw's *Adventures* reworked these early literary models, but as we shall see, the 'intertextual' quotations did not stop there. The great writer's visit to South Africa stimulated literary activity in at least one other quarter. Within two years of its publication in Britain, the *Adventures of the Black Girl in her Search for God* itself became the model for a further satirical narrative, this time written by the Ghanaian woman writer, Mabel Dove, whose prolific literary output in the 1930s and 1940s has only recently started to be appreciated by academics (see Opoku-Agyemang, 1997). The latter part of this chapter will focus on Dove's fascinating, playful reply to Bernard Shaw's text, entitled *The Adventures of the Black Girl in her Search for Mr Shaw*: this story was serialised under Dove's pseudonym, 'Marjorie Mensah', in the 'Woman's Corner' of *The Times of West Africa* between September and October 1934, and it has yet to be considered by literary scholars. An examination of Dove's appropriation of Shaw's *Adventures* sheds light on the function of western 'intertexts' in early West African literature, and greatly assists in our understanding of the role played by early Ghanaian readers in the reception and regeneration of European literary texts.

In his own version of Bunyan's and Voltaire's narratives, Shaw transforms the landscape and the protagonist, creating an African setting and an African girl to convey his challenge to the 'pseudo Christianity of the churches' (p.18). The intelligent and curious heroine of Shaw's tale has been taught to read the Bible by an incompetent missionary and, frustrated by her teacher's intellectual limitations, has set off alone in search of the answer to her question, 'Where is God?'. The heroine's experiences 'could hardly have happened to a white girl', the author explains in his Preface to the 1934 edition, for 'the missionary lifted her straight out of her native tribal fetichism into an unbiased contemplation of the Bible with its series of gods marking stages in the development of the conception of god' (p.18). In the manner of Bunyan's pilgrim, she carries the Bible on her journey (the pages are torn out by the wind with the passing of each stage); to symbolise her racial and ideological difference from white Christianity, and to inject humour into the narrative, she also carries in the other hand a small South African weapon, a *knobkerry*, with which she attacks and destroys all of the false Western gods and false Western prophets set up in the jungle by European Christians. Only the last and latest version is spared, for here God is conceived as 'an eternal but as yet unfulfilled purpose' (p.69). This Marxist-Hegelian idea is described by a red-haired Socialist Irishman who bears more than a passing

71

resemblance to Shaw in his youth, and whom the black girl marries at the end of the story.

These themes encapsulate the message about Christianity which Shaw repeatedly delivered to South Africans during his mission in the country. The black girl is a walking, talking resolution of many of the issues raised by the author in his interviews and public speeches. Fully aware of the mainstream Christianity practised by urban whites, Shaw made 'true religion' the theme of his visit. His public statements were peppered with Christian metaphors, and he took every opportunity to reinterpret Christian doctrine from a revolutionary perspective. In 1930s South Africa, he argued, the primary tenets of Christianity had been distorted, for 'no one believes here that the black man is the equal of the white, that the professional man is the equal of the retail shopkeeper, equal in the sight of God' (*CT*, 12 Jan 1932: 9). By contrast, he told reporters on *The Cape Times* that 'Jesus Christ was a very good Communist', and 'true religion ... is to be found only in Russia', where the principle of universal equality can be seen to prevail in all sectors of society (*ibid.*). This Christianised version of Russian Communism must have met with some general acceptance in South Africa, for *The Cape Times* devoted an entire issue of its illustrated supplement to images of Russia on 17 March 1932.

Shaw brought to South Africa a radically egalitarian conception of Christianity, especially designed to challenge the moral foundations of the racial and class categories that existed in the country. Of the particular reforms he proposed, the most controversial was inter-marriage between whites and blacks as the ideal solution to the 'race problem'; he also proposed the replacement of urban slums with quality accommodation which should be suitable for habitation by the white elite who would be expelled from their villas in the revolution. The former theme was especially distasteful to many in his 1930s audience, given the increasing racial segregation in South Africa and the influence of pseudo-scientific Nazi ideas about race purity. In addition to erasing these physical and material markers of difference, during his time in South Africa Shaw repeatedly prophesied the elimination of the wealthy white class. Whilst he did not go so far as to predict black revolution, perhaps fearing the repression that might arise from such comments (Holroyd, 1997: 643), he repeatedly argued that, in the master–servant dialectic that characterised this society, the coloured worker had started to possess a 'dangerous' capacity to transform the master into 'an idler and a parasite, a weakling and an imbecile' (*CT*, 8 Feb 1932: 10). Given the degeneracy of the dependent, wealthy class, Shaw warned that on the day of reckoning a virile black civilisation would rise up in place of white (*ibid.*).

Neither colonialism nor mission Christianity on the continent as a whole was explicitly criticised by Shaw during his South African tour. Nevertheless, his comments reverberated northwards through British-occupied territories, reaching the pages of newspapers in Nigeria, the Gold Coast (Ghana) and Sierra Leone. In particular, Shaw's promise that 'the next civilisation will be a Negro civilisation' went down well with anti-colonial nationalists in West Africa whose cultural struggle was entering a new phase in the 1930s (*CT*, 8 Feb 1932: 9). Fully aware of Shaw's outspoken anti-racism, journalists in Anglophone territories expressed the hope that, on his next visit to the continent, 'Mr Shaw will include West Africa in his itinerary. We have been much maligned in the past and in the present by [writers such as] Mr Ward Price' (*TWA*, 29 Sept 1934: 4).

Shaw's egalitarian ideas about religion, race and class are embodied in the heroine of *The Adventures of the Black Girl in her Search for God*: the 'black girl' is an emblematic protagonist who possesses all of the intellectual vitality and rebelliousness of other Shavian heroines. She responds to her teacher's Christian doctrine with 'unexpected interrogative reactions' and, in a spirit of dissatisfaction, strides 'right off into the African forest in search of God, [taking...] the bible with her as her guidebook' (p.22). Each of the images of God she encounters along the way tries to persuade her that it is the true Christian deity, but falls foul of her questions and is destroyed or chased away.

While preserving the didactic tone of the spiritual quest narrative, Shaw also historicises the Bible and creates separate characters from its various conceptions of God. In this way, he makes the Holy Book answerable to humanity. Abstract religious concepts are made into 'real' men who, when pressed on ethical issues, become ludicrous or detestable. For example, at one point the heroine encounters a group of people carrying heavy churches on their backs, bowing under their burdens as in Dante's *Purgatory* and Bunyan's *Pilgrim's Progress.* Rather than accepting their sins and seeking the removal of their burdens, however, these characters throw stones at one another, defending their cargoes, each crying 'mine is the true church' (p.44).

The comic aspect of Shaw's tale is the manner in which diverse doctrines and representations of God are incarnated as human characters and then subjected to cross-examination by the sceptical black girl. The pageant develops: we meet the stereotypical Old Testament God, 'a well-built aristocratic looking white man with handsome regular features, an imposing beard and luxurious wavy hair' who kills the black mamba which has been his loyal messenger and insists that the black girl sacrifice her first child on his altar (p.23); the second image is that of an 'oldish gentleman' with a 'soft silvery beard and hair, also in a white nightshirt', who invites reasoned debate with the heroine, but becomes furious at the first hint of criticism (p.25). When humanised in this way, Christian gods are exposed as flawed, petulant and autocratic old men with no sense of human rights or equality. 'There are too many old men pretending to be gods in this forest', says the black girl who increasingly occupies the status of messiah in the text (p.27). Each time she raises her *knobkerry* to smash another idol, the wind whips thirty more pages from her Bible until finally she is faced, like Candide, with the earthy reality of a vegetable patch, and with her marriage to the red-haired Irishman and the demands of her 'charmingly coffee-coloured' children (p.69).

Shaw's heroine is the product of a European literary tradition: she resonates with references to similar tales of singular adventurers in hostile environments. The black girl is a Sancho Panza in a world filled with Don Quixotes; she is the isolated sceptic who exposes the flaws of European Christianity; and she is a misfit in the parable of which she is protagonist, for she takes biblical concepts literally and tests them by attempting to realise them in her own empirical world. Despite the tale's immersion in European literature, the heroine is not a 'godless' or 'savage' African in the manner of Joseph Conrad's natives, for she is shown clinging tightly to her Bible and *wanting* to find the true religion. In fact, the black girl's moral strength is shown to derive from her racial difference, which is symbolised by her *knobkerry* and vividly revealed by the illustrations which accompany each scene. Physically at least, this heroine is obviously African, described as 'a fine creature' who makes the 'white missionary folk seem like ashen ghosts' (p.22).

There is only one explicitly 'political' moment in the *Adventures*, when the black girl condemns a group of white explorers for their invasion and enslavement of Africa: 'you are heathens and savages', she cries, usurping their imperialist vocabulary to describe the European involvement with the continent (pp. 46–53). Except for this diatribe, however, colonialism is not addressed in the text and race seems to be more symbolic than real. The heroine's racial difference signifies her religious neutrality rather than the plenitude of her *own* local culture: she is an individual who is unincumbered by two thousand years of Western ideas, but she seems not to be encumbered with distinctive ideas of her own.

The Adventures of the Black Girl was published in time for Christmas 1932, containing elegant illustrations by John Farleigh, with a cover designed to resemble a greetings card. Massively popular and controversial in Britain, the first print-run of 25,000 sold out immediately and was followed by five additional impressions before the end of 1932. Sales had reached 100,000 by the summer of 1933, and copies had reached worldwide readerships; the book attracted a banning order in Ireland on grounds of indecency and obscenity, and was praised by Gandhi, who admired its spirituality (Holroyd, 1997).

Besides the debate it caused in its own right, one of the most remarkable side-effects of the *Adventures* was the successor it generated in 1934. Several thousand miles to the north-west of Knysna, where Shaw's heroine was conceived, the Ghanaian journalist Mabel Dove (also known as Dove-Danquah) responded to the book by writing her own version of it, superimposing her own 'black girl' onto Shaw's template. However, in the process of mimicking Shaw's tone and adopting his episodic structure, Dove also challenges the very text that gave her inspiration, for as we shall see, her heroine critiques Shaw's character in a variety of ways.

Mabel Dove was the only woman in the Gold Coast, if not in West Africa, to publish newspaper articles on a regular basis throughout the 1930s.[2] As with many other newspaper correspondents at the time, she was not a professional journalist, continuing to work throughout the decade as a clerk in the offices of

---

[2] Dove achieved another 'first' in 1954 when she was the only woman to be elected to the new Ghanaian National Assembly, having won the Ga Rural Constituency for Kwame Nkrumah's Convention People's Party (CPP).

various European shipping firms, producing her daily column in her spare time (see Denzer, 1992).[3] All of Dove's work for *The Times of West Africa* was produced under cover of the pseudonym 'Marjorie Mensah', a name that was created for the women's page in 1931 by the managing directors of the company.

An acrimonious court case brought against the *Times* in May 1934 by Kenneth MacNeill Stewart, former editor-in-chief of the paper, reveals that 'Marjorie Mensah' was used simultaneously by at least two journalists between 1931 and 1933 (see *TWA*, 11 May 1934: f.p.). MacNeill Stewart's case was precipitated by the release in the United Kingdom of an anthology of 'Marjorie' articles entitled *Us Women*, and he claimed the royalties and proceeds from sales on the grounds that he was the author of *all* items appearing in the 'Ladies Corner' since its inception.

One of the merits of the court case was that evidence was furnished – in the form of original manuscripts by Mabel Dove – which proved that MacNeill Stewart was responsible for the production of only one-eighth of articles for the women's page in 1931, averaging less than one per week: his sweeping claim to the authorship of *all* 'Marjorie Mensah' articles was thus disproved (*TWA*, 11 May 1934: f.p.). In addition, given that MacNeill Stewart was in Togoland for a considerable proportion of 1932 and 1933, the court also concluded that he would have been hard-pressed to produce material for the women's page for much of this time, leaving 'other writers, especially Miss Mabel Dove', in charge of the column (*ibid.*).

'Marjorie Mensah' may have been invented by press-men and partially controlled by the editor-in-chief, but clearly she was 'vocalised' by a woman journalist for a substantial proportion of the years between 1931 and 1933. By early 1934 MacNeill Stewart had left the staff for good, leaving Mabel Dove solely responsible for occupying and fleshing out the heroine of the piece. 'Marjorie Mensah' gained a massive following in the country with her ethical essays and didactic commentaries on gender morality: 'what has Marjorie got to say today?' often preceded enquiries about the content of editorials (*TWA*, 10–11 July 1931: 4). In fact, readers were so willing to believe in the physical body behind the name that she continued to receive (and rebuff) proposals of marriage from readers long after the court case in 1934 had established that she did not actually exist.

'Miss Marjorie Mensah', as developed by Dove, is a flirtatious, opinionated, highly educated member of the African elite who has studied literature at Girton College in Cambridge and music at the Royal Academy in London in addition to attending many pleasant soirées at rural mansions owned by the English gentry.[4] Given these 'English' cultural reference points, it is not surprising that she expresses strongly anglicised views about monogamy, 'culture' and good

---

[3] The column was entitled the 'Ladies' Corner' until April 1933, when it was renamed the 'Women's Corner'.

[4] 'Marjorie Mensah' makes these claims in the *Times of West Africa* on 30 April 1931 (p.2). There is, however, no record of any West African woman at Girton College between 1914 and 1930. I am indebted to Kate Perry, the archivist at Girton, for making available many decades of College records and photograph albums.

manners, but she is neither a snob nor an anglophile: her upper-crust morality does not undermine her politically located insistence on the importance of racial and sexual equality throughout colonial West Africa. Dove's persona castigates the racism of European women on the West Coast of Africa (*TWA*, 30 April 1931: 2); she calls repeatedly for women's equal rights with men in the Gold Coast education system; she criticises colonial governors for their repressive ordinances; and she regularly rails against the exploitative behaviour of local dandies – 'slim dreadfuls', as she calls them – who seduce young ladies with promises of marriage, then abandon them to the stigma of unmarried motherhood (*TWA*, 1 May 1931: 2).

As with the 'literary and social' clubs that burgeoned in Ghana in the 1920s and 1930s, initiated by secondary school-leavers bent on improving their life-chances, Mabel Dove's column promoted educational self-help, for women in particular. 'I have observed with some degree of dismay, that many of our young girls are taking to reading books that can do them no earthly good, and I think that while it is yet early the practice should be discouraged', she writes (*TWA*, 26 Jan 1935: 2). Constantly bemoaning the absence of women-only debating societies, and complaining vociferously about local women's preference for romantic novels and 'penny dreadfuls', 'Marjorie Mensah' sets forth to be the new role model for women, to be the prototype of literary cultivation who will fill the culture-gap in Ghana and save it from the shame of colonial 'backwardness'.[5] 'To be well-read is to be as conversant with many worth-while books – books written by the masters of literature all over the world', she insists (*TWA*, 30 June 1934: 4).

Concerned less with imparting news stories than with achieving the intellectual improvement of her readership, Dove chose English-language literature as her educational tool, and created in the character of 'Marjorie Mensah' a larger-than-life schoolmistress figure who set forth to refine readers' literary tastes and impart literary appreciation skills to them. 'I would like to see our girls reading more of the works of the really classical authors', Marjorie writes, setting forth a reading list for Ghanaian women which includes *Jane Eyre*, *Pride and Prejudice* and *Wuthering Heights* alongside poems by Ella Wheeler Wilcox and Phillis Wheatley (*TWA*, 22 Jan 1932: 2). Such literature is praised for being 'true to reality and worthy of emulation', containing 'none of the false heroine sort of stuff like such things that we read of in the Penny Dreadfuls' (*ibid.*).

Combined with Marjorie's reverence for British institutions such as the aristocracy, Cambridge University and Selfridges, reading activities such as those

---

[5] Marjorie's success as role model and motivator of women is revealed in a letter she received from a young woman who has clearly grappled with great hesitations about her own literary abilities before writing to the *Times of West Africa*. 'Even as I write now I feel almost sure that some wheels shall tread this my little attempt', she begins, quickly gathering confidence as she praises women who 'are holding up their own in spheres of Law, medicine, teaching etc': the letter concludes by claiming that the 'literary activities' of Gold Coast women 'are, I venture to say, superior to some of the men' (*TWA*, 11 May 1931: 4). Another female correspondent praises 'the nourishing manna from Marjorie' which is created 'to improve and educate us – the women folk in this country' (*TWA*, 11 Aug 1932: 3).

described above seem to bear the hallmark of colonial subservience to the metropolitan culture. As with her author, 'Marjorie Mensah' clearly belongs to that class of Africans who had, in J. E. K. Agovi's words, 'been educated and trained to uphold the best in European civilisation in the Ghanaian environment. Hence whatever the whiteman did, they could do the same, if not better' (1990: 249). To this end, in an article on dress, Marjorie proclaims without embarrassment, 'We should at least try to imitate our white friends, if it is our intention to follow fashion and be always in the correct way of things' (*TWA*, 8–9 April 1932: 2). Similarly, her summaries of British novels and elegant discourses on the beauty of poetry seem to be a confident promotion of the colonial culture, designed to activate what she represents as Ghanaian readers' underdeveloped aesthetic sense. Such texts will, she argues, 'give us a fine institution [i.e., instruction] in certain phases of life that are true to reality and worthy of emulation' (*TWA*, 22 Jan 1932: 2). At no point in the daily literary appreciation classes staged in the Women's Corner does Dove's persona praise indigenous cultural productivity. As with Bernard Shaw's black girl, 'Marjorie Mensah' seems to be a heroine with no cultural foundations of her own, a figure keen to carry others' churches because she has no spiritual load of her own.

What prevents 'Marjorie Mensah's' literary activities from conforming unambiguously to this model of mimicry and subservience is the *pedagogic purpose* which drives Dove in her use of English literature. Rarely are literary texts simply reviewed or summarised in the column, treated as autonomous works of art existing for the reader's pleasure. 'All writing should aim at being instructive and should be a model in style', readers are informed on a regular basis (*TWA*, 27 Feb 1935: 2). To this end, English literary classics are used as Marjorie's starting point whenever she wishes to stir up opinion and provoke debate about contemporary local issues: and she practises what she preaches, writing in 'stylish' English and always emphasising the 'instructive' elements of her selected texts.

Marjorie makes a habit of praising her chosen authors, but she also quietly develops her own range of value judgements based upon the primary material. Discussing Dickens, for example, she applauds his 'sublimity of wit and marvellous wealth of humour', and considers his writing 'unsurpassed in the history of English literature'(*TWA*, 19 Feb 1932: 2). Crucially, within a few weeks of this commentary she has located living, local examples of a Dickens character: in criticising Ghanaian women who lack the ambition to work, she remarks, 'There are many of us who are just resting on our cars waiting, like that imperishable character in Dickens, Micawber, for something to turn up – preferably a good offer at the altar' (*TWA*, 7 April 1932: 2). At other times she cites from *The Pickwick Papers* in order to advise readers on the benefits of forgiveness. Here we are witnessing a distinctive form of intertextual quotation in which the source text is used as a model to *license* the personal opinion which follows in its wake. 'Marjorie Mensah' can pass moral judgement on local women *because* she has Charles Dickens at her fingertips; in addition, she seems to assume, a priori, the existence of a shared local aesthetic in which narratives exist *in order to be* extended by readers and applied to their social lives (see Chapters 1 and 2).

Dove perfected 'Marjorie Mensah's' quoting technique over the years, and Marjorie took on the characteristics of a reviewer and critic, offering synopses of the novels she had read. As the months passed by, her column became a fascinating storehouse of resumés and commentaries with a distinctly local flavour. When Dove's character holds forth about local issues in her essays and intervenes in debates about morality and social change, her opinions are expressed *via* the British literary canon. In this process of 'working over' her favourite texts, she extracts only those episodes and characters that are relevant to her own argument about her own local culture. Metropolitan narratives are treated as envelopes containing slips of wisdom and moral lessons to be extracted and appreciated by readers. Such an interpretive mode reveals the existence of a complex, locally determined process of reader reception which is far removed from a slavish promotion of colonial literary culture (see Chapter 1).

Beyond the 'mimicry' of Western values described by critics such as Agovi, a number of more detailed cultural and aesthetic points arise from Dove's choice of master-texts. Does Dove's preference for specific authors and genres also imply the existence of distinctive local practices for reading and responding to foreign material? Repeatedly, readers of the women's page are reminded that 'good', valuable literature must be that which is useful and relevant in their daily lives, for novels, 'although purely fiction, still must have some resemblance to similar attitudes in every day life. If it has no such element about it in fact, it loses its interest and colour and, of course, we will not be able to derive anything from it' (*TWA*, 2 Feb 1932: 2).

In her non-fictional (and semi-fictional) commentaries on literature, 'Marjorie Mensah' embellishes and personalises narratives by drawing them into local debates, thus performing an active, creative role in the reception of English-language material.[6] By and large, the type of text which lends itself most readily to her process of assimilation is non-realist: didactic, structurally fragmented, poetic or polemical texts are referred to repeatedly in the column. Alongside these formal features, in thematic terms the literature recommended in the Women's Corner tends to be morally engaged with issues of social reform and sexual exploitation, staging characters' struggles for equal rights in societies sharply divided by race, class, or gender discriminations.

Such structural and thematic qualities lead us full-circle back to Bernard Shaw's *The Adventures of the Black Girl in her Search for God*, which can now be

---

[6] Such appropriations appear perfectly acceptable locally, if only because of the lack of correspondence on the issue: 'Marjorie Mensah' received a large post-bag and her readers were willing to send in negative as well as positive comments about her articles. In fact, in one instance of large-scale reader commentary on one of her early serials, readers complained about the *lack* of relevance of the story to their daily lives. Marjorie was compelled to offer an interpretation of the tale which placed it in terms of the local environment. 'To begin with', she writes, the protagonists 'represent two characters that we meet in the streets [in] every day life. The setting, I may mention, is purely African, and we of the soil are consequently better in a position to follow the trend than persons not acquainted with indigenous idiosyncrasies' (*TWA*, 9 June 1931: 2).

appreciated as an ideal text for inclusion in Mabel Dove's column. Parabolic, episodic, moralistic and non-realist, Shaw's text lends itself immediately to Dove's critical method. Shaw's egalitarian, revolutionary politics also must have appealed to the writer whose constant injunction to her readers was 'Act Now!'. Interestingly, Shaw's narrative has *already* been appropriated and reworked by the time it is first mentioned in September 1934, in the first of the series entitled *The Adventures of the Black Girl in her Search for Mr Shaw* (*TWA*, 25 Sept 1934: 2). Shaw's text becomes Dove's daily template for the next seven weeks, as she shifts away from her usual activity of summarising plots to the activity of *constructing* a new narrative from (or upon) an original text.

In a brief preamble before the story-proper, 'Marjorie Mensah' criticises her mentor's heroine, stating at the outset that, 'The "Black Girl" as represented by Mr Shaw corresponds with a very old type long gone out of date' (*TWA*, 25 Sept 1934: 2). While the didactic, episodic form of Shaw's *Adventures* is retained, Shaw's symbolic heroine cannot be admitted into the vicinity while a whiff of 'native tribal fetishism' lingers around her (Shaw, 1934: 18). 'The object of my present attempt', Marjorie continues, 'is to give a picture of a *modern* black girl – as she is *today*, the product of a missionary school with some considerable English polish, who after having read Bunyan's *Pilgrim's Progress*, and to be more *up-to-date*, Mr Shaw's "Black Girl In Her Search for God", considers also undertaking a similar search for Mr Shaw' (*TWA*, 25 Sept 1934: 2; emphasis added). As the triple reference to western 'modernity' indicates, there is nothing 'tribal' about this educated, urbane Ghanaian heroine. Gone is the *knobkerry*, with which the original black girl made sport amongst the European gods: in its place the heroine carries a tennis racquet, symbol of her cosmopolitan sophistication, which she flourishes under the noses of the Europeans she meets, 'as though in imitation of a famous stroke lately in vogue at Wimbledon' (*TWA*, 9 Oct 1934: 2). Gone too is the Bible, as carried by Bunyan's and Shaw's travellers: rather blasphemously, it is replaced with a copy of Shaw's *Adventures*, a text which the heroine 'treasured nearly as much as the Bible' and which again signifies her 'up-to-date' tastes (*TWA*, 26 Sept 1934: 2).

In Shaw's *Adventures*, the ignorance of Christian educators in Africa was exposed in the opening satirical portrait of the white missionary teacher. While upholding Shaw's disapproving tone, the new narrator's critique of mission Christianity is deeper and more complex, revolving around issues of race rather than of doctrine and faith. As in 'Marjorie Mensah's' non-fictional writings, in the new *Adventures* European and Christian values are shown to be thoroughly intertwined with *positive* social goals such as literacy, 'progress' and 'modernity'; and, from the outset, the narrator highlights and praises the local language work of the Basel and Bremen Protestants in West Africa, describing 'the extreme pleasure of reading the wonderful thoughts of the famous evangelist and writer, John Bunyan', whose *Pilgrim's Progress* had been 'translated into the vernacular by the German Missionaries' (*TWA*, 25 Sept, 1934: 2). 'I shall never forget the impression that reading about Christian leaving his wife and family had on my mind', the narrator continues, drawing attention to the intellectual stimulation to be gained from the act of reading (p.3).

As with Shaw's 'black girl', whose reading skills are detached from and used against the Christian educational system, in Dove's text the heroine's literacy is rapidly separated from the doctrinal context in which it was learnt, and mission Christianity is subjected to radical questioning. For both writers, the acquisition of literacy seems to signify the liberation of Africans from their mental shackles: for Shaw, the heroine's ability to read confers on her an arch-sceptical mode of thinking; for Dove, the black girl's literacy leads her to challenge the racial servitude demanded of Africans by white colonialists to sustain their ideological system. Continuing her response to Bunyan's text, Dove's narrator comments:

> I thought at first it was a very wrong thing for a man, a great Christian, to desert his wife and family and try only to save himself ... I asked a missionary friend I had about this. She told me I should only read the story for the beauty of the literature and not occupy my time with questions that would only perplex my mind and lead me to nowhere. At the time I quite agreed with her. I had a perfect regard for criticisms coming from my superiors at least Europeans (*TWA*, 25 Sept 1934: 3).

Moral values are intrinsic to the heroine's act of literary appreciation, for she cannot savour the beauty of the *Pilgrim's Progress* until the matter of Christian's apparent selfishness has been resolved. The aesthetic abstraction of the 'missionary friend' is unsatisfactory given the practical question posed by the narrator, who is concerned to preserve the Christian family value of conjugal co-residence over and against selfish individualism. The 'extreme pleasure of reading' described by the black girl cannot be divorced from the everyday issues raised by Bunyan's text.

Despite her tennis racquet and frequent indications of familiarity with English culture, Dove's black girl is not the de-nationalised product of a European education system transplanted into African soil. Indeed, her 'reader response' to the *Pilgrim's Progress* is a perfect example of the local interpretive mode recommended by 'Marjorie Mensah' in her daily column. Having summarised the missionary's aesthetic advice, the narrator shifts immediately into a didactic space of her own which, in itself, disallows the European's view of art: 'We are taught to have a wonderful belief in all that the European, man or woman, may say to us', she states, 'In short, we are taught, out here, to accept everything as gospel truth. And I certainly did until I started to think for myself' (*TWA*, 25 Sept 1934: 3). The narrator's discontent with Bunyan's *Pilgrim's Progress* has made way for this contemporary political comment about the problem with education 'out here'. The black girl's dissatisfaction with the recommended mode of reading – her refusal to submit to European words and texts as 'gospel truths' – leads directly to these comments about the racism underpinning the colonial relationship.

Where Shaw's heroine journeys through the African jungle carrying her *knob-kerry*, 'Marjorie Mensah's' heroine is hard-pushed to find any forests in the locality. The largest patch of vegetation described in the tale is the 'small stretch of wild country' separating the black girl from the first missionary compound she visits at the start of her search, 'tennis racquet in hand, which is a perfectly right thing to do in these modern days' (*TWA*, 26 Sept 1934: 2). In fact, the landscape she moves through – filled with churches, bookshops, harbours, and customs warehouses filled with cocoa and commodities – is remote from Shaw's timeless setting, for it closely resembles the city of Accra in the 1930s. It is as if the symbolic forest described by Shaw is too ideologically loaded as a setting, saturated with colonial writings by authors such as Joseph Conrad, Ward Price and Rider Haggard, for whom the West African forest represents all that is 'dark' and 'primitive' and 'savage' in Africa.

While Shaw's 'black girl' is a common-sensical character, she is, nevertheless, the heroine of a parable which is set in a symbolic landscape. Each new episode is opened by the repetition of her question, 'Where is God?' and closed with the swing of her *knobkerry*. The comedy of Shaw's protagonist is her ardent physicality within this obviously abstract setting, for she charges through the forest wrecking an entire history of Western spiritual concepts. Dove's heroine, meanwhile, retains the insolence and irreverence of Shaw's heroine, but, as with the landscape, is more realistic and profane than her predecessor.

Nevertheless, the model provided by Shaw's text serves to license Dove's own black girl, being a constant point of reference within the second version. The new black girl refines the behaviour of her prototype, adopting the symbolic gesture of 'waving my tennis racquet in the air in the same manner in which the Black Girl brandished her "knobkerry"' (*TWA*, 28 Sept 1934: 3). Dove's heroine demonstrates the superiority of the literate over the warlike lifestyle, in that her literacy has conferred on her the power to challenge and overthrow colonial prejudice and narrow Christian doctrine. She always answers back, defending her reading of the original *Adventures*, and repeating her belief in Shaw's qualities as a prophet, capable of delivering truths to Black Africa: 'To me, he appears to be such a man of great, new ideas, that I feel positive that he is in a position to make some great utterance in the interest of the Negro race' (*TWA*, 1 Oct 1934: 3).

Dove adjusts the primary theme of Shaw's text by prioritising the 'interest of the Negro race' in the colonies above an exploration of theological concepts. In this way, she is reading and responding to Shaw's *Adventures* by writing her own text into and upon his narrative: in particular, she inserts anti-racist and anticolonial commentaries where Shaw focused predominantly upon spiritual faith. Dove's heroine lays into racial prejudice and colonialist sentiments with more verbal ferocity than the original 'black girl'. 'You paint Christ on your big ornamented Frescoes and in your Bible white', she blasts at the Anglican Bishop in Accra, 'Nothing of goodness is black; we see nothing but white everywhere ... Why all this deception? And why do you encourage segregation in the Church – the supposed House of God?' (*TWA*, 8 Oct 1934: 2). Such violent outbursts have been licensed in a fundamental way by Shaw's black girl, but far surpass the sentiments she is capable of expressing.

Shaw's master-text is embellished constantly by its new author. For example, as the 'black girl' embarks on her search for the 'wonderful Irishman who wrote this wonderful book', she suffers a series of comic interruptions, particularly from her mother, a narrow-minded village woman who brilliantly inverts and exposes the racial prejudice experienced on a daily basis by Africans in the colony: 'She told me that the Irish are not good people; that they are people with very pronounced prejudices and hatreds' (*TWA*, 26 Sept 1934: 2). Frequent digressions such as this allow the borrowed narrative to be 'fattened' with didactic sentiments about religion, literature and reading in Ghana, many of which are drawn directly from recent 'Marjorie Mensah' essays. For example, while waiting for the first character, an Irish missionary, to awaken from his siesta, the heroine visits a bookshop in town. The shop is packed out with 'choleric' European women, all 'highly interested in buying absolute tosh' (*TWA*, 27 Sept 1934: 2). Such a scene allows 'Marjorie Mensah' to reassert her views, firstly, about the racial arrogance of European women on the West Coast, and secondly, about the effects of 'penny dreadfuls' upon women's moral sensibilities. Shaw's original text assists the narrator to illustrate these points with a vivid visual image: 'one of the women who had a face very similar to one of the caricatures in Shaw's book came up to me and said, with a peculiar twinkle in her eyes: "Excuse me. Reading Bernard Shaw? Rather difficult for you is it not?"' (*TWA*, 27 Sept 1934: 2). After a lengthy condemnation of Shaw's *Adventures* as a danger to the natural racial hierarchy which keeps colonialism in place, this laughably 'bad reader' concludes, '"Black people have no right whatsoever to question the superior discretion of the white man. God knows what is right for the world and the whiteman knows what is right for the African. I am a missionary"' (*ibid.*, p.5). In a mocking exposure of her antagonist, the heroine, 'took out my book of Mr Shaw's "Black Girl in Her Search for God" and consulted the drawing. "What are you looking at?" asked my missionary friend. "Oh, nothing", I said. "I was only comparing notes"' (*ibid.*, p.5; see Plate 5.1).

This is a complex intertextual moment, for Dove has incorporated her master-text *into* the narrative as a tangible entity. Shaw's *Adventures* exists in its own right as a book within the book (within the bookshop), treated by the 'black girl' as a reference text to be consulted whenever she meets manifestations of its characters. In addition, everyone she meets has read the story and formed strong opinions about the racially mixed utopia which forms its finale. For example, several of the holy-men to appear in the narrative fall to their knees at the very mention of Shaw and pray fervently, crying out that the black girl is 'lost' (e.g., *TWA*, 1 Oct 1934: 2). By contrast, the black girl declares, 'I would like to find Bernard Shaw. I have read his book and I have been greatly impress[ed] by his brave new utterances. I am the daughter of a downtrodden race' (*TWA*, 8 Oct 1934: 2). Hence, not only does Shaw's book lend structure to Dove's *Adventures* in a formal sense, but it is also employed *within* the text to assist readers in their interpretation of characters.

In self-referential moments worthy of high postmodernist literature, Shaw's

5.1 The 'black girl' confronts her antagonist. Illustration, 'The Caravan of the Curious', by John Farleigh (Shaw, 1934: 47)

own characters come to the forefront of Dove's text in order to comment nega-
tively on the 'false and absurd' notions of 'Mr Shaw, in that silly book' about the
black girl (*TWA*, 27 Sept 1934: 2). The isolated voice contesting these 'bad'
readings is that of the black girl herself, who has clearly also read Aldous Huxley
and holds to her view that 'Mr Shaw is in favour of a brave new world and a fine
new and durable religion' (*TWA*, 27 Sept 1934: 5). The narrator of the new
Adventures also rearranges the order in which Shaw's European characters appear,
selecting items that will assist in the explication of local ideological issues. Clearly,
the episodic nature of Shaw's 'original' – and the episodic nature of *his* primary
texts – permits these moments of expansion, digression and reorganisation.[7]

The authorship of this extraordinary tale is attributed, not to the 'real' writer
Mabel Dove, but to 'Marjorie Mensah', that is, to a personality without substance
who is already the chief character of her own daily text. Thus, not only is Dove's
narrative embedded in Shaw's text, but its 'author' is already a well-known local
character embedded in her own newspaper column. The first-person narrator
provides an additional layer separating Mabel Dove from her narrative. The
author's identity is thus covered over with the intertexts and voices provided by
Bunyan, Shaw and 'Marjorie Mensah'. One effect of these layers is that the
narrator can be more outspoken and outrageous than is usual in the Women's
Corner.

A possible explanation for the concealment of the 'real' author behind so many
masks is the existence of the Criminal Code Amendment Bill (the Sedition Bill),
a recent and detested colonial ordinance which the Governor forced through the
Gold Coast Legislative Council in February and March 1934. In spite of
unanimous African opposition and a cross-party delegation to London, Governor
Shenton Thomas refused all requests to abandon the bill, responding to his critics
by making cryptic comments in public speeches about the entry of 'dangerous'
and 'subversive' literature to the colony: 'I say that the people of this country are
being threatened to-day by a danger of which they know little or nothing, and it
is my bounden duty to protect them against it', he pronounced ominously in a
Minute issued to the press on 21 February 1934 (*GCT*, 3–10 March 1934: 3). He
seemed to believe that by stemming the flow of imported 'seditious' literature, he
would also halt the growing anti-colonial struggle in the country.

At the peak of this controversy, Dove deployed 'Marjorie Mensah' deliberately
to test the limits of the new censorship rules, hurling playful personal insults at
the Governor and ridiculing the bureaucratic belief that seditious sentiments
could be banned: 'I cannot imagine that his Excellency really means to shut me
up one way or the other. After all, he is an attractive gentleman', she writes,
adding flirtatiously, 'If wrinkles appear would that be sedition?' (*TWA*, 9 March
1934: 2).

Aside from references to the Governor's wrinkles, one suspects that, at the

---

[7] Isabel Hofmeyr's current research into John Bunyan in Africa and African readings of the *Pilgrim's Progress* is immensely useful for understanding the importance of episodic texts in Africa.

very least, Bernard Shaw's publications would not have been welcome in British West Africa given his Communist sympathies and prophecies that a black civilisation would rise up in place of white in Africa. Dove's *Adventures* therefore continues the process of provocation in a more serious manner, for its vehement exposé of European racism in the colonies is inspired by and infused with Shaw's revolutionary politics. Unsurprisingly, all of the white characters in Dove's narrative regard Shaw's *Adventures* as a dangerous text which Africans should not read, and they issue continual warnings 'against Mr Shaw and his false doctrines' (*TWA*, 28 Sept 1934: 2). The prevailing view amongst whites in Dove's text is that, 'In Europe, people can read what they like, because they have the understanding to distinguish the chaff from the wheat. You have not that understanding out here' (*TWA*, 1 Oct 1934: 2). The irony, of course, is that Dove's black girl is the *only* competent reader furnished by the entire narrative in which she features, for the Europeans surrounding her prefer to read 'tosh' and 'moth-eaten books', and give vent to the narrowest racist opinions at the merest mention of Shaw's publications.

Unsympathetic whites proliferate in Dove's narrative to the same degree that the 'savages' howl and throw spears in Joseph Conrad's *Heart of Darkness*. Racists are shown to dominate every religious institution in West Africa, and they fill the boat and train during the heroine's long journey to Bernard Shaw's house in London. Here, at the very centre of the British Empire, in a room overlooking the House of Commons, the black girl meets the man behind the name, the source of the anti-racist texts that have so impressed her in West Africa. Intertextual and parodic to the end, she inquires, 'Mr Shaw, I presume?', of the man who enters the room (*TWA*, 15 Oct 1934: 2).[8]

The political context surrounding this closing episode is vital, for Ghanaian readers would have been perfectly aware that, in the real historical time outside Dove's story, a delegation of men from diverse political interest groups in the country had united and travelled to Britain to campaign against the Sedition Bill and to petition political power groups in Westminster. While they failed to secure the repeal of the ordinance, the coalition succeeded in another respect, achieving popular support in the UK and helping to generate consciousness of 'national' issues on a mass scale back in Ghana (see Sheng-Pao, 1970). By having her heroine look out of the window at the Houses of Parliament from the revolutionary, Communist political space represented by Shaw, Dove closes her narrative with a utopian anti-colonial gesture. In a sense, however, this final scene also signifies despair at British legislative processes, for in rejecting the Ghanaian

---

[8] Alongside its intertextual references to Shaw, Dove's narrative contains repeated references to Aldous Huxley's *A Brave New World* (1932), published the same year as Shaw's *Adventures*. Part of Huxley's narrative depicts the appalled reaction of a 'savage' whom the hero has brought to London – the 'brave new world', transformed by an experiment in social engineering – from a New Mexican Reservation. Huxley's parable contains a similar vision of cultural difference to Shaw's, featuring an unnamed, non-European 'Other' who exposes Western ideological distortions, and who figures as a force for moral purification. Dove plays upon both of these representations in her depiction of the black girl's visit to London.

delegation the political class in Britain had prioritised colonial domination above freedom of speech and failed Dove's compatriots in their moment of unity.

Dove's *Adventures* fulfils the desire of its heroine – one of the most persistent 'fans' in West African literature – who justifies her epic search for Mr Shaw with the comment, 'I have read his books and there are some points that I would like to discuss with him' (*TWA*, 3 Oct 1934: 2). These needs are satisfied as the heroine sits down to tell her mentor how his books have been suppressed in Africa in order 'that we may long remain in a state of mental coma and ever helpless and at the mercy of the nations who thirst for territorial possessions overseas and invade our shores under the banner of Christ' (*TWA*, 15 Oct 1934: 2). Tragically for the contemporary reader, the last instalments of *The Adventures of the Black Girl in her Search for Mr Shaw* are not available in British, American or Ghanaian archives. It has proved impossible to trace the *Times of West Africa* for 17 and 18 October 1934. Presumably, these issues contain Bernard Shaw's advice to his African visitor on the subjects of revolution, race and religion in Africa. Given that the Criminal Code Amendment Bill was operational in Ghana by the end of 1934, it is conceivable that the colonial censors suppressed these final instalments. Perhaps the issues have not been preserved for other reasons. The 'wind' has torn these pages from the tale, and in a manner that 'Marjorie Mensah' would no doubt applaud, we are left to generate our own version of the concluding episode. Even without the full final text, however, the story has succeeded in 'discussing some points' with George Bernard Shaw, for from the very outset the narrator's digressions have served to 'dialogise' Shaw's *Adventures* and bring to the fore an anti-racist reading of the original text.

Dove's writing for the women's page reveals the extent to which 'intertextuality' is a culturally specific practice, guided by aesthetic values which are located and learnt. 'The object of all writing', comments 'Marjorie Mensah', as if offering a natural, common-sensical view of the world, is 'to curb certain moral tendencies in us and make our society beautiful, pure and perfect' (*TWA*, 16 March 1933: 2). Such an aesthetic is locally determined and, as I hope to have shown, in her choice of literature for appraisal and analysis, Mabel Dove 'naturally' incorporated particular literary models above others.

An examination of Dove's *Adventures* in the light of Shaw's original raises fascinating questions about the manner in which literate West Africans in the 1930s read and responded to British literary forms. What emerges in Dove's *Adventures* is a complex relationship with 'metropolitan' literature, for the method by which she reads, responds to and rewrites Shaw's *Adventures* does not simply display subservience to colonial cultural norms. For a start, in order to convey her message, she chose *Shaw's* version of Africa above that developed in previous decades by other colonial writers. In this she chose a politically controversial writer, an ardent supporter of Home Rule for Ireland and an opponent of British colonialism (see Holroyd, 1997).

The concept of 'intertextuality' needs to be politicised and contextualised if we are to appreciate the cultural and aesthetic subtleties which, as far back as 1934, guided writers such as Dove in their choice of literary models. As a politically engaged, locally positioned West African writer, she chose to *write over* or *write into* a contemporary text which was oppositional and radical, which was critical of the imperialist context within which it was produced. Shaw's text made possible Dove's questioning, but from this starting position she generated a narrative which localised and 'discussed certain points' with the master-text: the result is a direct, non-deferential critique of racism in West Africa.

6

The 'Book Famine'
in Postcolonial West Africa

In order to define what is 'popular' about local publishers' output in modern-day Ghana, Western preconceptions about popular publishing need to be displaced in favour of production models that are not bound to late-capitalist industrial societies. Western popular publishing is characterised by mass-production, mass-marketing and mass-consumption, and titles are sold to readers as cheap, dispos-able commodities, available alongside confectionery and tobacco in supermarkets and newsagents. As previous chapters have demonstrated, West African 'popular' texts, on the other hand, tend to be published in small print-runs and distributed within the locality, a process often paid for by the authors themselves.[1] Non-textbook publishing in West Africa is intricately intertwined with economic con-ditions in the region. The cheapest new releases sell the most: often only pamphlets, they are sold in bookshops and on market bookstalls, where one can also buy well-thumbed novels by James Hadley Chase, Bertha M. Clay, Frederick Forsyth, Ngugi wa Thiong'o and Chinua Achebe.

Cost is the most significant element in determining a book's 'bestselling' status; the relevance of a book to the reader's life is also an important factor, as is the author's or bookseller's marketing ability. Between 1944 and 1949, for example, J. Benibengor Blay toured the Gold Coast, moving between shops and offices selling his novelettes in tens of thousands. Knocking on doors in well-to-do neighbourhoods and enlisting children and street-hawkers to be 'agents', Blay made enough money to fund his fare to the United Kingdom. In a short time, his publications were so popular that 'they were selling themselves' and he could afford to set up the Benibengor Book Agency, a publishing house staffed by five part-time employees (Blay, 1974).

[1] These comments are based on author interviews and discussions with Ghanaian printers and booksellers between 1995 and 1998.

Blay's sales figures demonstrate a hunger for literature among those Ghanaians who, while they might not have entered bookshops, responded positively to his direct sales techniques in the informal sector: *Emelia's Promise* (1944) sold 50,000 copies between 1944 and 1956; *Be Content with your Lot* (1947) sold 60,000 copies; *Stubborn Girl* (1958) sold 50,000 copies (Blay, 1974). As Asare Konadu says of his own popular fiction, which has sold in similar quantities to Blay's publications, the cardinal rule for an autonomous local publisher is that the price must be 'within reach of any person who wants to read' (Konadu, 1974). Since the mid-1960s, Konadu's 'romances and problematic stories' have undergone numerous re-prints, remaining affordable despite the rising price of imported paper and printing materials (*ibid.*).[2]

Nigerian 'market literature' commands the most impressive sales figures to date. It was produced in bulk by small printer-publishers who, in the 1950s and 1960s, bought disused newspaper presses and government printers, and also imported reconditioned letterhead presses from Europe (see Obiechina, 1973). Market literature fed the voracious book-hunger of young urban Nigerians. In Ibadan, Onitsha and Enugu, print-runs of 10,000 pamphlets followed swiftly upon one another and, as in Ghana, pamphlets often were sold in the informal sector as well as in local bookshops. Ogali A. Ogali's *Veronica My Daughter* (1956) sold 60,000 copies within a few years of its release and remains available today on the bookstalls in Onitsha market; amongst others, *How to Speak to a Girl about Marriage* (Abiakam, 1964?) can still be purchased, as can *How to Make Friends with Girls* (Abiakam, 1971a) and *The Game of Love* (Abiakam, 1971b). Since 1990, a new and strikingly similar brand of 'market literature' has emerged in northern Nigeria. Cheap, privately published *soyayya* books circulate in large numbers around Kano. Like their eastern and southern forebears, *soyayya* authors write about romantic love, parental interference in marriage plans and relationship problems (see Larkin, 1997). The vital difference in the north is that authors write in Hausa, liberating popular literature from the English-language stronghold which still prevails over popular literature in the south of the country.

The impressive sales figures for locally published Ghanaian literature in the 1940s contrast with the prevailing belief amongst scholars that literate school-leavers in West Africa have not developed a 'reading habit' for fiction. Numerous articles on indigenous publishing industries in Africa contain the lament that there is no local interest in leisure-reading. According to commentators, the problem lies in Africans' pragmatic attitudes towards the printed word: 'Africans read for utilitarian purposes, in virtual exclusion of all else', writes S. Kotei (1987: 180); rather than choosing to read fiction, 'the less educated take to textbooks to improve themselves occupationally', writes S. Amu Djoleto (1985:

[2] E. K. Mickson can be added to this list of bestselling authors, although the Ghana Publishing Corporation was responsible for distributing his publications. *When the Heart Decides* (Mickson, 1966) sold 40,000 copies immediately; in the years that followed, each subsequent print-run of 10,000 would sell out within a month (Gyedu, 1976: 73).

31). Reading for personal achievement rather than for fantasy or pleasure, Africans have what T. Gyedu terms a 'textbook mentality', selecting educational texts in the hope of acquiring knowledge for social or professional advancement (1976: 69–75). 'Less than one per cent of those who read, do so for reasons other than formal preparation for an examination, or a career', Solomon Unoh says of Nigerian readers (1993: 108). Likewise, the Ghanaian author Isaac Ephson dismisses 'the average Ghanaian' as being 'interested in beer, dances, frivolous life; they are not interested so much in reading, except those at school, to whom certain textbooks have been recommended' (1974). Even if there were a willing readership, these commentators continue, high production costs have created a 'book famine' in all but the African textbook sector (Crowder, 1986; Walsh, 1991).

The commercial success of Blay, Konadu and the travelling book-vendors in Ghana undermines the belief that Africans are unwilling and unable to buy fiction. Many of the scholars cited above have ignored the submerged but vibrant informal sector of the market. In addition, commentators' laments seem to derive from a belief, firstly, that local publications should be *non-didactic*; secondly, that leisure-reading should be produced by *national* publishing houses; and thirdly, that fiction should create for the reader a wholly *imaginary* world, set apart from reality. According to these preconceptions, creative writing is not 'fiction' if it presents scenarios that are edifying and educational. As previous chapters have revealed, however, locally published West African books and magazines are marketed most often in a way that emphasises their status as 'problem-solving' texts, as quasi-fictions which are relevant and didactic. Sales figures can soar when the covers of texts promise that 'this story will excite any couple involved in the endless search for harmony in marriage' (Nwoye, 1993: n.p.). Authors and book-hawkers alike appeal to potential customers' personal interests, emphasising the moral knowledge to be gleaned from reading and, as Chapter 3 revealed, many Ghanaian readers expect literature to fulfil precisely this didactic function.

Since the 1950s in Ghana and Nigeria, the covers of local Anglophone texts have advertised themselves by promising to reveal truths to the reader about money, love, women, marriage, and parenthood. The covers of bestsellers are scattered with promises: *Never Trust all that Love You* (1961), still sold in Onitsha, declares, 'The world is so Corrupt that it has become difficult to Trust All People', 'Love All But Trust Few', 'If You Like, Take My Advice: A Word Is Enough For The Wise' (Abiakam, n.p.). Critics are not necessarily wrong in their assessments of readers' utilitarian attitudes towards reading material, but they are misguided in presuming that West African readers will not purchase fiction because, in itself, fiction is not 'educational'. Popular novels, as most authors declare on their covers and as most readers agree, must be included among the range of 'educational' texts that a reader might purchase.

Not all commentators on the publishing industry in Africa support the idea that there is a 'book famine'. A separate strand of research into the indigenous non-textbook sector acknowledges that large quantities of popular literature *can* be purchased locally from 'author-cum-publisher-cum-printer-cum-bookseller

pioneers' (Ike, 1993: 137). Often, however, this indigenous production is dispar-
aged or condemned, particularly in Nigeria. For example, Jibril Aminu complains:

> There is no shortage, and there never was, of junk books and magazines, some
> of which are probably better banned from the shelves of booksellers and
> libraries since they are motivated solely and simply by financial reasons. ...
> The authors of these books, if they can be so called, do not bother to check the
> grammar, let alone the facts and the logic. (1993: xxxvi)

Concerned about the 'recent upsurge' in Kano market literature, or *soyayya*
books, Sani Abba and Jibril Ibrahim also complain that:

> The writing is conceived and executed in a rush. The author is usually the
> printer/publisher ... these young authors, equipped with relatively low educa-
> tional standards, are putting to shame the serious Hausa literary establishment.
> (Abba and Ibrahim, 1995: 3, 5)

Rather than putting 'serious' literature to shame, these privately published
novelists can be seen to be 'filling a vacuum that conventional publishers have
allowed to grow' (Dekutsey, 1993: 72). The established publishers in West Africa
have neglected local authors and readers in their enthusiasm to compete with
multinational publishers for the guaranteed school textbook market.

   Many local author-publishers, particularly in Ghana, operate outside conventional bookselling networks, complementing rather than competing with their
national and multinational rivals. Employing street-vendors and office workers, or
visiting head teachers personally with copies of their novels and textbooks, these
authors have adopted unofficial channels to promote their publications. Often,
their 'agents' take the product directly to the customer rather than trusting the
customer to visit a bookshop: 'we take the books to them', Konadu commented in
an interview (1974). As well as supplying urban bookshops in the 1970s,
Konadu's publishing house, Anowuo Educational Publications, recruited post-
masters, librarians, headmasters and government accounts clerks to act as bookselling agents. The latter group were especially efficient, for they could deduct
money directly from a worker's salary if he or she refused to pay for a book
(*ibid.*). Starting from nothing and entering a fragile leisure-reading market, many
of these local author-publishers have had 'nerves of steel', for their survival or
failure has depended upon their own marketing skills (Gyamfuaa-Fofie, 1995).
Confronted by escalating costs and slim profit margins, they have been responsible for the entire production process, from the conception of each book to its
printing, storage, distribution and publicity.

   A market exists for locally published literature, but it is not always visible in
urban bookshops, which tend to reserve a small rack for fiction while the surrounding shelves are stocked with school textbooks, foreign second-hand fiction,
Bibles and religious readers, all of which are relatively safe publications for a
ready market. The dynamic 'informal sector' is where much of West Africa's
reading public can be located and it is here that popular literature circulates, on

the second-hand bookstalls, in crowded buses and 'trotros', on the streets beside market stalls in urban areas and on the client lists of small publishers' agents.

Numerous economic and infrastructural obstacles prevent small Ghanaian publishing houses from accepting 'general interest' manuscripts by local authors. Since the early 1970s, import duties have escalated on ink, spare parts for printing machinery and paper. Except for the church presses, most sub-national publishers cannot afford in-house printing equipment; nor can they hold large stocks of paper in reserve, having to rely instead upon independent jobbing presses which are, in turn, largely dependent upon imported supplies of paper (see Plates 6.1–6.8). Prices for print-runs can soar at short notice as supplies dwindle and duties increase. In these conditions, few publishers will risk accepting titles unless sales can be guaranteed. In the face of competition for government textbook contracts from western multinational companies and their semi-privatised subsidiaries, autonomous local publishers are unlikely to gamble capital on non-textbook ventures. Similarly, without a book-buying public regularly seeking to read for leisure, sales of novels can be slow or stagnant.

In the 1970s, the governments of both Nigeria and Ghana sought to stop the outflows of foreign exchange to foreign publishing companies, which dominated the lucrative textbook market. Both countries passed 'indigenisation' decrees. In Nigeria, multinational publishers were required in 1973 to enter 40 per cent share-holding partnerships with private entrepreneurs. Currently managed wholly by locals, who have inherited the parent company's warehouses and distribution networks, the Nigerian subsidiaries now commission educational material from local authors, and the multinationals grant licences to publishers who apply for permission to reprint their own lists of titles.

In Ghana, the situation for multinational companies in 1976, the year of 'indigenisation', was different from Nigeria where there has never been a parastatal publishing house. The Ghana Publishing Corporation (GPC) had been set up in 1965 to take control of the entire school textbook market from the religious presses that had, until then, dominated the sector. The vast new printing press at Tema was filled with the latest offset technology and the Ministry of Education, in a controversial partnership with Macmillan, supervised every aspect of school textbook publishing, from commissioning, editing and printing to sales and distribution. Only 30 per cent of Ghanaian bookshops survived the commercial impact of the GPC, which deprived them of September textbook sales, 'the "bread and butter" of the retail trade' which sustained them through the year (Tauber and Weidhaas, 1984: 128).

The GPC was necessitated by the expansion of education after 1951, including the introduction of free, universal education at primary and middle-school levels in 1961 and the Free Textbook Scheme, introduced in 1963. Entirely dependent until 1965 upon local jobbing presses which were unable to undertake large print-runs, and upon imported foreign textbooks sold through regional bookshops, the Ministry of Education was faced with the consequences of its schemes: millions of schoolchildren urgently needed millions of prescribed texts.

Critics argue that Macmillan played an important role in the GPC's refusal fully to indigenise its school textbook production. Rather than helping to commission *local* material for the expanding and profitable market, Macmillan, it is claimed, used its professional expertise and 40 per cent stake in the GPC to secure a stronghold for its own titles, posing a 'cynical threat' to 'free enterprise' by monopolising the market until the partnership was cancelled in the early 1970s (Hill, 1992: 51).

Set up to encourage local creative talent and sustain the schoolchild's full range of educational needs, the GPC rapidly became congested with new manuscripts, commissioned and typeset in the Publishing Division but abandoned in a five- to six-year queue at the printing press in Tema. A 'chronic shortage' of printing materials, spare parts and paper meant that by 1980 the Corporation had a backlog of over 150 manuscripts awaiting publication and the Printing Division had to place an embargo on the commissioning of new titles (Djoleto, 1985: 79). The dwindling output of locally-authored material is reflected in the GPC's production figures for the period between 1978 and 1982: output declined from twenty-nine new titles in 1978, to seven in 1980, one in 1981 and three in 1982 (*ibid.*). Local authors have given up on the GPC as a potential publisher, preferring to establish their own publishing companies to ensure the quick release of their own titles (Gyamfuaa-Fofie, 1995). Ironically, these independent author-publishers often dispatch titles to the Tema printing press, which offers a relatively efficient service to private entrepreneurs and prioritises cash-paying customers above the sluggish remittances from its own Publishing Division (Abbam, 1974; Konadu, 1974).

Despite the indigenisation decrees in Ghana and Nigeria, the marketing of non-textbooks remains easier for multinational companies and their subsidiaries than for autonomous sub-national publishers. Macmillan, Heinemann and Longman operate on economies of scale and have the advantage of established, extensive book distribution channels in Africa.

In the last fifteen years, Macmillan has re-styled its approach to the African non-textbook market, developing collaborative projects that are coordinated from its headquarters in Britain. Perceiving a gap in the African literary market-place in the late 1970s, the company commissioned local authors to write thrillers, detective stories and romances for the new *Pacesetters* series. (Not to be outdone, Longman followed swiftly with its *Drumbeat* series and Heinemann with its *Heartbeats* series.) The *Pacesetters* are heavily edited, written in compliance with the publisher's generic specifications, printed and bound in Hong Kong, exported to African bookshops and advertised in Macmillan Education's colourful, glossy catalogues which are produced in Basingstoke, Britain. The company has utilised its distribution networks in Africa to promote the series on a large scale and the titles are immensely popular with young readers. Such a commissioning, editing and mass-marketing style makes the *Pacesetters* series thoroughly 'popular', but only in the Western sense of the term.

Few contemporary indigenous publishers have the capital to commission or mass-market series of generic novels and few West African readers have the

Printing presses in Kumasi,
Ghana, 1995–1998

6.1 (*above*) The Ghanaian author-
publisher, Akosua Gyamfuaa-Fofie
with Wilson Asare, Manager of
Wilas Press, Kumasi.

6.2 (*right*) Typesetting by hand
continues to be a common practice
when smaller jobs (e.g. posters,
leaflets, short pamphlets) are
undertaken at Ghanaian printing
presses

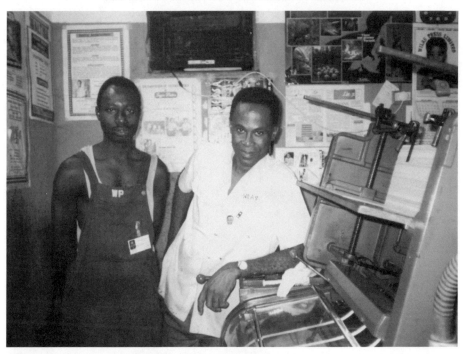

6.3 & 6.4 The preparation of receipt books using reconditioned 30-year-old Heidelberg machines imported from Germany by the manager of Wilas Press.

6.5 & 6.6 Exercise books are printed, collated and stitched at Wilas Press, Kumasi, in preparation for the beginning of the academic year in 1995.

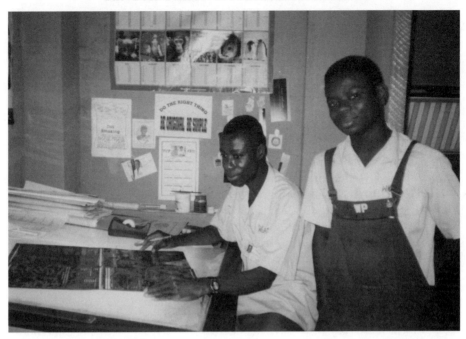

6.7 Preparing lithographic plates.

6.8 Computerized desktop publishing has replaced hand–typesetting at Cita Press, one of the larger printing presses in Kumasi.

resources to purchase popular literature on a regular basis. Small print-runs of romances, detective stories and marriage guidance pamphlets often are paid for by authors-turned-publishers, or published by small companies with no in-house stylesheets to specify the content or structure of particular genres. In fact, unlike Macmillan's *Pacesetters*, the locally published 'popular' text in West Africa can be defined as that which circulates *outside* the very structures that characterise popular literary production in late-capitalist economies. Operating outside official publishing channels, local creative writers and publishers have adopted the role of artisans, as in pre-capitalist Europe, crafting books for a limited market and relying upon external support rather than producing potentially profitable commodities for mass-circulation to pre-arranged outlets (see Radway, 1987: 20–45).

Undeterred by the immense infrastructural constraints, there are several successful publishers of popular literature in West Africa, particularly in Western Nigeria, where Onibonoje Press, Fagbamigbe Publishers and Spectrum Books are leaders in the market. Releasing romances and thrillers alongside examination crammers and imprints of foreign popular novels, they have carved out a sustainable niche in the leisure-reading market. 'Our publishing policy', declared Onibonoje's publicity flyer in the early 1980s:

> is to develop and use indigenous talents, personnel and resources. To produce books which are fully responsive to Nigerian and African needs and aspirations. ... Our *African Literature Series* conceives of African literature as a dialogue between the African author and the African reader. (cited in Kotei, 1981: 81–2)

These indigenous publishers, like the artisanal author-publishers who operate beside them, release less generically conventional popular novels than Macmillan. Circulating within a geographical radius determined by the publisher's or author's mobility, these texts occupy a tangential position in relation to western generic classifications.

As we have seen, the absence of editorial input into locally published literature has caused concern about the diminishing quality of books entering people's homes and schools (Aminu, 1993: xxxvi; Abba and Ibrahim, 1995). This very absence has also lent a certain freedom of creative movement to those authors and publishers who possess sufficient finances and marketing skills to release non-textbooks into the West African market place. Whether it is fictional, religious or instructional, locally published literature represents, as Per Gedin says, 'a quite different kind of new African writing, which shows an independence of the ... European-oriented writing and which may become much more of a starting point for an autonomous literary development' (Gedin, 1984: 104).

In fact, as I hope to have shown, the 'starting-point' anticipated by Gedin can be located many decades ago. Local authorship has been stimulated by the keen local readership, by the travelling book-vendors who touted (and continue to tout) texts in the informal sector, and by the multitudes of small publishing houses that have sprung up and vanished throughout the region since Independence.

7

'Two Things May be Alike but Never the Same'
E. K. Mickson's parodic techniques

Since Blay and Abedi-Boafo first popularised local literature in the late 1930s, there has not been a 'book boom' in Ghana to match the rise of locally published literatures in Nigeria, but there has not been a 'book famine' either, as some commentators claim. Both the 'reading habit' and the market are present and, as the publishing tycoon Asare Konadu (1974) says, 'the only thing has been choosing the right material, aiming [it] at the Ghanaian reader' and making sure the price is within the means of 'any person who wants to read'.

Reprints of the most popular novels from the 1960s are still widely available, masking the shortage of new titles. E. K. Mickson's 'Lucy' pamphlets, which will be explored in this chapter, and full-length paperbacks by Asare Bediako (pseud. Asare Konadu) remain favourites with readers. The information printed inside the front covers of these old publications tends to suppress the book's age: while the date of 'this edition' is usually proclaimed, its original publication date is rarely included. Publishers seem to be aware that book-buyers in Ghana might be put off by thirty-year-old narratives, that readers are seeking relevant, contemporary stories containing 'great lesson[s]' and 'fore-warning[s] ... against heart-breaks' (Mickson, 1966: 5).[1]

Richard Priebe (1978) is one of the few scholars to have studied Ghanaian popular literature in detail, writing as the publishing industry went into a decline from which it has not yet recovered. Priebe notices a preoccupation with personal hygiene in novelettes published after the fall of Kwame Nkrumah in 1966. In response to the stains that had spread through Nkrumah's government in the

[1] This is also the case in eastern Nigeria, where the most popular pamphlets from the 1950s and 1960s are still on sale in Onitsha market. Love-letters dated 1959 or 1961 in original editions now read '1983' or '1986'. Imprints of Bertha M. Clay novels, first published over a century ago, also remain on sale in Ghana and Nigeria, published and distributed since the 1970s by Fagbamigbe Publishers in Akure, Nigeria.

early 1960s, Priebe argues, authors turned in on their communities, translating corruption at a national level into a 'puritanical' sexual ethic directed particularly against promiscuous women: female sexuality, when misused, is represented as a threat both to the male body and to the body politic (1978: 413–16). The character types to be found in popular fiction are connected with political realities by a direct 'text-context' relationship and a 'serious moral' impulse can be located in the most raunchy romance (p. 410). The protagonist's moral cleanliness is used by authors to symbolise a political desire for a morally clean nation-state: in apparently apolitical texts one can therefore find 'serious and very conservative statement[s] about the moral health of society' (p. 411).

In Priebe's reading, popular novels are vessels containing authors' frustrated political hopes. Requiring release, these sentiments are formed into 'polluted' character types – most of which are female – created in order to symbolise how the polity has degenerated. According to this interpretation, when the unfaithful heroine of E. K. Mickson's 'Lucy' pamphlets is punished for her sexual promiscuity by having her leg severed at the knee and 'her neck stiffened to the left' (Mickson, 1967: 99), she in fact represents a symbolic resolution of Ghanaians' frustrations about their newly formed nation-state.

By emphasising the submerged political themes attaching to protagonists such as Lucy, Priebe attempts to retrieve local publications from the dismissive standpoint of critics who set popular novels against 'serious' African literature and complain that the former lack political engagement (see e.g. Ikiddeh, 1971; Ehling, 1990).[2] However, in the process of politicising domestic scenarios, Priebe underrates the value of characters like Lucy as didactic 'proverbial' types, used by authors to make judgements about men's and women's *personal* relationships. While the authors Priebe interviewed in 1973 and 1974 certainly endowed their protagonists with symbolic and metaphorical functions, political meanings were never mentioned as reasons for the success of particular stories: 'As the traditional stories were actually woven around morals and the day-to-day problems', Asare Konadu (1974) explained, 'I also wrote these stories around day-to-day problems of the Ghanaian youngman or worker'. Fiction opens up an intimate, advice-giving space, where the author can explore 'youthful marriages and problems in developing communication' (*ibid.*); Konadu says he is 'taking the marriage problem and writing from that level and maybe posing to the youngman the problems that he is likely to face if he goes in to get married' (*ibid.*). In Konadu's comments at least, the 'text–context' relationship seems to be more intimate than allowed for in Priebe's framework, for the author is fictionalising 'the marriage problem' and handing it over to the 'youngman', who can produce lessons from the story that will be relevant to his own private life.

As previous chapters have illustrated, Lucy's character type and the template for her downfall existed in Ghanaian narratives long before Mickson's pamphlets

[2] Indeed, Priebe is one of the few scholars to have undertaken a non-dismissive contextual study of Ghanaian popular literature in the 1970s; his article contains valuable details about the local publishing industry in Ghana.

were conceived. The promiscuous young woman is relevant and meaningful in novels published as early as 1938, when authors had radically different expectations for their African leaders and different perspectives on decolonisation (see Abedi-Boafo, [1938] 1946). Another difficulty with Priebe's argument as it stands, then, is that it does not fully account for the existence of morally 'stained' female character types in Ghanaian literature prior to Nkrumah's period in power.

Priebe's interpretation can perhaps be accommodated if we regard Mickson and his contemporaries as *inheriting* and *reapplying* popular character types which have been circulating around West African cultures for many decades. In fate at least, Mickson's Lucy echoes the numerous good-time girls in Nigerian pamphlets who die 'miserable, lonely and lamentable death[s]' after lives spent exploiting young men (Maxwell, 1959: n.p.). It is important to emphasise that Lucy's derivations as a literary figure are confined to her appearance. If the deceitful, promiscuous young woman is a familiar figure in West African literatures, she is also an internally dynamic type, reconfigured by individual authors and instilled with specific, local preoccupations about gender (or politics, if one accepts Priebe's argument). These good-time girls are culturally specific, filled to the brim with the concerns of their authors and readers. Each time the good-time girl is invoked by an author, she retains her familiar appearance but is adapted and transformed. Latched onto diverse morals and messages, this popular character type validates a wide array of meanings.

In a large number of Ghanaian 'romances' written since the 1960s, a rift has split this type of heroine so radically that her two parts appear to be irreconcilable.[3] Single and newly-married women are depicted as temptresses and *also* as genuine lovers. Morally degraded and sexually exploitative, they nevertheless adore their partners with a romantic passion which preserves the ideal that, were they to marry, their households would contain all 'the wonders of love' (Mickson, 1966: 57).

Ghanaian authors in the 1960s tend to oscillate between violent punishments of young heroines and constructions of the same characters as tragic heroines deserving sympathy. E. K. Mickson's durable, best-selling pamphlets about a good-time girl called Lucy exemplify the ambivalence of narrators towards the representation of women. *When the Heart Decides* (1966) and its sequel *Who Killed Lucy?* (1967) first appeared in Ghana a generation later than Abedi-Boafo's and Blay's novels, and are still widely available in bookshops today, remaining enormously popular with readers.

A young, male first-person narrator testifies to Lucy's betrayal of Frank in *When the Heart Decides*. Frank's closest companion, Seth, frames the romantic narrative with his own comments as he pieces together the fragments of his friend's relationship. Seth operates at one remove from the rhetoric of his friend: when Frank enters his 'chamber' and brings out a gold ring given to Lucy by one

---

[3] Locally published romantic novels generate their own conventions in Ghana and, as Chapter 10 will explore in more detail, the romance cannot be defined according to the rules of the genre in Europe and America.

of her lovers, Seth asks, '"What is this?" … in a rather careless manner, sipping my beer, with my legs crossed' (Mickson, 1967: 18).[4] While Frank recalls the 'tender kisses', the 'greatness of our love' and the 'unbelievable fondness and devotion' he shared with his 'Sweetie' (p. 11), the narrator takes up a position *outside* the language of love. Rather than sympathising with the 'romantic hero', Seth uses the story of Frank to exemplify how 'love' can be misdirected and badly formulated, and he warns readers continually against emulating his friend's type of passion.

Like Don Quixote and his down-to-earth companion, Sancho Panza, the two characters communicate their different beliefs in different language registers. Speaking always 'in a careless manner' (*ibid.*), Seth is Frank's ideological counter-point in the novel. He exposes the reality behind the hero's romantic rhetoric by letting forth streams of cynical comments about Ghanaian women's incapacity to be romantic heroines. 'I concluded that anyone who ever trusted a woman was the world's biggest stupid idiot, a fool', Seth informs readers, after hearing Frank's evidence of Lucy's betrayals (p. 27); 'God forbid', he comments at the suggestion that he would ever love a 'modern' woman, for 'I can't stand their unsteady flir-tations and the quantity of provisions they consume' (p. 28). Throughout the narrative, Seth's comic rejection of his friend's romantic sentiments is spliced into Frank's account of his tragic experiences in love.

By adopting an 'everyday' language register and using it to highlight the contrasts between Lucy's promises of love and her actual infidelities, Seth ironises the lovers' romantic discourse. The difference between his tone and Frank's creates a critical distance between Frank and the reader. As the frame narrator with responsibility for narrating the entire story, Seth's judgements of Frank have an authority denied to the character whose story he hears. Rather than allowing readers to identify and sympathise wholeheartedly with the romantic hero, his interruptions to Frank's story and his interpretations of 'modern girls' undermine Frank's type of love. In fact, each instance of 'romantic' language is mediated by Seth's interventions. For example, when Frank goes into his 'chamber' and fetches out a large bundle of love-letters, Seth comments humorously on the lovers' prolific output, 'But how many times do you want to write to yourselves [i.e. each other] in a week when in fact you meet every day?' (p. 9). At the end of the pamphlet, Seth isolates quotations from these love-letters, further ironising their 'high' romantic sentiments. Concluding the story with a moral addressed directly to male Ghanaian readers, he says:

[4] Alcohol features prominently in *When the Heart Decides* and *Who Killed Lucy?* Throughout the latter text, both Lucy and Frank drink heavily. Genuinely repentant, Lucy drinks alone with the specific aim of driving away her worries (Mickson, 1967: 19). 'Three sheet[s] in the wind (drunk), as they say', she becomes more miserable with each sip of brandy (p. 24); Frank, meanwhile, is shown sitting alone, 'drinking his head off' (p. 19), seeking, without achieving, escape from his misery. Alcohol has been appropriated by these youths from their elders, who once would have publicly asserted their seniority through the controlled use and distribution of alcohol during customary ceremonies (see Akyeampong, 1993). In Mickson's texts, alcohol is linked with youth, 'modernity', nightclubs, depression and the pre-marital love of adolescents.

I hope that from this, you and the whole modern world will agree with me that anyone who ever trusts a woman and earnestly gives his heart, mind, soul and all to her just because the woman 'loves' him, or is 'beautiful', is the world's biggest stupid idiot, a fool. (p. 84)

By placing the key concepts of romantic love in quotation marks, and by repeating his judgement that a man like Frank is 'the world's biggest stupid idiot, a fool' (*ibid.*), Seth increases the critical distance separating readers from the literary genre in which the protagonists have operated for the duration of the novel. Seth's 'everyday' language exposes the *literariness* of heroines like Lucy. He has extracted the figure of the beautiful romantic heroine from her genre and dressed her down in the language of the 'real' Ghanaian world.

Ghanaian fiction is replete with the figure of the male first-person narrator who claims authority to narrate a 'real' person's life-story (e.g. Konadu, 1989; Amarteifio, 1985). Sometimes these narrators play no major role in the development of the plot; or they are intervening authority-figures like the fathers and priests in Kwabena Antwi-Boasiako's novels (e.g. 1994, 1995). Whatever their function in the plot, first-person narrators are full-bodied, named characters in numerous novels by Ghanaian men. Occupying voyeuristic vantage-points, they offer moral assessments of protagonists and provide readers with interpretive pivots for the judgement of characters. Authors make every effort to filter stories through these narrators, struggling, in some instances, against an omniscience necessitated by the plot.

Why should limited narration be chosen above omniscient narration? In prefaces and publicity material on the covers of novels, authors often declare that their texts will teach readers how to differentiate between false and authentic friendships, between a woman's cunning intentions and her passionate words of love: *When the Heart Decides*, Mickson writes, 'will make bare in its natural perspectives, how cunning, wicked, very dangerous and killing some girls – sincerest of lovers – can be' (1966: 5); the front cover of Antwi-Boasiako's *Not this Time Mercy* (1982), which is another first-person narrative, reveals this to be a 'sensational and romantic novel which describes an unscrupulous woman who deserted her poor husband mysteriously to become a prostitute in a foreign country' (n.p.). Omniscient narration would appear to be ideally suited to this didactic project, working in favour of readers by exposing the contrasts between the thoughts and actions of a character. Readers would be provided with access to a character's mind at the very moment when her devious plans are hatched.

Why then should Ghanaian authors be attracted to the convention of limited narration? First-person narrators tend to be close relatives or confidantes of young protagonists, listening to their dilemmas, commenting freely on the situation and counselling characters on appropriate responses. Narrators attempt to intervene in and halt the fragmentation of marriages or romances. Crucially, they hold recognisable social positions in the social networks created within texts, as close friends, fathers or priests, functioning as problem-solvers in the lives of protagonists. A further social role attaches to first-person narrators: they are storytellers, narrating events which have passed. Where omniscience allows a narrator to gain access to each character's thoughts and intentions, the storyteller takes up a position where interiority is not as important as interpretation. Ghanaian narrators are socially embedded *interpreters* of plots and characters. The guiding 'I' provides an identification point for readers. Through narrators like Seth, Ghanaian readers are able to assess the behaviour of characters while remaining at several removes from them. Prevented from over-identifying with protagonists, they can project their own views into the narrative.

Suspense is also absent from these locally published romances. As in Nigerian market literature, plots and character types tend to be revealed in advance, summarised on the covers of novels and in authors' introductions (see Newell, 1996). This 'spoiling' gesture changes the nature of the reading process. By providing detailed foreknowledge of events, authors endow readers with privileged interpretive positions in relation to the plot, allowing them to contemplate the narrator's moral evaluations rather than to read for revelations about what will happen next.

When the Heart Decides revolves around a dossier of Lucy's love-letters, each of which is read aloud by three other characters: Seth, Frank and Lucy's friend, Lily. Letters play so crucial a part in the progress of the novel that Frank substitutes Lucy's letters for verbal explanations. Asked why he is terminating the relationship, he collects 'a bunch of letters and handed one of them to me [Seth]. "Read this part", he said', pointing to the words, 'SINCERE LOVE' (Mickson, 1966: 11; author's emphasis). Lucy's duplicitous character can only be discovered through the retrieval and exhibition of her letters. Somehow Frank has obtained Lucy's letters to her many other lovers, with whom 'she had been in frequent secret correspondence ... Here are also some of the young man's replies to Lucy's letters. You may wonder how I got them, but that is immaterial at this moment' (p. 18). Extensive written documentation is required to prove Lucy's disloyalty. She has written her own life-sentence, condemned herself by using the language of monogamous love with more than one partner.

Reading and writing are pivotal to the progression of *When the Heart Decides*. Throughout the narrative, Frank can be found 'tensely seated behind his writing desk, writing very fast' (p. 7); or he is rushing into his bedroom – site of sleepless nights and tear-soaked pillows – to collect more of Lucy's love-letters. The expression of romantic love is inextricable from the figure of the literate individual, or the writing body. This emphasis on written love occurs, of course, within the framework of the written text, setting up a close connection between literacy and romantic love (see Plates 7.1 and 7.2).

In place of an epigraph, the pamphlet opens with a reprint of Frank's letter to Lucy, in which he ends the relationship: 'let us put an end to our love affair as from 8pm this fateful Wednesday', Frank writes, 'I ask you to pardon and forgive me for any inconvenience, suspense or unhappiness you might have experienced through me during the course of our love' (p. 6; see Plates 7.3 and 7.4). Frank's letter of 'resignation' is reprinted in full twice more in the pamphlet, italicised

E. K. MICKSON. Author of this book. His other works are: *"Who Killed Lucy?" "Now I Know"* and *"The Violent Kiss. "Woman Is Poison"*

The close connections between literacy, the act of writing and romantic love are demonstrated by these images of romance-writing.

7.1 The author E. K. Mickson, as pictured inside the front cover of *When the Heart Decides* (1966).

I have therefore been compelled . . . to ask you to let us put an end to our love affair as from 8 p.m. this fateful Wednesday.

7.2 This image appears to derive from the portrait of E. K. Mickson, depicting the romantic hero, Frank, writing the letter that finishes his affair with Lucy (Mickson, 1966: 85).

Dear Lucy,

"It has been said that when everything, has been done and the die is cast, no amount of witchery or prayers can ever prevent the crossing of Rubicon.

"I have therefore been compelled to go against the very dictates of my heart to ask you to let us put an end to our love affair as from 8 p.m. this fateful Wednesday.

"This decision has come to me not only as a blow but also with the sting, as it were, of a scorpion. But having realised from both past and present circumstances that you have cast the die, it is evident that the crossing of Rubicon will follow as a matter of natural sequence.

"And as wise old men have always maintained that prevention is better than cure, I have no alternative than to arrive at this decision.

"While thanking you heartily for your love for me during the times past, I ask you to pardon and forgive me for any inconvenience, suspense or unhappiness you might have experienced through me during the course of our love.

"I assure you that I have no bad feeling against you and will ever remain as friendly as I can with you.

"I finally wish you the best of luck, success and happiness in your next love affair and pray that your next LOVE may have for you the kind of love I had for you.

Thanks
"Frank"

7.3 & 7.4 *When the Heart Decides*
(Mickson, 1966: 6, 8)

... But there was Franklin tensely seated behind his writing desk, writing very fast, words which, judging from the greatness of the love existing between them, could easily mean suicide to either or both of them.

106

each time and physically isolated from the surrounding narrative. In it, Frank adopts an 'official' register to end the love-contract, and his language is contrasted immediately with Seth's less formal style as he reacts to the news with shock (p. 7). Like a businessman cancelling a meeting, or a white-collar worker resigning from his office job, Frank names the exact time and day of the separation and apologises for 'any inconvenience' caused.

In reacting to the letter, Seth draws attention to its distinctive language, asking Frank 'what prompted him to write such an "unwarranted and highly unjudicious" letter to no other person than "Sweetie"' (p. 10). By placing the formal words and the romantic appellation in quotation marks, Seth highlights the distance between the language used for letter-writing and the language of everyday life. In addition, Seth creates a neologism, 'unjudicious', when he might have used the 'correct' form of the word, 'injudicious'. This misusage of English, whether intentional or not on the part of the author, could be seen as a *subversion* of the official discourse that is being quoted. Readers perceiving the error in Seth's quotation are likely to experience a further increase in the distance between themselves and the 'official' language that is adopted whenever the romance is referred to in the novel (see Hutcheon, 1985).

In her theory of parody in postmodern literature, Linda Hutcheon (1985) argues that authors might employ a range of parodic techniques within a single text: while some forms of parody criticise or satirise the parodied text (or set of literary conventions), other forms might ironise their target without necessarily ridiculing it (pp. 11–12). When target-texts are inverted or exposed, authors are not always writing 'at the expense of the parodied text' (p. 6). Mickson fits this framework, for he does not employ parody simply to ridicule his 'target' genre, for the 'ridiculing' type of parody is confined to Lucy's love-letters. Romantic language is both a target *and* a tool in *When the Heart Decides*. When the language of Lucy's letters seeps into the couple's 'real' encounters, Mickson seems to be upholding romantic love as an ideal, mourning the impossibility of its realisation in a society filled with deceitful women, but preserving it 'as an ideal or at least a norm from which the modern departs' (Hutcheon, 1985: 5). Parody which ridicules its target is only one of several types of parody: other parodic techniques may be more ambivalent, preserving the authority of the parodied conventions in the very process of transgressing them (p. 69).

At a stylistic level, in Lucy's love-letters to Frank one can find implicit, unmarked quotations from the Victorian sentimental literature that was imported into Ghana in the 1920s and 1930s and can still be purchased in urban bookshops today. Bertha M. Clay's *Beyond Pardon* (1977), first published in Britain in 1884, was, and still is, enormously popular with West African readers. 'Oh Elinor!', cries Clay's hero in a letter to his wife:

> Is it I who write or the fiend that has taken possession of me? As I write these lines to be read by your pure and loving eyes, I avow myself the most pitiful fellow, the most abject coward that ever lived. Oh, Elinor, beautiful, beloved,

faithful wife, good-bye for evermore; I go out into the darkness of death; good-bye. (1977: 14)

The authentic remorse conveyed in this type of letter is appropriated by Mickson and transposed into the 'remorseful' letters written by his duplicitous young heroine. 'Well, Sweetie', reads one of Lucy's letters:

> This letter is written while tears are fast flowing from my eyes. My heart is sore and my soul has regretted for loving you so deeply ... Darling, to tell you the truth, I can NEVER NEVER bear to leave you ... With shaking hands am I writing this note to you. My face is worn out and I am really tortured in my heart. I follow the song which says 'I wish I had never been born'. Ah! Where is my Romeo? Is he gone? ... Darling, I am restless, I am seriously sick at heart and I do not know what to do now ... I am now so weak that writing is just no more possible for my weak body to continue. (Mickson, 1966: 14; author's emphasis)

The letter is signed 'Sorrowful' and contains a postscript in which Lucy threatens, for the fifth time, to commit suicide if Frank does not forgive her for her most recent affair (*ibid.*). By having Lucy, the most deceitful of Ghanaian character types, emulate Clay's language and style so perfectly, Mickson makes the European model into a target for criticism and distances his readers from the Western romance.

Extracts from Lucy's letters are read aloud by Seth and Frank, forming quotations which are repeated time and again in the novel, cited as evidence to reveal the contrast between the romantic heroine's written sentiments and her actual behaviour towards her lover. Mickson seems to be alerting readers to the dubious nature of Lucy's discourse in relation to the rest of the narrative. Her letters constantly are being recontextualised and ironised through this process of extraction, quotation and application to the non-'literary' world that is created within the text.

Lucy's letters are intertextual, containing chunks of other romantic narratives. The range of quotations in them is so dense that they acquire a separate textuality from the rest of the novel. The letter printed above contains two explicit quotations: the first, 'I wish I had never been born', is from a popular love-song; the second, 'Where is my Romeo?' is a common misquotation from Romeo and Juliet.[5] Mickson is using the 'quoting mode' to demonstrate his authority as an adviser to young, urban, literate readers who may be familiar with the quotations he uses but unable to combine and apply them in a didactic way. Despite his skill in citing from the European literature of love, this quoting mode is not an unambiguous attempt to gain status for himself through the imitation of European texts. After all, Lucy is not a Juliet but a *parodic inversion* of Juliet. She is an unfaithful lover who exploits the resources of a Western romantic canon in order

---

[5] As in Seth's misquotation of the word injudicious, Lucy's Shakespearean reference can be seen as a subversion of the source text, arousing readers' suspicions about the imitated discourse.

to fool her fiancé. Mickson's 'romantic' quotations are radically recontextualised by Lucy's application of them to her own relationship.

Mickson both draws upon and disallows the ideological authority of European romances. By incorporating quotations from Western authors, he establishes his authority as a proficient quoter, well-versed in the European literature of love. At the same time, he parodies the 'imitated' genre, demonstrating the impossibility of applying it to the 'real' world. The love-letter forms a genre of its own within the novel, providing Lucy with a licence to emulate a European, literary version of love: but when Seth, Frank and Lily contrast the contents of her letters with her actions, the European model is radically subverted. *When the Heart Decides* contains a heroine whose mimicry of the Western romance is so excessive that she *parodies* the entire genre. As her practical aunt comments, 'Lucy has been to hospital for heart-break, she has tried suicide by drowning herself in the sea and she has tried suicide by poison – all this for "REAL LOVE". What kind of unusual love is this? NONSENSE' (p. 61; author's emphasis). Meanwhile, the heroine phones Frank's workplace twenty-three times in the space of ten minutes (p. 62), swoons in her lover's arms (p. 70), threatens suicide five times in a single letter (p. 14) and reels off romantic phrases which are so densely packed together that her meaning is submerged (pp. 43–6). Despite the swathes of purple prose contained within the narrative, *When the Heart Decides* is not therefore an unambiguous copy of European romantic templates, mimicking without transforming the genre in which its protagonists are immersed. If he is borrowing a style and a genre from the West, Mickson seems to be doing so in order to *parody* the European master-texts.

In negotiating with the Western romance, Mickson exhibits what might be termed a desire to 'refunction' the quoted form, using its codes and conventions in order to generate an alternative marital ethic for young Ghanaian readers (Hutcheon, 1985: 4). 'Two things may be alike but never the same', Frank says when he reflects upon Lucy's romantic language in *Who Killed Lucy?* (1967: 15): likewise, in parody, two forms may be alike, but they are never the same. *When the Heart Decides* introduces subtle alterations into the 'imitated' genre and manifests a faith in the reader's ability to recognise the parody and participate in the critique of romantic love. In order to comprehend Mickson's parody of romantic quotations, readers need to share an understanding of the codes of love and be able to perceive their distortion or exaggeration (see Hutcheon, 1985: 25). Within the text, Seth fulfils a vital role in helping readers to recognise this process: he repeatedly alerts readers to the way that 'modern' Ghanaian women will achieve their goals by imitating European romantic discourse. His rejection of the romantic register helps to create the critical distance that is required if the parody is to be recognised as such.

As Mickson's preface makes clear, *When the Heart Decides* has not been composed to provide fantasy resolutions to readers seeking an escape from the problem of finding suitable marriage partners. The story is aimed at educating readers about 'real' women's behaviour in Ghana (1967: 5). Yet Mickson has created a generic romantic hero and heroine, both of whom express their love in a 'literary' language. In addition, their authenticity as lovers is largely confined to the written word: their love is shown by Seth to be no more than a literary style, incapable of being replicated in the reader's own world. As we have seen, whenever Lucy is transposed out of her literary genre and into the 'real' social world represented by Seth, her 'sacred pledges' (p. 73) are inverted and transformed. Ultimately Frank himself finds that 'the beautiful, fair coloured, tall and stately girl called Lucy, and who for love's sake I affectionately called "Sweetie", is a love pirate and a swindler, playing fast and loose' (p. 18). The effort to *apply* her to (or realise her in) the local world fails each time, for her letters promising endless fidelity are revealed to mean the opposite.

Mickson is not simply rejecting the literary codes and conventions of romantic love. Although the language of love allows Lucy repeatedly to deceive Frank, Frank expresses his own genuine love using the *same* romantic register as Lucy. Male romantic love is construed as authentic and constant, for men 'give their hearts, souls and bodies wholeheartedly' to their lovers (p. 5). Frank embodies the ideal that Lucy violates, and he promotes romantic love as the sole criterion for a successful marriage. 'Love in its magnificence and splendour', he cries at one of their reunions: 'love, pure, fresh, natural, sincere, real and solid. Love greater than that of Romeo and Juliet, love stronger than any mortal being can think of; Oh! love in the real sense of the word' (p. 57). Curiously, Seth also describes this reconciliation scene without a trace of the irony he usually reserves for the lovers. The framing devices have been stripped away and readers witness:

> a warm warm embrace of affectionate tenderness, and long passionate and involved kisses, portraying nothing short of love that is unique and ideal, that characterised the reunion of the two lovers under the 'forget-me-not' tree. (p. 70)

An excerpt from Seth's commentary is quoted again in the caption beneath the illustration of this scene.

Mickson seems unwilling ultimately to jettison the ideology and rhetoric of romantic novels. Although it is ironised by its contrast with subsequent events, Frank's outburst of passion celebrates the possibility that love can indeed be 'real and solid' (p. 57). For the duration of the narrative, this ideal remains preserved and unsullied in the figure of the hero, who mimics without mocking the language of love: he embodies one half of an unattainable whole, dependent upon a woman who rarely practises the concepts that she preaches and who uses romantic discourse as 'one of her persuasive and once effectively convincing tricky traps' (p. 83).

The idea that Mickson is using parody to reject the European ideology of romantic love is also complicated by the way in which he represents Lucy's experience of romantic love, for on occasion, love halts the sexually deviant heroine in her tracks and introduces ambivalence into her type. In one of the rare moments when readers encounter Lucy in an unmediated form and enter her consciousness, her love for Frank seems to be genuine enough. With eight betrayals to her name, Lucy stands waiting for Frank under the 'forget-me-not tree':

> 'Glory be to God and Hallelujah to the Angels in heaven', she kept repeating *within her* with joy ... All her *thoughts* were then filled with ideas – grand ideas – of how to prepare to meet the life-giving apple of her soul – Frankie – at the appointed time. (1966: 51; emphasis added)

An omniscient narrator testifies here to the authenticity of Lucy's love. When Frank appears at a subsequent meeting, Lucy runs 'wild up the [line of] pine trees with all her radiance, shouting "Sweetie, Frank"' (p. 69). No wonder the whole nation is thrown into confusion when her infidelities emerge!

When the Heart Decides is split by these contradictory representations of romantic love. Lucy's loving thoughts and feelings reveal a romantic passion that complicates the construction of her as a deceitful woman and the lovers' reconciliation scene, narrated without irony by Seth, appears to be an unambiguous endorsement of the very ideals that flounder repeatedly in the novel. These contradictions need not be seen as signs of Mickson's confusion about the ideology of love, nor as signs of his failure to emulate Western romantic conventions. Rather, the very ideals which are exposed by Lucy's promiscuity and rejected by Seth seem to subsist in the novel, retaining their value as images of a perfect love.

When the Heart Decides can be read as a space-clearing narrative which explicitly parodies one genre in order to prepare the ground for the alternative ideologies offered in the sequel, *Who Killed Lucy?* Mickson has 'come to terms with the past' through parody in the former text (Hutcheon, 1985: 101), using his hero and heroine to re-read the Western romances that have filled the shelves of Ghanaian bookshops since the 1930s. *Who Killed Lucy?* explores more practicable models of marriage for young Ghanaians. While Frank still loves Lucy in the sequel, he has realised that, to preserve his integrity, he must be more rational about his choice of partner and 'end his love with Lucy' (Mickson, 1967: 19). Mickson's parody in the first part of the story thus gives way to local, resynthesised versions of 'love' in part two.

The introduction to *Who Killed Lucy?* repeats much of the preface to *When the Heart Decides*, adding that 'we shall carefully follow the development of events (after the delivery of that fateful letter), till the end of this great, gripping, suspensive and educated story' (p. 8). As in part one, the 'gripping, suspensive' elements of the story are revealed in advance, allowing readers to take up critical positions in relation to the characters. Frank's 'resignation' letter is reprinted in full once again at the start of the first chapter, preceded this time by two illustrations with captions disclosing the outcome of the tale (see Plates 7.5 and 7.6). Seth opens the narrative by repeating his cynical stance towards 'modern' Ghanaian women: 'Oh! men', he exclaims:

> if you would but pause for a moment to ponder over the cunningly fraudulent intrigues of the girls of this generation, you might perhaps have been a little

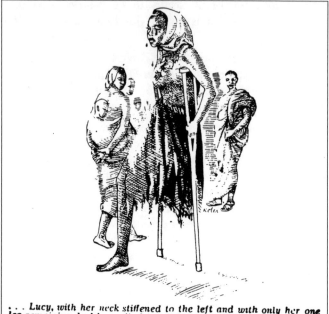

... Lucy, with her neck stiffened to the left and with only her one leg remaining, had been discharged from hospital and was living a most wretched and miserable life ...

7.5 & 7.6 *Who Killed Lucy?* (Mickson, 1967: 3, 5)

Sometime later, somebody ... placed a tomb-stone between the graves of the two lovers with the inscription: "HEREIN LIE THE REMAINS OF A WORTHWHILE LESSON"

wiser and the girls would consequently also have considered you when planning their tricks on you. (p. 18)

Mickson does not include many quotations from European literature in the second part of the story, nor does he retrieve and redeem the language of romantic love. Instead, he positions his protagonists within alternative ideological frameworks. The 'madness' of love has left Frank (p. 27); the narrator now quotes and applies Akan proverbs to the relationship; Seth and Lily even set up an arbitration court in their effort to bring about a reconciliation between the couple. The romantic hero now addresses his ex-lover as 'Lucy' rather than calling her "'Sweetie, My Love, or My Own". ... This was very significant to Lucy. Frank had NEVER addressed her by her name before' (p. 25; author's emphasis). Most important of all, Lucy is deprived of the romantic discourse she exploited in the first part to deceive her lover. Although she has 'in all sincerity changed for the better' (p. 26), Lucy now has no language with which to express her inner transformation:

> But how was she to utter it? She had in the past played all sorts of tricks on Frank into believing whatever she said. And now that she was in earnest, she did not know what to say for Frank to believe her again. And so, in silence she continued her tears. (*ibid.*)

Cast out of her genre, the romantic heroine feels genuine love but remains lost for words for much of the sequel. The entire tone of Mickson's narrative is altered by this silencing of the romance: in its place, *Who Killed Lucy?* contains repeated reconciliation attempts, as Seth and Lily join forces to intervene, facilitate dialogue and 'settle the differences' between the estranged couple (p. 32). Local arbitration procedures displace the ideology of romantic love, fundamentally changing the orientation of the narrative away from its references to 'literary' sentiments.

Since the mid-1960s, arbitration scenes have recurred in Ghanaian novels. Arbitration seems to represent an authoritative, culturally legitimate alternative to the ex-colonial High Court, where marriage cases would be judged by the terms of the colonial Marriage Ordinance (see Vellenga, 1983). A variety of different juries become involved in domestic 'trials' in Ghanaian fiction, as attempts are made to mediate between husbands and wives. In numerous novels, friends, parents, parents-in-law, priests, landlords or co-tenants adopt official, culturally sanctioned roles and participate in formal arbitration cases (see e.g. Konadu, 1989; Antwi-Boasiako, 1994).

Tom McCaskie (1995) describes arbitration in pre-colonial Ashanti as, 'the resolution of conflict by discussion and consent rather than by the unilateral imposition of authority' (p. 77). The fact that arbitration scenes permeate novels written since the 1960s demonstrates the ongoing relevance and adaptability of pre-colonial legal processes in Ghana. An active Africanisation of the romance seems to be taking place in these narratives, for within a single text, diverse mediators will intervene in domestic disputes. These efforts are, however, rarely matched by successful outcomes. Again and again, the customary arbitration model fails in Ghanaian fiction.

In *Who Killed Lucy?* the arbitration process is never concluded successfully. Seeking to reunite the couple, Seth becomes the 'chief arbitrator' and Lily becomes the 'linguist' (p. 56). As the 'case' opens, Seth warns, in language vested with authority, 'that anyone who would show the least sign of non-cooperation or impertinence to us the arbitrators would be accordingly penalised to pay some fees or kill some fowls in pacification' (*ibid.*). The reference to fees, fowls and pacification establishes Seth's authority: he has adopted the role of a senior man and quoted from an 'official' customary discourse in order to open up a space for the resolution of the couple's problems.

During the formal 'case', the defendants refuse to comply with the rules and they reject the decisions imposed by the court. Neither Lucy nor Frank will recognise the authority of the mediators who are, after all, their friends and peers. The negotiation process should encourage dialogue above the airing of grudges, but it is usurped, firstly by Frank and then by Lucy, both of whom use the opportunity of having an audience to narrate in detail their partner's mis-behaviour. The arbitrators have merely triggered a catalogue of grievances from Frank against Lucy (p. 58) and Lucy remains 'proud', refusing to accept the court's decision that she should admit responsibility, apologise to Frank and 'appease him with two fowls and twenty-four eggs' (p. 60). When it finally occurs, the reconciliation is imposed upon Frank. Forced to co-habit after the second arbitration attempt, Frank and Lucy remain alienated from one another; ultimately the arbitrators' success in achieving a reunion causes the death of Frank, whose 'heart has decided' against Lucy, but whose head is swayed by his friends' imposition of a judgement.[6]

Lily and Seth struggle to accommodate the couple's recriminations during the hearing, and *Who Killed Lucy?* charts the failure of the customary system to accommodate the rifts that occur in a 'romantic' liaison. The dialogical structure of arbitration seems to conflict with the fact that Lucy – if she is judged by a court filled with 'modern' young lovers – has betrayed the cardinal rules of romantic love: true love should be permanent and self-regulating, characterised by an instinctive obedience to the law of monogamy. Arbitration, it seems, is too lenient a cultural model to be able to deal with Lucy's violation of these principles. As in other narratives published in the 1960s, *Who Killed Lucy?* demonstrates the failure of reconciliation when the woman involved is promiscuous and insubordinate (see

---

[6] Frank dies after being imprisoned mistakenly for the attempted murder of Lucy. The narrator makes it clear that, had Frank held fast to the decision of his heart and refused to take Lucy back, he would have been free from suspicion: 'Before the jailers led Frank away to begin his five-year term of imprisonment', Frank says to his friends:

You remember I told you with tears during the last [arbitration] meeting over this Lucy affair in my house that you should never forget that it was for your sakes that I had been compelled to have Lucy back ... Don't ever forget also that it is because of you that I suffer these things today, innocently enough. (p. 99)

Antwi-Boasiako, 1995; Konadu, [1966] 1989). Mickson has explored the potential of arbitration, but it seems to be too forgiving a procedure to apply to the good-time girl: negotiation and reconciliation do not fulfil the promise of the preface, where readers are told in advance that the story will 'serve as a reprimand and perhaps a "purgative"' to morally deviant women, who will be punished for their sins (1967: 7).

Having been rendered speechless by the loss of her romantic vocabulary, mid-way through *Who Killed Lucy?* the heroine is endowed with a new voice and a new character type. 'I have sinned against God, sinned against my neighbours and sinned against myself', she says, kneeling before Frank, 'There is no doubt that it would be most appropriate if my name Lucy were changed to read "Sinner"' (p. 72). Mickson has not let his heroine return to romantic discourse, where her appellations were 'Sweetie' and 'My Darling'. Instead, she is given a new identity and positioned within a Christian moral framework. Through Christianity, Mickson can redeem the errant good-time girl by reconstructing her as a repentant sinner. As a Christian, Lucy is transformed into a tragic victim suffering punishment for her past sexual sins. Readers are assured repeatedly that her conversion is authentic, for 'in truth and in fact, she had changed' (p. 75); 'Lucy now was not the Lucy of old. She was a completely changed Lucy' (p. 74); 'Lucy was now a really good girl, changed completely from her bad morals' (p. 77). This does not prevent her violent punishment at the end of the novel, but it does perhaps allow readers to adopt a compassionate standpoint towards her downfall and to understand how Lucy's life might have been different had she altered her behaviour.

Mickson uses the 'completely changed Lucy' to generate a model of feminine behaviour based not on romantic love, but on a strict adherence to Christian marital codes. He places his heroine into another 'master discourse': in so doing, he explores an ideological alternative to the arbitration which required only an apology from Lucy and thus failed to punish her or exact moral justice. Christianity also represents an alternative to romantic love, which has been shown in part one to conceal more than it reveals about women's intentions. Having tested out Christian discourse, however, Mickson does not seem to settle upon it as a feasible alternative to romantic love.

Who Killed Lucy? concludes with a sudden influx of different plots and endings, which intermingle in the final pages, complicating rather than resolving the author's project to offer 'a great lesson, in fact, a fore-warning, to many a young man desperately in love' (p. 7). Heterogeneous narrative templates are introduced in the final chapter. After Frank has been 'compelled' by his friends to take Lucy back (p. 73), he is transformed from a romantic hero into a proto-typical unfaithful husband who goes drinking in hotels with his girlfriends. Readers familiar with this scenario might expect Lucy to respond by becoming the prototypical ideal wife who quietly tolerates her husband's infidelities and waits for her husband to return. Lucy, however, conforms to a different popular character type. She pursues Frank's mistress down the street and beats her up in public, bringing shame upon herself and her husband. Immediately after this scene, Mickson introduces an unresolved murder-mystery plot in which Lucy seems to have been killed. She is found lying in a pool of blood after her ex-lovers have, one by one, sworn revenge. This plot is abandoned, however, for Lucy is revived in order to be written into another familiar and far more didactic plot: she lives on, physically disabled, until she 'degenerated into something that defied description' (p. 101):

> so she remained, wretched, worried and unhappy cursing her early life, her morals and above all her 'foolish and stupid pride', scorned and despised by all till she died, five years later, at the age of twenty-two with no mother, friend, child or dear one to mourn her, or even place an ordinary leaf on her grave to honour [her]. (*ibid.*)

To drive home the moral directed at promiscuous women, Lucy must be portrayed as a social outcast, shown to suffer for and regret the behaviour which caused her downfall. Had she died in the 'murder-mystery' plot, this message would have lost some of its impact, for Lucy would have had no time to contemplate her moral defects. Meanwhile, Frank is written into a different popular template. Mistakenly judged guilty for the attempted murder of Lucy, he emerges from prison as a destitute man: unemployed and homeless, he wanders aimlessly around Ghana until he dies in isolation (see also Amartiefio, 1985).

By the final page of *Who Killed Lucy?* the generic 'romantic' hero and heroine of *When the Heart Decides* have been fragmented and complicated by numerous plot templates. The author seems to be rummaging through Ghana's archives of popular narratives, seeking an ending and a genre that he can apply to his characters in order to stabilise the moral of the tale. He has tested out, but not rested with, ideological replacements for the all-consuming love expressed in *When the Heart Decides*.[7] Having parodied Western romantic literature in part one, he turns to the model of customary arbitration, but it fails to punish Lucy adequately or to settle the protagonists in a workable marriage. The model of Christian repentance is then applied to the heroine, but it does not make her into the good wife who remains silent and submissive while her husband strays from home. Both the customary and the Christian marital models fall foul of two protagonists who remain, to the end, tainted by the failure of their romantic ideal.

The gravestone on Frank's and Lucy's shared funeral mound is etched with the moral of the tale, which is both emphatic and ambiguous. Remaining open to a diversity of interpretations, the epitaph reads, 'HEREIN LIE THE REMAINS OF A WORTHWHILE LESSON' (p. 102; author's emphasis). Readers must

---

[7] Similar observations have been made about the fragmentary nature of Yoruba narratives which, as in *Who Killed Lucy?*, are not necessarily *meant* to offer stable conclusions to plots (Quayson, 1995; Barber, 1987, 1995a). In their openness and multiplicity, such 'endings' offer space for readers and audiences to enter into discussions of the character types and scenarios, to draw their own lessons from the scenes they have witnessed. Indeed, as we saw in Chapter 2, within *Who Killed Lucy?* there is just such a scene of spectator participation in the penultimate chapter.

compose the 'worthwhile lesson' for themselves: it is the reader's task to produce a coherent moral from the heterogeneous narrative fragments contained in the final chapter.

In the 'Lucy' pamphlets, Mickson problematises the ideology of romantic love. He does so initially by drawing readers' attention to the writtenness of Lucy's love-letters, which license sentiments that cannot easily be experienced in everyday relationships. Romantic love takes the form of an unattainable ideal in these novels, but Mickson does not finally abandon it in favour of an alternative model. Arbitration procedures are simultaneously employed and disappointed in *Who Killed Lucy?* and Lucy's shift from a romantic to a Christian language register cannot retrieve the relationship. Romantic love continues to exist in the 'Lucy' pamphlets as a quixotic literary dream. Unlike the women writers to be explored in Chapters 9 and 10, for Mickson romantic love is something which determines the protagonists but is impossible to realise in his tragic version of the 'real' Ghanaian world.

8

'Those Mean & Empty-headed Men'
The shifting representations of wealth & women in two Ghanaian popular novels

By the end of the 1970s the Ghanaian economy was in a state of 'extreme turbulence', even collapse, and this condition persisted well into the 1980s (Nugent, 1995: 17). During the price-boom years of the 1950s, cocoa farmers had operated in an economy in which large-scale producers could amass wealth and transform their social status from 'commoners' to 'Big Men' (Assimeng, 1989; Nugent, 1995). By the late 1970s, however, excessive taxation of cocoa producers had led to smuggling and decreasing production levels in the cash-crop sector; rapid inflation had set in, rising from 10.1 per cent in 1972 to 116.5 per cent in 1977, causing shortages of fuel, consumer goods, spare parts and imported commodities (Nugent, 1995: 26; Boahen, 1989: 9). Economic mismanagement and natural disasters at home combined with political instabilities in the region to create a climate of uncertainty: the social effects of inflation, drought and forest fires were compounded in 1983 by the forced repatriation of over one million Ghanaians from Nigeria. Where their parents and grandparents might have accumulated savings as cocoa producers, as commercial brokers for foreign merchants or as educated professionals, Ghanaian workers now found their forebears' routes to wealth blocked by the recession. Clearly, the potential sources of wealth available to Ghanaians had shifted over time.

This chapter explores the manner in which the changing economic climate in Ghana has been accompanied by shifts in the ways wealth and women are conceptualised within locally published novels. These narratives actively recreate the variety of moral meanings that are commonly attached to the accumulation of wealth. Generating new meanings and incorporating residual attitudes towards wealth, Ghanaian novelists are 'reading' and responding to the economy through their protagonists and plots.

A simple 'text-context' relationship cannot be found in the novels to be explored here: fluctuations in global cash-crop prices, for example, are not reflected unambiguously in a protagonist's attitudes towards farming and agricultural wealth. Rather, authors are engaged in an ongoing process of constructing symbolic economies: they convert and transform real economic relationships into symbolic ones and help to generate explanations of (mis)fortune that will touch the experiences of their readers. Real economic conditions are absorbed into the symbolic space of popular fiction. The economy is converted into a textual 'event', attached to character types through whose experience moral messages about money can be conveyed and, finally, transformed by this process into a complex, sometimes contradictory set of interpretations of wealth in contemporary society.

Popular interpretations of the origins and uses of immense wealth have changed significantly since Independence. Through a comparative study of two locally produced Ghanaian novels, published twenty years apart, this chapter explores the ways in which specific economic conditions have generated different conceptualisations of wealth. As we shall see, Ghana's 'real' monetary economy is not erased in this process: it is translated into 'money moralities' in which an individual's struggle to make and invest capital is equated with his or her moral worth.

Victor Amarteifio's *Bediako the Adventurer* (1985), which we have encountered already in Chapter 2, was first published in the Twi language in 1967 and Kwame Osei-Poku's *Blood for Money* was first published in English in 1989. Both novels depict commoners seeking elevation to 'Big Man' status, and both have the generation, retention and investment of wealth as their central concerns. However, the potential money-making opportunities available to an ambitious Ghanaian 'youngman' are configured very differently in the two texts. In discussing the reasons for these differences, I will be suspending textual analysis at regular intervals and using the narratives to open up a situational analysis of the specific economic and cultural contexts within which they were composed.

After periods of price-rises, wage decreases, inflation and social unrest between 1939 and 1948, the sudden and seemingly limitless influx of foreign exchange during the cocoa-boom years of the 1950s allowed Nkrumah to nurture the image of Ghana as a land of plenty. He announced in a speech:

[Our goals are] the total abolition of unemployment, malnutrition and illiteracy, and the creation of conditions where all our people can enjoy good health, [and] proper housing, where our children can have the best of educational facilities and *where every citizen has the fullest opportunities to develop and use his* [sic] *skills and talents.* (cited in Robertson, 1984b: 39; emphasis added)

Nkrumah's comments imply that through hard work an ordinary man one day will be able to harness the new forms of wealth, increase his purchasing power and perhaps become a man of status in his community. The country's substantial foreign exchange reserves had, however, been depleted by the mid-1960s. Ghana's downward economic spiral started at this time, when Nkrumah's government failed to respond to the slump in international cocoa prices or to stem the individualistic appropriation of national resources by corrupt officials (Rimmer, 1992). Surrounded by a population suffering from unemployment, high inflation and scarcities in imported goods, the Big Men in Nkrumah's government cut themselves loose from the very communities in which they distributed their wealth and acquired recognition (Robertson, 1984a; Akyeampong, 1993).

Published the year after Nkrumah's fall, *Bediako the Adventurer* (1967) opens with an accusation which inverts the President's vision of an egalitarian society.[1] A young man indirectly suggests that Bediako has acquired his wealth in the manner of a corrupt official, through speculation and hoarding rather than through productive hard work. When three youths catch sight of Bediako's 'posh two-storeyed house', one of them comments that, to be able to afford such luxury the owner must be 'one of those mean and empty-headed men who never struggle much, yet get richer and richer to a point where they don't know what to do with themselves' (p. 11). Contained within this comment is the presupposition that readers will recognise a contemporary social type, for Bediako is alluded to as 'one of *those* … men'. Positioned thus, little more needs to be added about the source of Bediako's apparently unearned wealth. The speaker is interpellating a local reader who will be able to interpret the insinuation and connect it with a popular belief about Big Men's malpractices in Ghana.

Also embedded in the young man's comment – in an unmarked form – is an archaic reference to an individual's personal destiny, which cannot be reined in or controlled. Regardless of individual agency, an amoral force appears to have helped Bediako to get 'richer and richer' (see McCaskie, 1995). If such a reference to Bediako's auspicious destiny is present, however, it is absorbed into a far more specific opinion about the Big Man's moral laxity: the youth situates Bediako in a popular moral economy in which immense wealth is equated with 'meanness' towards his community, laziness and a lack of 'struggle'. These interpenetrating perceptions of wealth contest Nkrumah's futuristic image of a time when human agency – hard work, skills and talents – will generate health and housing for the masses. Instead, money seems to have fallen from nowhere onto the 'happy' man.

The young men's negative judgements spring from the sight of the rich man's house and it shows their sense of alienation from the conspicuous symbols of a Big Man's status. Instead of manifesting his hard work and auspicious destiny, Bediako's money supplies are infused with the onlookers' concerns about the struggle to survive in the 1960s: like a speculator on the commodity markets, his wealth seems to stem from self-generating sources and not from productive labour.

The youths voice common opinions about the economic transformations that had occurred in the final years of Nkrumah's government. On a microeconomic scale, during Nkrumah's period in power the cocoa-farming commoners and

---

[1] All subsequent references to *Bediako the Adventurer* will relate to the English translation, published in 1985.

entrepreneurial 'youngmen' who had, for generations, been able to gain wealth and status in the cash-crop sector, experienced dramatic shifts in the sources of possible wealth. Trade and commerce had largely centred upon productive activities until the mid-1960s, when fluctuations in the world market price for Ghana's monocrop altered the potential sources of wealth. Money-making opportunities shifted at this time towards speculative activities (Nugent, 1995). The ebbs and flows of cedis that speculators played with were linked to Ghana's trading status as a producer of cocoa, the price of which producers could not control; in addition, foreign exchange was largely contained within a small, politically well-connected class of men who did indeed appear to be getting 'richer and richer' without creating or marketing a visible product (Davidson, 1973).[2]

The protagonist of Amarteifio's novel is keen to distance himself from the young men's presuppositions about the source of his wealth. Bediako invites the boys into his house and narrates his life-story to them, and the entire novel is built around an effort to justify this Big Man's moral worth. He tells his internal audience at the start of his story:

My advice to you is that wherever you may go and whenever you find any person who in your opinion, is more successful, wealthier or happier than you are – as I assume you think I must be – don't be tempted to say that he has had an easy life all the way. (Amarteifio, 1985: 18)

An alternative money morality is created in the course of the novel to resist and displace the values applied by the youths. Repeatedly, Bediako insists that the vacillating money supplies in an individual's life are *divinely* regulated, and that a man's income is decided ultimately by God, who sits in judgement of his social behaviour: 'It is only God who ... knows all about us, and what the future has in store for us', he says, adding that, 'If we follow the teachings of Christ, we shall always succeed; it is only when we turn against the ways of God that we find life so bitter and not worth living' (p. 116). Bediako emphasises that God distributes and takes away money, and humans can only regulate their incomes by conforming to Christian moral precepts. The important point, here, is that God becomes a kind of divine speculator in this moral economy, investing large sums of money in individual 'goods' and watching them fail or succeed in realising their moral value.

Bediako's sin, remorse, repentance and final acceptance of his social responsibilities as a husband are paralleled in the morally equivalent realm of money: abject poverty strikes when he evicts his wife from the house and enters an adulterous relationship with a 'good-time girl'; money 'flees' from him when he enters a period of purgation, wandering aimlessly through the Ghanaian borderlands

---

[2] This point should not be overemphasised, nor should privately accumulated wealth be seen to originate in the impact of a Western capitalist ideology. For centuries, West African traders have speculated by hoarding goods, or purchasing commodities in one region to be sold in areas of scarcity. What distinguishes the mid-1960s from previous decades is the scale of speculation and the public perception of it as a corrupt, individualistic activity depriving people of essential commodities.

with no social roots or family connections; and enormous wealth descends as if from nowhere when he has repented and accepted responsibility for his sins. A superior, aloof force seems to be intervening each time, tossing money to and fro before depositing it in the passive protagonist's lap. The author rationalises and moralises this extreme, almost amoral force which is all-giving and all-punishing, blind to human systems of justice. Amarteifio seems to have applied the Christian idea of God to the residual Ashanti concept of an uncontrollable, whimsical force which directs a person's fate or destiny. In pre-colonial Ashanti, *Onyame* signified the 'withdrawn God', a 'remote and allocative rather than approachable and flexible judge' (McCaskie, 1995: 107). The power of *Onyame* has been preserved, then, but it has been translocated into Christian doctrine and attached to the Christian God.

As we saw in Chapter 2, a 'trollop' initiates Bediako's financial downfall: the 'captivating', 'irresistible' young woman tempts Bediako away from his marriage and gains access to all of his hard-earned cash (Amarteifio, 1985: 58). While his pregnant wife is staying with her mother, Feli arrives from an unknown location, 'and brought about, in my happy and prosperous life, a change quite startling in its suddenness' (p. 52). An explicit parallel is thus established between a man's loss of control over his wealth and his sexual abandonment to a woman.

Feli is not a simple character into whom Amarteifio pours the final responsibility for his protagonist's downfall. She is a transitional and catalytic figure in the narrative, opening the door to a universe which contains multiple punishments sent directly to Bediako from God. Immediately after meeting Feli, in a realm that cannot be disconnected from his infidelity, his money gains a momentum of its own: having let go of his masculine status as a husband and householder, Bediako is punished in the material world. In the space of two pages he is sacked for defrauding his company, thieves ransack his house, debt-collectors insist upon repayment and Feli disappears from the relationship leaving outstanding debts (pp. 67–8). Left without status or resources, Bediako is nothing as a human being.

Feli embodies a set of warnings aimed at men about the dire social consequences of sexual irresponsibility. She is significant to the moral economy of the novel, for it is *through* her that Bediako loses control of his conscience, savings and social status, and once he has been cast out of society for his sexual sins, large quantities of money start to appear and disappear at whim. A 'miserly' uncle leaves his secretly hoarded wealth to Bediako, but the extended family intervenes, reclaims and redistributes the money (pp. 140–3); thrown into extreme poverty, Bediako climbs a tree to hang himself, only to witness two members of his family bury his uncle's treasure-box, which he retrieves as his rightful inheritance (pp. 146–7); simultaneously, friends arrive with the good news that his cocoa plantation has yielded an enormous harvest and made him a rich man (p. 147). 'Now, my friends, what had I discovered?', Bediako asks his audience of young men as he begins to interpret these sudden inflows of wealth, 'The very Saturday that I felt that luck had forsaken me and that all was lost and life not worth living, God revealed himself once more to me in the most astonishing manner' (p. 150).

Wealth does not come from nowhere, and a man does not get 'richer and richer' for no reason. Bediako is explaining his good fortune by linking 'luck' – or his new-found ability to harness wealth – with the principle of divine intervention, which is manifested on earth through money.[3] 'Let us now go back to your original statement that money runs easily', the hero concludes. 'Sinner as I am, God has always had mercy and pardon for me' (Amarteifio, 1985: 153). Human agency is excluded from this money morality. By situating his protagonist within a Christian discourse, Amarteifio has disconnected the Big Man from the domestic economy and conceptualised his wealth in terms of divine punishment and forgiveness. Immense wealth is thus legitimised and rationalised through Christianity, for the Big Man's material goods are manifestations of God's reward to individuals who live according to abstract Christian values.

The lack of control over money that emerges in *Bediako the Adventurer* is not connected to the concept that cash is 'evil'. Quite the reverse: there are several clearly differentiated sources of wealth in the novel, both earned and inherited, and none of them is unambiguously 'good' or 'evil'. Money is an elusive, contradictory substance in the novel. Amarteifio instils this slippery resource with 'good' or 'bad' qualities by leashing it to a religious pole, but, in itself, it has no essential moral meaning. Through Christianity he is able to create the impression that cash-flows are divinely regulated and that money is the earthly sign of the value God places upon an individual's life. Any political critique of the Ghanaian Big Men who became rich during the 1960s is made irrelevant by this image of God. Bediako's explanations thus resist the young men's insinuation that his wealth has political sources.

Viewed in the context of the corruption and cocoa slump occurring in Ghana when the novel was first published, it becomes possible to see how economic conditions have infiltrated the narrative, only to be reconceptualised by the author. Amarteifio has recognised 'those men' who hoard Ghana's resources, but he has managed to legitimise certain other types of wealth by having his protagonist

---

[3] Close parallels can be found between Ghanaian narratives containing money symbolism and Yoruba texts produced during the oil-boom years and subsequent oil-recessions in Nigeria. Karin Barber (1982) finds that in popular Yoruba theatre performances since the 1970s, solutions are proposed to the problem of ordinary workers' exclusion from the oil-rich sector of the economy. Political criticisms of corruption and nepotism in the country are 'displaced sideways onto armed robbery and magical money' narratives, both of which are the experienced or imagined 'by-products of the petro-naira economy' (p. 449; see Watts, 1994). In their efforts to resolve the audience's experience of poverty in the midst of visible national wealth, the plays frequently promote a hard-work ethic, combining it with the Christian missionary principle that 'one should be content with one's lot' (Barber, 1982: 448). These popular performances are thoroughly ambivalent: on the one hand, plots partially reject the cultural legitimacy of the cash-rich millionaire by attributing his or her wealth to black magic or criminal activities; on the other hand, the plays express ambitions for the Big Man's social status, which is valued immensely in Nigeria. The plays thus manifest a great *desire* for 'boundless' wealth, but they also portray the dubious means by which unearned, 'baseless fortunes' are gained. As in the Ghanaian popular novels I have chosen to discuss, in the plays studied by Barber, suspicion is introduced into the means by which 'ordinary' individuals have obtained their immense fortunes (*ibid.*).

123

reject the accusation that he is a self-motivated speculator. An alternative money morality is promoted which resists the young men's opinions. By situating his protagonist within a noticeably non-political discourse, Amarteifio retrieves the possibility that, despite political corruption, a poor man can still become a Big Man if he conforms to strict moral precepts based upon sexual self-control and Christian family values.

Between 1972 and 1977, Lieutenant General Acheampong's regime increased the domestic money supply by 80 per cent, creating uncontrollable inflation. The economy was saturated with new cedis, described by Mike Oquaye as 'loose money in a few hands' (1980: 29), and giving 'the impression that the government was printing money at whim' (Robertson, 1984b: 42). Appearing as if from nowhere, the freshly minted currency made ordinary workers' incomes worth less by the day and generated widespread malpractices. The salaried middle classes, composed of professionals and civil servants, were forced to supplement the fixed amounts they earned each month with entrepreneurial, farming or smuggling activities. Teachers turned their cars into taxis after work; civil servants left work early to tend subsistence crops or, if well-connected, they imported spare parts and consumer goods for sale on the black market; and some market women aggravated the scarcity economy by hoarding produce and waiting for prices to rise (Clark, 1994; Robertson, 1984b).

Most of these practices were basic survival strategies undertaken by men and women facing desperation at home. For over a decade, traders and white-collar workers alike suffered massive hardships as commodity prices soared and their purchasing power diminished. Meanwhile, the new Big Men and wealthy women who had access to sources of hard currency increased their expenditure on prestige goods such as Mercedes Benzes and large purpose-built houses, illustrating in a concrete manner the gap between the wealthy and the poor. Openly parading their wealth at funerals, weddings and other status-conferring occasions, the Big Men of the 1970s, like their newly rich predecessors, would publicly distribute cash and consumer goods. Through these 'social investments' they sought social recognition and support, vital requirements in the maintenance of their status (see Ekejiuba, 1995).

Inevitably, popular attitudes towards wealth and accumulation have been affected by these new modes of money-making in Ghana. A great deal of recent anthropological research has focused upon the connections between West Africa's fluctuating economic status in relation to regional and global markets, and the shifting representations of accumulated wealth in popular discourses about money (see e.g. Parry and Bloch (eds), 1989; Guyer (ed.), 1995). The moral and symbolic values placed upon accumulation are not static or singular, for within the diverse cultures that constitute West African nations, multiple meanings attach to money at specific historical moments. Money has been circulating in West Africa for centuries, and economic fluctuations have generated complex narratives about the origins of fortune and misfortune (Barber, 1995b; Ekejiuba, 1995; Meyer, 1995a, 1995b).

Some individuals accumulated immense amounts of wealth during the Ghanaian economic crises of the 1970s and 1980s. As ordinary workers watched the successful few parade their wealth and enhance their power within their communities, a new economic practice was diagnosed, gaining popular currency as living conditions worsened for the masses: newly rich individuals were labelled '*kalabule* operators'. Describing men and women whose wealth derived from illicit sources, the term *kalabule* contained a network of negative references, all relating to the moral peril of money-making and its individualistic uses. Perhaps deriving from the Hausa expression *kere kabure*, meaning 'keep it quiet', *kalabule* referred to individuals who had abandoned productive labour in favour of speculative activities such as smuggling and hoarding, or who had accepted 'commissions' from corrupt officials in government agencies (Oquaye, 1980). *Kalabule* operators were profiteers who had access to Ghana's hidden stores of wealth. Rather than converting this currency into socially acceptable investments, they were believed to be hiding their stores from the rest of society, converting it into essential commodities which they would withhold, ready to sell to needy locals at inflated prices.

As a new and popular classification, *kalabule* conveyed a significant shift in popular conceptualisations of wealth and accumulation. The label became so widespread as a description of the newly rich that by the early 1980s it had permeated and transformed the established category of 'Big Man'. This latter type is a far more favourable figure in Ghanaian popular typologies, emerging in the late nineteenth century to describe educated, business-minded 'youngmen' who engaged in trading and brokering activities with European cocoa firms (McCaskie, 1995). Challenging the ranks of chiefs and elders, the Big Man gained economic power by his own hard work, and his vast reserves of accumulated wealth were seen to derive from legitimate sources. As we have seen in the figure of Bediako, the Big Man works hard and is also blessed with an auspicious destiny. This social type is an individual who has managed to discover the source of money and harness it for his personal use: he only retains a hold upon the slippery material, which might leave him at any time, by making substantial 'social investments' involving the distribution of large gifts at community events (Barber, 1995b; Manuh, 1995).

Paul Nugent (1995) points out that during the fiscal crises of the 1970s and 1980s, almost any kind of brokering activity in Ghana was regarded as a *kalabule* operation: 'Whereas the successful entrepreneur had once been the object of praise and emulation, his or her activities were increasingly regarded as both underhand and parasitic' (p. 28). By 1981, as Flight Lieutenant Rawlings took power for the second time and pledged to cleanse society of financial malpractices, 'the popular critique of speculation came close to offering an indictment of the dominant class as a whole' (p. 35). It was as if the majority of the population, having struggled to produce the smallest of incomes, were acknowledging the demise of the Big Man as a type with relevance to their own lives and admitting the impossibility of their ever attaining Big Man status in contemporary Ghanaian society.

By the early 1980s, the term *kalabule* had been 'gendered' as feminine. Women traders in Accra's main market started to be blamed for the country's 'moral decadence and economic degradation' (Nugent, 1995: 80). By focusing on local women rather than abstract fiscal policies, the accusers – journalists, politicians and members of the public – were isolating real bodies from Ghana's uncontrollable economy and holding them responsible both for 'immorality' and for the population's financial hardships. Market women were homogenised and stereotyped, and this process allowed a compound of meanings to be attached to their physical bodies. With popular support and the backing of President Jerry Rawlings, soldiers raided and destroyed Makola No.1 market in Central Accra; price controls were imposed on the market women's produce, and 'small boys' from Rawlings' People's Defence Committees (PDCs) were installed to regulate their sales; when they tried to demonstrate at Burma Camp, the market women were chased away by groups of angry 'youngmen' (*ibid.*). Symbolic qualities had been attached to a particular class of women and, in this way, collective frustrations about the unfair distribution of wealth in Ghana could be projected onto the traders.

Another type of woman also was accused of cashing in on Ghana's unevenly distributed 'loose money' supplies at this time (Oquaye, 1980: 29): *unmarried young women* were held to be responsible for damaging the economy, and they too were singled out in the media. In a book published at the time of these accusations, Mike Oquaye (1980) describes how, during Acheampong's regime, young women would sexually manipulate men in order to secure contracts and 'commissions'. In a lengthy and exclusively woman-centred critique, he writes:

> Young women obtained millions of cedis worth of import licences which they often resold at three times the value. ... Big-turbaned, pretty women bought and sold every conceivable item. ... These *kalabule* women rode in the choicest cars and attended parties on end with commissioners, top military men and their associates. (pp. 17–18)

As Oquaye's economic analysis demonstrates, one of the problems with an exclusive emphasis on women's role in African 'money moralities' is that *men* tend to be neglected as generators of illicit wealth.

Unmarried young women and market women might be familiar, recurrent figures in explanations of (mis)fortune, but other more ambiguous character types also surface in Ghanaian popular discourses on the subject of wealth. As in the numerous 'satanic possession' testimonies produced within charismatic Christian churches, women feature as temptresses and the Devil's minions, but ultimately it is *male* protagonists who choose the unholy route to wealth and status in many contemporary narratives (see e.g. Uzorma, 1993; Eni, 1987).

Kwame Osei-Poku's *Blood for Money* is described on the back cover as 'an attempt at exposing to the reader the problems and troubles that result from the craze for quick money' (1989: n.p.). The protagonist, Diawuo, takes 'a short cut to riches. Though very rich, he realizes that he was comparatively happier as a poor man than as a rich man' (*ibid.*). Here we find a man who contrasts with Bediako in that he turns to *juju* (rather than Christianity) for his supply of money. As in the opening of *Bediako the Adventurer*, where three youths used an insinuation about 'one of those men' to air their suspicions about a specific type of accumulation, the synopsis on the back cover of *Blood for Money* contains contemporary euphemisms about individuals who have chosen illicit forms of wealth. The phrases 'the craze for quick money' and 'a short cut to riches' lack specificity, but this very vagueness implies that they contain allusions to other popular narratives. Loaded with dynamic potential meanings, these euphemisms presuppose the reader's familiarity with the plots and resolutions of other satanic wealth stories, where the 'craze for quick money' and the 'short cut to riches' signify specific types of malpractice.

Narratives about the 'short cut to riches' are also quoted visually on the front cover, where a cartoon portrays the ritual items commonly associated with witchcraft, *juju* and satanic temptation: a cartoon calabash stands on a tripod and a snake emerges from it, spewing wads of Bank of Ghana notes onto the ground; blood-red liquid bubbles out of the calabash, flowing up to the title-word 'Blood'. This image is polysemic. Like the euphemisms on the back cover, it resonates with numerous intertextual allusions to ritual objects, beliefs and ceremonies. Ghanaian readers might recognise the calabash and tripod as a parodic representation of *nyame-dua* ('God's tree'), described by Tom McCaskie as the 'ubiquitous household shrine dedicated to *onyame*' in pre-colonial Ashanti, made from the forked branch of a tree and supporting a vessel into which ritual offerings are placed (McCaskie, 1995: 110–11). The snake signifies a whole complex of meanings, including (in)fertility, illicit wealth, the form taken by Satan and the form taken by witches (see Meyer, 1995a: 300). The Bank of Ghana notes which the snake vomits, neatly packaged and bound, might be a symbolic representation of the public perception that uncontrolled money supplies are circulating among the wealthy few in Ghana; the bank notes might also contain a symbolic reference to the time, in the mid-1970s, when Acheampong's government increased the money supply by 80 per cent and appeared to be 'printing money at whim' (Robertson, 1984b: 42). Some readers might immediately make the image cohere as a totality by positioning it within a manichean Christian discourse, for since the first missionaries arrived in Ghana, many of the ritual objects associated with *juju* have been regarded as real and translated as 'satanic' (Meyer, 1995a).

Gathered together in a single, saturated image, these symbols depend upon the reader's prior knowledge to make them cohere. Archaic references have been reconfigured into a resonant contemporary image of illicit wealth in Ghana. However, it is important to emphasise that the cartooning style and garish colours on the cover suggest that these references are also being parodied. The cover is ambivalent: it seems simultaneously to endorse *and* debunk its references by representing 'blood for money' narratives in the form of a sensational cartoon.

On the first page of *Blood for Money*, Diawuo (whose name translates as 'murderer') is shown entering into a diabolical pact with the shrine priest Abakah in order to gain immense wealth. A false friend has tempted him with the promise of a 'short cut' to personal riches, and Diawuo makes the conscious decision to sacrifice one of his wives. In conformity with the moral economy of other 'blood for money' narratives, he is tortured by terrible dreams and mental anguish until his suicide at the end of the novel.

Birgit Meyer (1995a) suggests that this resilient template symbolises the contradictions between individual accumulation and 'pre-capitalist ethics' in Ghana (Meyer, 1995a: 249). In her discussion of popular pentecostal stories about the Devil and money in south-eastern areas of Ghana, Meyer distinguishes between individualistic consumption and the 'reversion to a pre-capitalist ethics which emphasises family and solidarity' (p. 305). Acquisitive individualism, she argues, is represented in the narratives as a by-product of 'life-destructive' capitalist transactions, which are, in turn, conceptualised as 'evil' or 'satanic' (*ibid.*). In the context of popular pentecostalism, where God and Satan are perceived to be real presences in an individual's daily life, poverty and wealth 'can be either godly or satanic', conceptualised differently depending upon people's interpretations of the sources and uses of an individual's wealth (p. 307). Secret stockpiles of cash, if they are used individualistically to purchase status symbols instead of being redistributed within the extended family, are represented as satanic in these 'blood for money' narratives: such '[i]ndividualism and indifference towards the extended family, though adequate in the context of a capitalist economy, threaten ... extended family relations' (pp. 304–5).

In communities where personal savings are vital for status-enhancing investments, individuals on low incomes experience constant pressure on their resources from their extended families. Meyer argues that the tensions between the desire for wealth and the dispersal of money through the family generate compelling stories in which people can express frustrations about their social obligations by reading about the symbolic killing of close family members; simultaneously, they can reaffirm the moral superiority of a community-centred order by witnessing the agony and downfall of the tempted individual. Attractive as it may be to the low-paid 'youngman' who resents the financial demands of his extended family, unearned wealth thus is shown to extract too great a price from the individual.

From the outset of *Blood for Money*, Osei-Poku problematises the morality of these 'blood for money' templates. Despite its title, the novel does not conform to Meyer's interpretive framework, because Diawuo's 'evil' wealth does not unequivocally jeopardise the future of his community. Instead, his life-destructive ritual endows him with the resources to make 'social investments' in his family and home-town. Significantly, after killing his second wife, Diawuo's very first public gesture as a newly rich man is to make a substantial donation at the funeral of his victim (Osei-Poku, 1989: 132). He is 'socialising' his illicit wealth in the manner of a contemporary Big Man, redistributing his resources within Kyeiwaa's family and attempting to gain status amongst the recipients of his wealth. Witnesses to Diawuo's rapid rise to prosperity also hail him as a legitimate Big Man. Having donated millions of cedis towards community projects in his home-town, his dream of social recognition is realised, for he is carried through his village on the shoulders of young men, passing through streets lined with cheering villagers (p. 221).

In her detailed exploration of popular reactions to currency instabilities in Nigeria, Felicia Ekujiuba (1995) comments that an individual's wealth symbolises more than the value of his or her personal savings account. Monetary wealth gains its cultural value in the dynamic *process* of its exchange, translation, or conversion, into 'social capital' (p. 134). In Nigeria, as in other areas of Africa, personal wealth gains meaning during the 'processes of increasing prestige and social status': individuals are 'creating, maintaining, and reproducing social relationships through gift giving, marriage payments, elaborate funeral expenses, and title-taking' (*ibid.*; see Barber, 1995b). Similarly, Ashanti funeral payments in Ghana have come to be regarded as 'a means of valuation' through which Big Men are 'investing in social institutions ... cementing existing social relations' and creating new social bonds (Manuh, 1995: 190). Such investments in the long-term social order will, of course, enhance the Big Man's personal status and acceptability, and gain him recognition. At the same time, in the process of redistributing a proportion of his capital, the donor's wealth will be symbolically converted from hoarded, private cash into a resource which sustains the ideal of an 'unchanging community' (Parry and Bloch, 1989: 24).

When he redistributes his money, Diawuo fulfils a vital transformative function. Parry and Bloch (1989) describe this process clearly, though somewhat reductively:

> the morally equivocal money derived from short-term exchange cycles is transformed by a simple symbolic operation into a positively beneficial resource which sustains the ideal order of unchanging community. (p. 24)

Applied to *Blood for Money*, such a theory reveals how, in the process of becoming a Big Man, Diawuo is transformed into a moral 'broker': he bridges the potential dichotomy between individual accumulation and long-term community values by re-channelling his money, changing cash acquired through equivocal transactions into investments which preserve the stability of his community. Even though the source of Diawuo's wealth is represented as 'evil', the author is not presenting his investments as anti-social. The *process* whereby diabolical money is converted into social capital is morally ambivalent, and the protagonist's hoard of money is not set in a neat opposition to the 'pre-capitalist' ethics of his community, as Meyer claims for other Ghanaian blood-money narratives (Meyer, 1995a).

The process whereby Diawuo's money is legitimised distinguishes popular narratives about men gaining illicit wealth from those about women. Women in Ghana have access to different, less public social investment opportunities than men, and perhaps it is the 'hidden' nature of their wealth that generates negative, suspicious attitudes towards the source of their savings. The fact that currently there is no female equivalent to the Big Man in Ghana implies that men can legit-imise their wealth and status more easily than women (Oduyoye, 1979; Nugent, 1995). As we have seen, rich men can socialise their savings through community investments involving the acceptance of long-term responsibilities for the welfare of others: Big Men might sponsor the education of youths in their home-towns, take titles, fund social welfare projects and distribute consumer goods through their extended family networks. While women can make considerable donations to their communities and achieve formal status, the channels through which they legitimise their wealth tend to be less ceremonial, less related to public projects and, therefore, less likely to create an atmosphere of acceptance. As a result, stories about women's illicit wealth – epitomised by witchcraft accusations – are seldom ambivalent about the moral value of that wealth (see Comaroff and Comaroff, 1993).

As in Amarteifio's novel, a complex and contradictory morality attaches to Diawuo's sudden influx of wealth. One need only compare Bediako's early 'investments' with Diawuo's to see how the moral boundaries are blurred between the sources and uses of these men's different kinds of wealth. Although Bediako has earned his cash through honest labour as a salaried shop assistant, when he invests it in the good-time girl he corrupts his earnings, for they have been used to fuel his lust and purchase Feli's sexual favours. When the good-time girl gets her hands on the hero's money it is transformed as a resource – or 're-sourced' – for it ought to have been reserved for transactions that would benefit his extended family. Diawuo, on the other hand, has acquired his wealth in a malevolent way by sacrificing his wife and committing himself to the on-going elimination of close family members. However, the manner in which he spends his satanic wealth partially 're-sources' it, for he invests it wisely in long-term business ventures and plans to 'invest it in his children to ensure a prosperous future for them and he would generously give to the poor so as to become popular' (Osei-Poku, 1989: 83).

Blood for Money does not seem to express the conflicts between the two distinct moral economies that Meyer attributes to 'blood for money' narratives in pentecostal circles (1995a: 249–305). Rather, two *parallel* value systems coexist in the novel, constantly contradicting one another and yet also inter-penetrating one another. On the one hand, in order 'to leave any name behind when you die', a man requires large sums of money for social investments (Osei-Poku, 1989: 69); on the other hand, the most abominable act is required to confer Big Man status upon an ordinary worker. These parallel value systems can be illustrated by the way in which Diawuo's secret 'shrine' is represented. Entry to the room contain-ing his money requires numerous quasi-religious rituals. Diawuo's incantations and vestments are explicit parodies of charismatic church practices: climbing into his red robes, he comments, 'I really look like Apostle Zebulum of the 51st Disciples Church, which is rather unfortunate because I have forever parted ways with them' (p. 150); the comic shock of this comparison is compounded when he chants, 'Glory be to Abakah, long live Abakah' three times upon entering the secret room (p. 142); and, after collecting his cash, Diawuo makes the sign of the cross and says, 'Lord God, thank thee for raising me from grass to grace through your faithful servant Abakah ... Amen' (p. 152). The secret snake-room is thus a parody: it both doubles and quotes from the discourse of the charismatic Christian Church. Blood-money and charismatic Christian values are forever connected by this representation, illustrating the contradictions faced by a poor man seeking prosperity and status in Ghana. Diawuo's choice to become a 'rich, haunted man' is represented in the very language of an institution which insists that it is better to wait for God's favour and to remain 'a poor, happy man' (p. 230).

Diawuo is a hard-working individual who has struggled to make ends meet but has been propelled towards evil by the economic situation in Ghana. His ambition is to command respect in his community, and yet his earnings slip away from him constantly; and his poverty renders him submissive to his wealthy wife, Kyeiwaa. What finally persuades Diawuo to consult the shrine priest is his friend Ansah's comment on the gender dimension to his poverty: 'Get it straight from me that any financial assistance from a woman is bad. You definitely mortgage your freedom and subordinate your rights and interests to hers' (p. 62). Immense wealth brings dignity and masculinity, for Diawuo has noticed that Ansah's wives call him 'my lord' and obey his commands (p. 69). Emasculated by poverty, he is 'compelled by circumstances much beyond his control' to sacrifice Kyeiwaa at Katatwo shrine (p. 1); 'Lord forgive my sin', he prays in an ironic appeal to God immediately after the ritual, 'for I've been compelled to do so. It is not my fault but that of poverty and degradation' (p. 106). The omniscient narrator does not comment on the flawed logic of this compulsion: instead, readers are reminded, 'Diawuo knew that whereas poor people had only hopes, the rich ... could undertake some meaningful projects so that they could leave an indelible mark before they died' (p. 83). The narrator exposes a paradox in contemporary Ghana, where corruption and speculation – symbolised here as diabolical wealth – appear to provide the *only* means of achieving the social ideal to leave behind a 'name' in one's community.

Blood for Money is morally ambivalent, for despite the heroic status Diawuo gains in his community, illicit wealth is by no means promoted. After Kyeiwaa has been killed, warnings are spliced into every moment of the hero's financial success. Diawuo is tormented by nightmares, moral anguish, guilt and the repeated realisation that, 'I have taken the wrong decision ... my presence on earth, *properly valued*, would be *worth more* than the money gained with all its attendant suffering' (p. 134; emphasis added). Ostensibly, he has selected incorrectly from the two parallel value systems described above and yet, as we have seen, these two systems are intertwined within a single ideology linking money with social prestige.

Given its ambivalence, *Blood for Money* can be read as a targeted critique of the money-making opportunities available to ordinary men in present-day Ghana. Diawuo's detailed business strategies and blood-money investments reveal the extent to which poor men's entrepreneurial abilities in Ghana are thwarted by their lack of capital. The informal sector workers who make up the text's society halt the plot repeatedly with stories about their struggles to survive.

A particular splinter in the moral body of the book is the life-story of Ansah, the 'false friend' who tempts Diawuo to visit the shrine priest. Honest and hard-working, he was a mechanic until malicious colleagues caused him to be sacked; pious but poor, he attended church – the 51st Disciples Church, no less – until the minister sexually assaulted his wife; at last, unemployed and without religious faith, he succumbed to temptation and visited Abakah at Katatwo shrine (pp. 27–39). These stories of men's frustrated potential serve as ironic comments on the economic optimism of the 1950s, when Nkrumah foresaw a nation 'where every citizen has the fullest opportunities to develop and use his skills and talents' (*op. cit.*).

By generating this 'blood for money' narrative and using it to explain the wealth of a *nouveau riche* man in the 1980s, Osei-Poku has found the means to express, explain and morally justify ordinary people's exclusion from money-making modes that require not 'skills and talents', but political connections and foreign exchange. Wealth is symbolised as that which requires secret handshakes and human capital. Entrepreneurial empire-building and blood-money are inex-tricable in the novel, to such an extent that the Chief Priest's devotees belong to a secret association that is called 'The Abakah Assisted Entrepreneurs Club' (Osei-Poku, 1989: 197). The ironic implication here is that, if he is to acquire immense wealth, a man requires the sponsorship of a powerful official. Osei-Poku has thus transformed the 'blood for money' templates that circulate around Christian groups in Ghana by leaving their central moral questions unresolved. In place of resolutions, he offers a sympathetic and often humorous account of the economic conditions 'compelling' men into this kind of covenant.

Bediako the Adventurer and *Blood for Money* attach diverse values to money, most of which are based upon the activity of exchanging, or 'socialising' cash. Firstly, the wasteful or productive *uses* to which money is put are vital considera-tions in the assessment of a character: as we have seen, the moral ambivalence of Diawuo stems from the social legitimacy of his investments, while Bediako's downfall is triggered by his 'sinful' expenditures on a 'peacock woman' (Amarteifio, 1985: 28). Secondly, secret hoards of money are not presented by these authors as being anti-social in themselves: what they symbolise depends upon the *intentions* of the hoarder, because the projects for which private savings are earmarked affect the moral evaluation of the money supply. For example, when readers of *Blood for Money* discover that Diawuo's first wife, Asoh, has been lying about her income and hiding her wealth from her husband to stop him from spending it, the omniscient narrator intervenes immediately to explain her intentions. Asoh's hoarding activities are not for selfish ends but for the sake of posterity: secretly she has purchased a plot of land in Kumasi with the intention of erecting a building for her children (1989: 24). Similarly, Diawuo intends to 'leave a name behind', and this is presented as the sole – though misguided – motivation for his temptation into a blood-for-money covenant with Abakah (p. 156).

The final, most important aspect of a character's moral value concerns the *social type* who does the spending. This area does not seem to have been explored in current publications on the subject of money symbolism. 'Proverbial' character types, as I have argued in Chapter 1, are reinvented constantly in West African popular narratives and filled with new moral meanings. The feminisation of the term *kalabule* and its attachment to Ghanaian market women and unmarried young women in the 1970s and 1980s reveals the manner in which new character types are continually re-constructed from human raw materials, and then inserted into the economy, used as figures through whom people's financial hardships can be explained.

In *Bediako the Adventurer* the moral evaluation of feminine types is illustrated by the way in which Feli, the 'trollop', is blamed by the hero for causing his downfall into financial ruin: 'The cause of all this is that baneful woman in my life – Feli', Bediako tells his audience of young men (Amarteifio, 1985: 100). When Bediako transfers his wealth to the good-time girl instead of investing it in his household and matrilineage, he is succumbing to a popular, proverbial character type who has been circulating in West African narratives for decades, warnings radiating from her seductive exterior. While his good wife, Fosua, 'had worked so hard to save for me' (Amarteifio, 1985: 66), Feli wastes his money on imported commodities acquired for her personal use. 'Now I was living with a woman who contributed nothing but spent a great deal of the money', Bediako complains (*ibid.*). Similarly, in *Blood for Money* the spending habits of Diawuo's two wives establish their 'types' and position them in a moral economy. Diawuo's first wife, Asoh, is 'good and devoted' because, like Fosua, she financially supports her husband in times of difficulty and invests her savings in the family (p. 8). Readers are warned against Kyeiwaa, on the other hand, because she comes from a moneyed family and hoards her own wealth: 'because she was richer than Diawuo, she had her own schedule and could not be controlled by him' (p. 84). Bridging the twenty year gap between the publication dates of these two novels is the persistent idea that a woman's moral worth can be evaluated by her expenditure, related always to its impact upon her husband's social stature.

The masculine figures in these two novels include the 'fallen husband' and the 'tempted man'. Like the female characters, the sources of their money are mediated by their intentions for it and the social types into which they are cast. In both texts, ordinary men coming into possession of immense wealth are explored through the category of the Big Man, making them more complex and morally ambiguous than the female character types discussed above. In Amarteifio's novel, while suspicions are aired about this character type, the Big Man is retrieved as a legitimate owner of uncontrollable money supplies. In Osei-Poku's novel, however, written for a readership situated in a post-Acheampong society, far more suspicion is cast upon the Big Man's activities. However, the way in which Diawuo 're-sources' his money complicates simple assumptions about the corruption of wealthy men, for his social investments preserve the possibility that this type of man still might be retrieved as a social ideal.

The central points I have sought to emphasise in this chapter are, firstly, that not all wealth stems from negative sources in West African narratives about money, and, secondly, that not all excessively wealthy individuals are believed to have abandoned their communities in favour of self-interested accumulation. While the 'commoner' protagonists of *Bediako the Adventurer* and *Blood for Money* take very different routes to Big Man status, both texts reveal that the good, amoral or evil 'sources' of an individual's wealth are not the only factors in the moral evaluation of a person's worth to his or her community. An exclusive focus on the origins of money as *either* godly *or* satanic neglects the vital processes and activities of *exchange*: as Parry points out, money is a transactional object, and the conversion of money into social (or anti-social) capital can signify different things, depending upon the type of exchange (1989: 66).

In *Bediako the Adventurer* and *Blood for Money*, we can see how the single word 'money' opens up a complex realm of moral evaluations in which money symbolism extends far beyond 'good' or 'bad' sources and uses. As Karin Barber points out, 'Money functions as a powerful organizing symbol, exerting a magnetic force on a whole field of discourse about social values, achievements, aspirations, and relationships' (Barber, 1995b: 207). By studying two Ghanaian novels in detail and situating them in specific economic and political contexts, I hope to have shown just how morally complex, dynamic and powerful that 'organizing symbol' can be.

9

'Reading the Right Sort of Books & Articles'
Kate Abbam's Obaa Sima

In an article entitled 'The absence of the African woman writer', Roseann Bell (1978) asks 'if the relative silence of African female authors is self-imposed, or whether it is generated externally' (p. 491). Molara Ogundipe-Leslie's (1987) reply is unambiguous: in Nigeria at least, local women have produced so few texts because, according to her, they have internalised Victorian gender inequalities imported by the British colonial regime; in addition, their creativity has been 'shackled' in male-dominated postcolonial societies (pp. 5–13). In a similar vein, Ifi Amadiume (1987) traces the decline in Igbo women's political power as the colonialists' rigid sexual categories, which privileged males, were adopted by Nigerian men, displacing the flexible gender positions that hitherto prevailed in Igbo societies (p. 15). Whatever the reasons for their lack of prominence, women writers continue to prove difficult to locate, particularly in Ghana. Many Ghanaian women's narratives are scattered through diverse collections, brought to the surface by committed African scholars (see Opoku-Agyemang, 1997). Often their work is uncatalogued, printed in small magazines and newspapers rather than in paperback by national or sub-national publishing houses.

In the 1930s, the journalist Mabel Dove-Danquah gained a foothold in the Gold Coast national press, writing short stories that were printed in the 'Ladies Corner' of *The Times of West Africa* (see Chapter 5). Critical of the political power of chiefs and the self-conferred superiority of men, Dove-Danquah often wrote women into 'trickster' roles, outwitting and punishing arrogant men (Opoku-Agyemang, 1997). National newspapers remain receptive to creative writers in Ghana, providing outlets for women who – with the exception of Akosua Gyamfuaa-Fofie – appear to have become almost extinct as locally published novelists in the 1990s. Established women's magazines such as *AWO* (*African Woman's Option*) and *Obaa Sima* (*Ideal Woman*), as well as newspapers and pentecostal magazines, also provide space for their writing.

Interviewed in 1974, the editor and pioneer of *Obaa Sima* spoke about her reasons for launching the magazine. Kate Abbam said:

> The aims were to produce an indigenous woman's magazine, a magazine which would seek to bring out all that is beautiful and good in the African woman and her environment, to educate as well as entertain her.

Abbam's comments echo the sentiments of numerous other locally published writers in Ghana, whose books offer 'education' alongside 'entertainment', promising practical guidance to readers about intimate aspects of their lives. While literary critics have been lamenting the 'silence' of African women writers, for over twenty years women writers in *Obaa Sima* have offered full-voiced moral assessments of society at large, prefacing their stories with warnings, judgements and promises, taking positions of interpretive authority with as much confidence as any male author of popular fiction. 'I decided to write this story', one regular contributor to the magazine declares, 'not because I am proud of it, but I am doing so hoping that young bachelor girls will learn a lesson from my experience' (Kofie, August–September 1973: 16); 'men are great deceivers', writes another female contributor, 'Doubt it? Then read this sensational short story' (Addae, July–August 1973: 12).

In her first editorial, entitled 'Why the Ideal Woman', Abbam issued a positive message to women readers, emphasising the hoped-for psychological consequences of the new magazine: *Obaa Sima* will, she proposes, meet the Ghanaian woman's needs 'and make her feel really proud of herself' (August 1971: 4). The longevity and popularity of the magazine testify to the fulfilment of these aspirations. Surviving the rising cost of paper and outliving many rivals, *Obaa Sima* seems to have hit upon a popular formula which changes with the times, which anticipates, co-creates and fulfils urban readers' expectations.

For several years after its inception, *Obaa Sima* was ideologically and generically unstable: household tips aimed at fully domesticated 'housewives' would be offered alongside biographies of successful businesswomen; articles advising wives about how to attract their husbands back from extra-marital affairs would be placed alongside short stories criticising women's submissive roles in marriage. The magazine was poly-generic at this time, spilling over the discursive boundaries that typify contemporary Western women's magazines: it contained short stories, children's features, factual information about the economy, medical information, gardening tips, polemical feminist essays, legal advice, a men's page and articles on issues ranging from abortion to divorce and inheritance rights. Clearly, the editor was reaching out to the widest possible market of readers in the first years of the magazine's life.

If there is an ideological umbrella unifying the disparate genres in *Obaa Sima*, it can be found in the emphasis on romantic love. Since the first issue appeared in August 1971, the concept of romantic love has saturated the magazine's problem pages, advice columns, short and serialised stories. In the 1970s, the articles and short stories printed in *Obaa Sima* presuppose a female thirst for knowledge and, in contrast to E. K. Mickson's ambivalent 'Lucy' pamphlets, they also presuppose the reader's investment in the ideal of marrying for romantic love. For over twenty years, creative writers in the magazine have offered happy-ever-after outcomes to tales in which heroines find marital and emotional fulfilment with the men of their choice. Kate Abbam (1974) associates interiority with romantic fiction: 'I like romantic novels', she comments, explaining that the genre allows authors to enter into people's minds to explore 'their thoughts and behaviour. With the romance format, I can bring in a lot of things.'

Women are encouraged to be choosy and proactive in securing their marriage partners. In the first of a series called 'What Every Woman Should Know', published in 1971, readers are told: 'First you have to *Find* your man ... Then you must *Attack Him* ... After this you have to make him have an *Interest* in you ... Then *Secure* him for your own ... Finally *Hold* him' (*Obaa Sima*, October 1971: 9; author's emphasis). Once a husband has been secured and a fulfilling relationship set in place, a woman's marriage will 'lead to wifehood and mother-hood – the two things which make every woman's life complete' (*ibid.*). 'What Every Woman Should Know' preserves the centrality of wifehood and mother-hood in women's lives, but it transforms the status of each partner within marriage. Having been told to participate aggressively in the selection process – for 'You can't sit at home and wait patiently for "Mr Right" to turn up' (*Obaa Sima*, November 1971: 9) – women readers must look for a man whose minimum qualifications include loyalty to his wife, a sense of humour, romantic love, good manners, neatness, intelligence, ambition and moral uprightness. Unmarried women readers are instructed to settle for nothing less than 'an ideal man' (*ibid.*).

The 'woman's magazine' genre seems to provide a space in which Abbam and her staff can contest the definitions of ideal husbands circulating in Christian marriage guidance pamphlets and in many male-authored narratives. The oft-quoted 'lord and master' model of masculinity is reimagined in *Obaa Sima*, for the ideal husband's moral uprightness relates to his abdication, and not his assertion, of domestic power. Romantic, sensitive and courteous, the new man imagined in 'What Every Woman Should Know' seems to exist as a utopian figure through whom the magazine can promote an image of wives as assertive and equal to men.

The 'ideal husband' of the 1970s is a resilient figure, for many of his charac-teristics resurface in the responses of single young women from colleges around Ghana, asked in January 1998 to describe 'the qualities that make an ideal husband'. The majority said they imagined marriage partners who were 'God-fearing, loving, caring and understanding, [who will] treat me as another human being created by God' (fL3, 1998).[1] No doubt after discussions with their room-mates, other women from this college cite the same list of features, writing them in

---

[1] The following referencing system has been used to differentiate between respondents: m – male; f – female; L – University of Ghana, Legon; C – University of Cape Coast; A – Accra Polytechnic; T – Bagabaga Training College, Tamale.

almost the same order as their friends: 'My ideal husband should be God-fearing, caring, loving, understanding, faithful and reliable, respectful, hard-working and responsible' (fL4, 1998); 'He should be hard-working, caring, understanding, considerate, respectful, must have time for his family especially [his] wife' (fL6, 1998). A man's emotional and financial commitment to his nuclear family features high on these women's lists of preferred qualities. As one student from Accra Polytechnic puts it, 'An ideal husband must be dedicated to his wife and kids, responsible, hard-working, caring, sensitive, respectful and should be capable of showing abundant love in all situations and circumstances' (fA1, 1998).

In *Obaa Sima* in the 1970s, 'Mr Right' and his assertive wife are offered as role models to unmarried female readers. Within a few months, when *post*-marital problems are explored in 'What Every Woman Should Know', a very different picture of marriage emerges. Confronted by the prospect that, once married, 'Mr Right' may turn out to be the prototypical unfaithful husband, the wife's responsibilities are redefined in a way that opposes the 'huntress' of previous issues. As in so many popular representations of male infidelity in the 1970s, when the 'ideal man' degenerates, it is the wife who carries most of the blame. In January and February 1972, 'What Every Woman Should Know' instructs the married woman to 'be feminine' towards her unfaithful man and to suspend her independent interests: if she suspects that her husband is having extra-marital affairs, the wife must respond by cooking his favourite meals, flattering him, expressing interest in his work and not criticising him. 'Yours is to entice him with your charm, your loveliness and your understanding', wives are told, contradicting the tone of previous issues, for 'Man has always been a "hunter" and woman the "hunted" – do not change this order of things' (January 1972: 9). As the column enters further into the field of marriage in subsequent issues, it undergoes further ideological shifts away from the model of pre-marital assertiveness. Wives are positioned within the home as housewives in perpetual curtsies to the egos of unfaithful husbands. These images of wives contrast with the 'hunting' terminology – the finding, attacking, securing and holding – that characterised the column when it addressed unmarried women's lifestyles.

Why should *Obaa Sima* represent women's pre- and post-marital behaviour in such a contradictory manner? Should we interpret the gulf separating the ideal man from the real husband to mean that Ghanaian feminism in the early 1970s can only describe an ideal, which is untranslatable into the real? When 'real' men and 'real' marriages replace the romantic ideals of previous issues, and when single women win the status of wives, *Obaa Sima* seems to lose its egalitarian orientation. The gender ideology becomes far more conventional, as assertive unmarried women become submissive wives.

The promiscuity of husbands is a major subject for debate amongst Ghanaian women, particularly in urban areas, and there is a striking degree of agreement between all classes of women when they comment on the issue. The single, white-collar women interviewed by Carmel Dinan in Accra 'accepted that it was hopeless to expect husbands to be faithful' (1983: 351). For economic reasons these young women chose to remain unmarried and to seek out sugar-daddies for short-term relationships. Aware that they would be expected to remain monogamous as wives, they preferred to reap the financial benefits of male infidelity by becoming girlfriends to married men.

Surprisingly perhaps, married women in Ghana express very similar views to the 'good-time girls' featuring in Dinan's research. In a recent survey of the reasons prompting women to seek divorce, the journalist and feminist academic Audrey Gadzekpo (1994) finds that male infidelity is accepted as an inevitable fact of married life in Ghana. Gadzekpo's interviewees say that violence and financial irresponsibility and not a husband's promiscuity would be their main reasons for leaving a marriage (1994: 13). Claire Robertson (1984a) also discovers a cynical acceptance of male infidelity among the Ga women she interviewed in Accra. Asked how she felt about her husband's several girlfriends, one woman commented with resignation, 'I did not mind as long as he fulfilled his financial obligations to me and the children' (p. 126). These women were opposed to male infidelity on economic rather than moral or religious grounds, arguing that it drained household resources. The women interviewed by Gracia Clark (1994) in her study of Kumasi market traders also were resigned to the idea that their husbands would have extra-marital affairs (p. 341). The majority of market women Clark spoke to in Kumasi distrusted their husbands, tolerating affairs but declaring that male promiscuity was the main reason for not establishing a joint bank account. If money was shared, the women commented suspiciously, their husbands would spend the family's hard-earned savings on girlfriends and wives would be forced to compete for scarce resources with 'outside' women (1994: 341–2).

Viewed in the light of these women's comments, 'What Every Woman Should Know' is presenting wives with strategies for coping with non-ideal marriages in the 1970s. To this extent, the advice preserves the proactive bias of previous issues of the magazine. The column was written at a time when a woman's adult status was largely conferred through marriage and motherhood, when divorced or unmarried women suffered widespread discrimination in Ghana (see Robertson, 1984b). Rather than defining wives as passive victims, the column intercedes in difficult marital situations and suggests actions that a woman might take to alleviate the crises. If we read the column sympathetically, the 'ideal husband' of previous issues might be seen to subsist as a powerful figure, for wives are being offered plans of action for 'enticing' or 'charming' husbands back into romantic love (*Obaa Sima*, January 1972: 9). The ideal husband imagined in the column can be seen as a comment on Ghanaian women's *frustrations* with the institution of marriage. The personality change required for their feminine enticements to succeed exposes the conflicts between women's expectations of husbands before marriage and their experiences of men within marriage. The ideal man described in earlier issues allowed women to imagine new roles for themselves: however, in the case of 'What Every Woman Should Know', the effort falls foul of the popular belief that a wife is to blame for her husband's infidelities by neglecting her appearance, failing to provide his favourite foods and failing to show an interest in his working life.

In 1973, Kate Abbam introduced a men's page, 'Mainly For Men', in response to pressure from male readers who had, in increasing numbers, been seeking advice from the Agony Aunt and writing short stories for publication. It is interesting to note that since the first issue of *Obaa Sima*, men formed the majority of respondents to the regular dilemma tale column, 'Food For Thought', and I shall discuss the possible reasons for this male-dominated reception process before moving on to explore more recent editions of the magazine. The 'Food for Thought' dilemmas provide fascinating gauges of readers' attitudes towards marriage in the early 1970s. The structure of each tale is the same: marital conflicts and infidelities are presented in the form of sparse narratives, and readers are then invited to send in their moral judgements. Letters flowed into the magazine each month, and male readers participated actively as commentators on a wide range of issues.

There is little character development in the dilemma tales, which read like bare templates containing familiar protagonists and popular plots. For example, in 'Food For Thought: No Tears For the Jealous Wife' (March 1972: 26), readers are informed that the husband, John, is having an affair with the beautiful Barbara while his wife, Mary, is out of town giving birth to their child. After discovering a love-letter sent to her husband, Mary sends a false telegram to Barbara inviting her over to the house: she then beats up the other woman and John responds by divorcing her. 'Well readers, who do you think was at fault?' the magazine asks, inviting them to take sides and to 'Send us your opinions' (*ibid.*). No narrator intercedes to apportion blame within the tale and, in itself, the plot contains no bias. The text is not neutral, however: the three characters – an errant husband, a betrayed wife and a good-time girl – draw from a popular 'proverbial' typology which is likely to generate specific moral standpoints among readers. In this particular story the betrayed wife, who would usually arouse respectful sympathy from readers, oversteps the limits of her type. By deceiving and beating up the good-time girl, Mary violates the good wife's character type, and the moral dilemma posed at the end is built around this complication.

A selection of responses was published in the June 1972 issue of *Obaa Sima* and most of the commentators identify themselves openly as men. Only one correspondent sympathises with Mary, though he disapproves of her violent reaction to the marital crisis. As for the rest, 'I blame Mary' is the common declaration (June 1972: 24). Mary is condemned for deliberately interfering with her husband's private life, for deceiving his lover and for humiliating him by beating up his girlfriend (*ibid.*). These letter-writers have fully utilised the public interpretive space offered by *Obaa Sima*, reacting to the characters and plot by producing definitions of good–wifely behaviour.

Again and again, male readers' sentiments predominate in the 'Food For Thought' column. The lack of female responses to the dilemma tale may be coincidental, or a result of editorial selection policy, or a sign of women readers' disinterest in the issues raised by the moral tableaux. The transformation of an apparently gender-neutral forum into an all-male display of moral authority in which wives are condemned repeatedly could, however, be seen to symptomise a deeper problem relating to women's authority as interpreters and moral arbiters in Ghana during the early 1970s.[2] Given the opportunity to express their opinions, women might be vociferous as oral commentators and audience members at concert parties, but they appear to have declined *Obaa Sima's* invitation to respond in writing to the marital dilemmas presented in the magazine.

If women remain hesitant about writing in to *Obaa Sima* with their views, a female interpretive community is prioritised within the magazine itself. While Abbam has always accepted material from male and female contributors, her editorials tend to ignore male readers and address a specifically female constituency of readers. Actively encouraging women to read and write, she emphasises the empowering nature of literacy:

> We want to expose the fallacy of those who told us: 'Hmm! Do you think these women will patronize this magazine? The Ghanaian woman as a rule DOES NOT READ!!!' We feel that given the chance and encouragement the Ghanaian woman CAN and WILL read. (October 1971: 4; author's emphasis)

Faced with a quiet majority of women readers, who were purchasing *Obaa Sima* without choosing to contribute to its discussions, Abbam defines her magazine as 'a medium for educating the women of Ghana and also ... a mouthpiece for them' (editorial, vol. 10, no. 1, 1981: 9). Unlike her less vocal readers, she has used the magazine as a loud-hailer to testify against gender discriminations in Ghana. After the death of her husband in July 1972, for example, Abbam utilised her 'mouthpiece' to write extensively about the injustices of matrilineal inheritance laws in Ghana. Within days of her husband's death, his matrikin had descended on Abbam's house to clear out the furniture and reclaim the capital; furthermore, these relatives rejected and humiliated the widow by refusing to allow her to participate in her husband's funeral (October 1972: 4). Abbam refuses to remain silent on this issue, returning repeatedly to Ghanaian inheritance laws in subsequent issues of the magazine, inviting experts and victims alike to testify against the government's lack of a legal framework to protect widows from their husband's matriclans.[3]

It is essential to emphasise that *Obaa Sima's* 30 years in print spans a period of great social and political change in Ghana, a period in which women's movements nationally have fought for equality, achieving recognition and power. Many of the sentiments expressed in the early 1970s have been discarded as irrelevant to

---

[2] Women emerged as romantic novelists in the 1970s, and their use of the genre to mount feminist commentaries on marriage and masculinity was addressed in Chapter 2. It is important to note, however, that when it comes to the giving of explicit advice on the issue of marriage, male authors predominate in the production of non-fictional texts.

[3] Colonial legislation entitling widows to inherit one third of their husband's estate was only altered in 1985 in PNDC Law III, a decree issued by President Rawlings.

today's readership. Since the early 1980s, *Obaa Sima* has manifested an increasingly coherent *feminist* agenda that contrasts with the diverse ideological positions to be found in early issues of the magazine. Dilemma tales and marital advice columns in the magazine have given way to weighty, politically engaged columns: Ghanaian women's economic situations are discussed in detail in the magazine; whole issues are given over to the analysis of world conferences on gender issues; Ghanaian legislative reforms and election campaigns are discussed in detail from a gender perspective. This shift in subject-matter parallels the emergence of gender internationally as an area of political and academic importance.

Today's *Obaa Sima* is more ideologically coherent than the fragmented, poly-generic magazine of the early 1970s. In the past, *Obaa Sima* survived by appealing to the widest possible constituency of readers, seeking to attract a diversity of urban consumers. The result was ideological and generic polyphony: different, divergent attitudes towards women would be expressed within a single issue of the magazine. Today's *Obaa Sima* exhibits a feminist confidence that was absent from it in the 1970s. An editorial in 1995, for example, states the case for a female President of Ghana (vol. 22, no. 2 1995: 3–4). Entirely dedicated to exploring this idea, the next issue of the magazine reiterates the argument and focuses upon distorted representations of women in the mass-media: it includes details of the Fourth World Conference of Women and concludes with a reprint of the rousing 'Woman's Creed', formulated at the Women's Global Strategies Meeting (vol. 22, no. 3, 1995: 32–41).

Obaa Sima's ideological coherence as a polemical feminist publication can be seen to reflect the emergence and rising confidence of a class of middle-income Ghanaian women who have the purchasing power to sustain its current bias. As the following chapter will explore in more detail, women's writing in contemporary Ghana manifests a feminist agenda that was barely thinkable in the early 1970s. *Obaa Sima* was the first of its kind in Ghana. Working initially with familiar, popular constructions of ideal husbands and ideal wives, the editor allowed other genres to emerge from the dynamic stock of characters and templates. During the course of its consolidation as a genre, this women's magazine has produced new generic conventions and has both serialised and influenced the work of important women writers in the country.

10

Uprising Genres
Akosua Gyamfuaa-Fofie's romantic fiction

Men, after they become rich and wealthy, always think that they can get whatever
they want with money. ... But love is one thing that money can never buy.
I mean genuine love.
(Gyamfuaa-Fofie, *Suffered Because of Love*)

In 1991 the Ghanaian author Ama Ata Aidoo published a novel entitled *Changes*,
subtitled 'a love story'. Before the love story commences, however, Aidoo seems
to apologise for it. Her ambivalence towards the genre within which she has
chosen to work is symptomised by the ironic retraction which opens the text:

> Several years ago when I was a little older than I am now, I said in a published
> interview that I could never write about lovers in Accra. Because surely in our
> environment there are more important things to write about? Working on this
> story then was an exercise in words-eating! ... It is not meant to be a contribu-
> tion to any debate, however current (n.p.)

Much of this disclaimer is repeated verbatim on the back cover, and so the
narrative is framed by these first and last words. Where Mills and Boon romances
offer free gifts of chocolate on their front covers, feeding readers' hunger for confectionery alongside their desire for romantic love, Aidoo, by contrast, uses the
flyleaf of her text to 'eat the words' spoken by her old self.

In commenting so ambiguously on the love story genre, Aidoo has admitted
the possibility that her readers might not engage seriously with the narrative, that
critics and reviewers might bring to the novel a prevalent negative stereotype of
romantic fiction. Aidoo therefore pre-empts such responses by labelling her story
non-discursive, stating that 'it is not meant to be a contribution to any debate,
however current' (*ibid.*). In this manner – which the subsequent story exposes as
thoroughly ironic – she seems to be apologising for producing a mass-consumable
type of text that readers will delve into and fatten their fantasies upon, but from
which they will learn little that is relevant to their own social experiences.

When we turn to women writers who publish *locally* in West Africa, we find
far less ambivalence towards romantic narratives and concepts. West African

women writers, this chapter will argue, produce genres which are 'uprising' to the extent that they contain surprising re-readings of romantic templates, in which the language and structures of Western romances are reworked in striking new ways. The local author to be discussed in detail here has not necessarily 'sold out' to or sought to 'mimic' mass-produced foreign texts. Rather, as we shall see, Akosua Gyamfuaa-Fofie is putting romantic discourse to diverse new uses.

In her discussion of Black women's experiences of and narratives about migration, Carole Boyce Davies (1994) argues that the most creative and disturbing discourses are those which occur 'outside' dominant genres, those which are as yet barely heard, which rise 'upward and outward from constructed and submerged spaces' in the metropolitan centres (pp.108–12). 'Uprising textualities', she continues, are those which signify 'resistance, reassertion, renewal and rethinking', qualities which characterise Black women's writing (pp.108–9). Positioned on the outskirts of the dominant (white, patriarchal, Eurofeminist) culture, uprising narratives and voices have not 'adopted' Western hegemonic ideologies, nor have they been silenced by anti-feminist agendas (p.108). This argument is persuasive, in that African women writers' creative differences from men are accounted for in terms of their social experiences and access to power, rather than in terms of their essential, symbolic and biologically determined status as 'mothers' (see Wilentz, 1992). Boyce Davies' argument might, however, be expanded to include 'uprisings' that occur *within* genres such as the romance, which has been labelled anti-feminist and patriarchal by feminist commentators (Anderson, 1974; Coward, 1984). When this dominant genre is put into operation by writers who are situated geographically and economically *outside* the centres of mass-production, then the gender conservatism commonly associated with the genre is detached: when authors who are neither mainstream nor canonical take on the romance, it becomes an 'uprising' form, capable of conveying potentially radical challenges to popular gender ideologies.

Readers in Ghana often regard printed narratives as learn-by-example discourses which relate directly to their own experiences with the opposite sex. When asked what he expected to learn from romantic literature, one trainee teacher replied, 'Morally I have learned to control myself when I am with a lady friend. Usually you are tempted to bring out certain secrets which may lead you into trouble' (mT11, 1998).[1] Another young man stated that, from his favourite novelist 'I learn about self-control in marital problems and also it gives me a lot of encouragement for the future' (mL1, 1998). Women readers also commented that when they read romances, they 'learn how to cultivate the right attitude' towards relationships and marriage (fC7, 1998): this respondent continued, 'when I'm in a relationship as a Christian lady, [I learn] how to be a good wife and maintain a good and loving family life and how to make my marriage work through the years to come' (*ibid.*). Another woman replied that when she read Akosua Gyamfuaa-

---

[1] The following referencing system has been used to differentiate between respondents: m– male; f – female; L – University of Ghana, Legon; C – University of Cape Coast; A – Accra Polytechnic; T – Bagabagen Training College, Tamale.

Fofie's fiction, she learnt 'how to go about with men because of the consequences and what to expect in future when I marry. In short the problems associated with marriage. How to live a model life which is worth emulating' (fT4, 1998). 'I learn about how deceitful the heart can be at times', commented a Danielle Steel reader:

> I learn that if you are to follow your heart most of the time, you would end in quite a large amount of trouble because the heart goes where it goes and this can be really serious because if you are not careful you could fall in love with about every man you come across. (fA2, 1998)

Interestingly, unlike the men I interviewed about their reading preferences, none of the Ghanaian women I spoke to mentioned the heroine's promiscuity as a significant aspect of a story. Quite the reverse. In Ghana, young women said they preferred to read about heroines who display loyalty to one man, intelligence and financial independence. In a reader questionnaire circulated in 1995 and 1996, women readers listed many of the same favourite titles as the male respondents, but 60 per cent of them said that the most important element in a novel was that the heroine remained faithful to her lover for the duration of the story. Rather than applying the figure of the promiscuous heroine to society at large, the women seem to be extracting alternative 'realities' from their favourite novels. Positioned differently prior to the act of reading, they actively generate their own meanings and morally judge the behaviour of characters.

Similarly, as we found in Chapter 2, women writers in Ghana do not problematise the ideology of romantic love to the same extent as their male colleagues, and I should like to expand upon this argument in the following pages. Romantic stories by Ghanaian women tend to be narrated from 'feminine' standpoints in which the language of love suspends gender inequalities. Loving couples are shown merging together in lifetimes of monogamous loyalty. If her heart misses a beat, or his touch is electrifying, if his gaze is captivating or his touch makes her dizzy, then readers enter a textual field in which, paradoxically perhaps, *conventional* feminine roles are erased. In magazines, religious pamphlets and novels, women writers seem to be using the romance to signify their dissatisfaction with existing popular narratives about marriage. Romantic fiction has become a tool enabling them to reconceptualise women's marital status. Through the ideology of love, a critique of 'masculinist' conceptions of marriage can be mounted, for the love-scenes portrayed by women writers convey utopian visions of relationships and marriage. Unlike authors such as E. K. Mickson, Ghanaian women seem to be re-reading existing, conventional gender roles *through* the romance, using the rhetoric of love implicitly to criticise the society in which wifely submission is promoted.

Akosua Gyamfuaa-Fofie exemplifies the process whereby local novelists re-utilise familiar genres, for she creates from romantic formulas a platform for polemical, pointed observations by a feminist narrator. In an interview (1997), she describes why she has chosen to develop this genre:

If I write about romantic [love], I make the women involved become independent. In our part of the world, tradition demands that the man takes the upper
hand in everything. I try to let women readers know that love must go with
reason, so they can love without necessarily giving themselves as slaves. They
must try to acquire a means of looking after themselves ... In my romantic
writings, most women characters are financially independent and they love not
because of financial gains.

Romantic writing gives Gyamfuaa-Fofie the space both to imagine utopian resolutions to young people's relationship problems and also to work for attitudinal
changes in Ghanaian society. The genre for her feminist ideals is the romance
because the concept of love allows her to promote women's free choice of partner
and to reject arranged marriage practices. Her own version of the genre allows for
the incorporation of strongly-worded opinions about the socialisation of women.

The opening pages of *The Tested Love* (1989) and *The Forbidden Love* (1990a)
are almost the same: love-smitten heroines are shown at home, weeping in their
bedrooms, attempting to write letters to their cruel lovers but unable to gather
enough strength to begin to express their feelings. Both heroines have been
wrongly accused of promiscuity and they are represented as tragic and passive in
the most intimate, familiar surroundings (see also Gyamfuaa-Fofie, 1996a).
Opening scenes such as these can be read as comments on young women's lack of
authority in their social and domestic environments. In the home, where women's
roles as daughters, wives and mothers are perhaps the most pronounced,
Gyamfuaa-Fofie's heroines lack the power or resources to deal with their
dilemmas. By contrast, men occupy positions of domestic authority in her novels
as husbands-to-be, fathers and boyfriends, controlling the emotional lives of the
heroines.

These heroines do not remain bound to the home, quietly awaiting the transformation of their lovers into sensitive husbands. Rather, they are shown breaking
away from the structures that confine them: the heroines of *The Tested Love* and
The Forbidden Love echo the 'migratory subjectivity' of Ayerley in *Beloved Twin*
(see Chapter 2). Crushed by circumstances beyond their control, these characters
escape from the situations that have ensnared them, leaving their home-towns to
become isolated strangers living on the outskirts of unknown communities: in *The
Tested Love*, Boahemaa leaves home after being accused of infidelity by her fiancé,
who is himself an unfaithful lover, and Yaa Agyemang, in *The Forbidden Love*,
flees from her father's house after becoming pregnant and being rejected by her
first love (he too is unfaithful to the heroine).

If they are labelled according to the most common character types in Ghanaian
popular narratives, Boahemaa would be the typical victimised wife, wrongly
accused and cast out by her fiancé; Yaa Agyemang, on the other hand, would be
the typical good-time girl, a promiscuous, impregnated woman who has been
punished and cast out of society. In a very real sense, then, these romances are
addressing the anxieties and fears that women readers might experience when

they attempt to assert their sexuality in domestic environments dominated by men.

Both Boahemaa and Yaa Agyemang are denied their hoped-for status as wives, yet both characters are shown to be partially empowered from their positions 'without' society. Gyamfuaa-Fofie demonstrates that women *can* survive independently in fluid, alternative worlds where they gain their identities not by conforming to familiar gender roles, but by exhibiting inner 'courage', 'determination' and 'boldness' (Gyamfuaa-Fofie, 1989: 25). In *The Forbidden Love*, Yaa Agyemang survives as a single woman in a world without men until the reconciliation scene at the end of the novel; in *The Tested Love*, after her period of isolation, Boahemaa embarks upon a marriage of convenience, remaining emotionally strong until she too is reunited with her lover. Robust and brave after their first brief outbursts of sobbing, these betrayed women recreate their lives, concentrating on earning independent incomes.

Interviewed in 1995 and again in 1998, Gyamfuaa-Fofie declared an appetite for Bertha M. Clay romances and also Mills and Boon novels: such books she regards as exemplary romances, influencing her own narrative style and themes.[2] Perhaps as a result of such influences, her romantic heroines have less control over their destinies than Awura-Ekuwa Badoe's first-person protagonist in *Beloved Twin* (1973), explored in Chapter 2. As in so many Mills and Boon novels, within the first few pages of Gyamfuaa-Fofie's romances, monogamous love is presented as eternal: as a result, her heroines lack the autonomy of Ayerley, who selected an ideal husband from a series of available men. In addition, the heroines of *The Tested Love* and *The Forbidden Love* spend the entire narrative yearning to be the wives of their unfaithful lovers, waiting patiently for reconciliations and showing no sexual desire for the other suitors surrounding them.

In the face of such passivity, Gyamfuaa-Fofie's omniscient narrators fulfil active, critical roles in each story. The progress of each romantic plot is suspended repeatedly by the narrator's intervention with moral assessments of masculine behaviour and comments about the position of women in contemporary Ghanaian society. These omniscient narrators actively 'read' the lives of protagonists, extrapolating from the heroines' experiences, re-constructing and criticising prevalent attitudes towards women. Heroines tend to be passive and abused in the plots, like the ideal-wife figures in popular plays; when one turns to the narrators, however, these instances of suffering open the door to forceful condemnations of men's behaviour as husbands, fathers and lovers.

As we have seen already in E. K. Mickson's 'Lucy' pamphlets, romantic formulas have not simply been transposed from European into Ghanaian narratives. Within Ghanaian romances one finds active, advice-giving narrators like Seth who offer commentaries – or critical meta-narratives – on the romantic templates that are employed in the plots. Similarly, when the unfaithful fiancé in

---

[2] In the latter interview, Gyamfuaa-Fofie commented that several of her romantic novels have been blacklisted by teachers at secondary schools in Ghana on the grounds that they contain sexually explicit scenes between young, unmarried lovers.

The Tested Love kneels before his lover to plead for forgiveness, the stern narrator delivers a moral warning against male promiscuity in a language that readers are likely to recognise from popular advice-giving genres: 'Love, trust, understanding and confidence are the backbone of every marriage', the narrator comments. 'Without these it [marriage] has but a temporary existence' (Gyamfuaa-Fofie, 1989: 76–7). In Gyamfuaa-Fofie's novels the narrator alights upon each deviation from the romantic ideal of monogamous, eternal love and extrapolates from it, making an example of each deviant hero by applying his behaviour to society at large. The heroines are passive, jilted and abused in the plots, but the treachery they suffer opens up a space for vocal feminist interventions by the omniscient narrator.

As with the ideal-wife figures in popular narratives about errant husbands, the heroines wait in the wings for the return of their lovers. Unlike these popular narratives, however, Gyamfuaa-Fofie constructs meta-narratives from her borrowed plots, commenting with great passion on men's misbehaviour as husbands, fathers and lovers. In *The Tested Love*, for example, the narrator engages directly with 'what men think about women', commenting:

> What many men think is that they have got licences in the name of their male organs with which to operate indiscriminately. They always want their wives to be virgins and innocent, but they on their part want to taste all the 'tasteables' before and even after marriage. (1989: 21)

Clearly, this interpretation of prevalent masculine attitudes is a biased construction formulated by a gender-positioned narrator who is 'reading' her society from a feminine perspective.

Utilising the narrator's voice for feminist ends, Gyamfuaa-Fofie frequently intervenes in this way, producing romances in which she can criticise male promiscuity in the 'real' Ghanaian society: however, ultimately she forgives male infidelity by incorporating it into her narratives, by *plotting for* it and explaining it. In the process of resolving the issues she raises, she seems to borrow from a popular Ghanaian plot in which husbands' infidelities are partially excused, for in each text, her fickle romantic heroes are transformed into ideal marriage partners at the end of the story. Unfaithful men are shown to become repentant and monogamous, returning at last to the outstretched arms of faithful heroines.

I argued in Chapter 2 that Gyamfuaa-Fofie does not simply reproduce existing 'masculine' templates about gender relations in modern Ghana: she also imagines utopian resolutions to political and domestic problems. Unlike *Because she was a Woman* (the utopian novel which formed the basis for the conclusions reached in Chapter 2), the myth of masculine redemption that circulates in Ghanaian popular narratives is not overthrown in her romances. Rather, the narrator's feminist interventions coexist with a familiar Ghanaian master-text in which the good wife's patience is rewarded with marital bliss at the end of the story.

Gyamfuaa-Fofie's romances are hybridised, open literary discourses, disengaged from the criteria set by multinational Western publishing houses which control and market popular fiction, issue guidelines to authors, set generic conventions and determine plot formulas. *The Tested Love* in particular is a generic hybrid rather than a simple 'romantic' novel. At the very moment when the young lovers are reconciled and the romance appears to have been concluded successfully, a wealthy, middle-aged bachelor called Kofi Jackson is introduced into the story; he insists upon marrying Boahemaa and kidnaps her to an isolated mansion in the middle of a forest.

Kofi Jackson's sudden appearance initiates a series of generic shifts in the novel. By invoking this character type, Gyamfuaa-Fofie recalls and rewrites the stock 'illiterate chief' figure, popular in early Nigerian literatures (see Newell, 1996). Drawing upon archives of narrative templates in which rich old men attempt to impose marriage on independent-minded young women, Gyamfuaa-Fofie reapplies the familiar character, setting him over and against the reformed but penniless 'youngman'. New concerns are injected into the proverbial male character type. Empowered by a belief in love and supported by her uncle, Boahemaa is explicit in declaring her freedom to choose, informing Jackson 'that she was engaged to somebody and nothing could convince her to break that engagement' (1989: 33). In response, 'he promised to give her a large sum of money to buy whatever she wanted' (*ibid.*). By ignoring her love-choice and offering a 'bride-price' directly to the heroine, the older man is shown to be inserting an outdated mentality into a contemporary situation, accepting Boahemaa's right to choose her own marital partner, but believing that cash can buy him this wife.

Kofi Jackson cannot be accommodated by the romantic storyline that precedes his appearance. His presence interrupts the genre, signalling the persistence of residual concerns that are difficult to erase. He is a 'baddie' drawn from non-romantic genres who, once activated in the context of the romance, becomes problematical. A significant generic shift occurs through Jackson, occurring at the very moment he appears. Perhaps because of his familiarity as a residual, stock character type appearing in popular West African narratives that compete with the romance, he seems to be a troubling figure that can be neither absorbed nor neutralised by 'romantic' discourse. In consequence, the narrative becomes hybridised, shedding the language of love and seeking resolutions to the problem of Jackson by moving into fairytale and 'adventure' genres.

Boahemaa is abducted by Jackson's 'evil-looking' henchmen, who drive her into a 'thick forest' and place her under guard in a 'lone and beautiful building', decorated lavishly with 'a double golden bed, an impressive wardrobe and the most beautiful rug she had ever seen on the floor' (1989: 41). This fairytale castle is overflowing with consumer goods, jewels and delicious foods, signs of the domestic lifestyle that Jackson has offered but Boahemaa has rejected in favour of romantic love. By framing such tempting commodities with the abduction and subsequent rape of the heroine, and by placing the mansion in a forest—site of witchcraft, magic and anti-social forces—Gyamfuaa-Fofie creates an ideological space in which women's fantasies of wealth can be expressed and also exorcised. Within this space, the reader's desire for riches is conveyed through Boahemaa, who gazes in awe at the house, tempted by the glistening commodities.

In a shrewd manoeuvre, at this very moment of consumer desire, Gyamfuaa-Fofie reintroduces romantic discourse in the form of a book. Having looked at the luxurious house, Boahemaa goes straight to a bookshelf 'and picked up Bertha M. Clay's *Woman's Temptation*' to read (p. 43). In itself, the title of Clay's novel pulls readers back from the brink of temptation. Additionally, by having Boahemaa select a well-known romantic novelist, readers are reminded of her resilience and primary position as the heroine of a *romantic* novel. In this way, through this subtle quotation of *Woman's Temptation*, Gyamfuaa-Fofie warns single young women not to succumb to materialistic desires. If the desire for luxury is a major obstacle which lures young women away from the economy of love, it is revealed here to stem from the most sinister forces plaguing society. Extreme wealth is tainted by evil, for Kofi Jackson is a drug-trafficker, rapist, murderer and juju practitioner who embodies popular beliefs about the illicit source of extreme wealth in Ghana (see Meyer, 1995a).

The 'adventure' genre allows Gyamfuaa-Fofie to sideline the tensions that coalesce around the figure of Jackson. With the help of a guilt-stricken member of the kidnapping gang, Boahemaa stages an escape; she is chased through the forest by a lion and stumbles upon a military landrover whose occupants are hunting Kofi Jackson. Loaded with suspense and action, staged in a simple manichean universe where good can be distinguished easily from evil, this section of *The Tested Love* depends upon the reader's acceptance that Jackson is an evil criminal rather than a potential husband. Constructed thus, his ambiguities are denied and, once caught, he is executed by a firing squad. Similarly, in the face of relationship problems that are too complex to untangle at the end of the novel, Gyamfuaa-Fofie puts Boakye through a sensational adventure: during the search for his lost love, he is thrown into jail on false charges, abducted by a shrine-priest in Nigeria, and he narrowly escapes being offered as a human sacrifice before being reconciled with Boahemaa for eternity (1989: 93–100). The contradictions triggered by both male characters are therefore circumvented through a generic shift into 'adventure' and away from the romance, and as in Mickson's *Who Killed Lucy?*, multiple narrative threads remain loose at the end, requiring readers to actualise lessons for themselves.

Genre is an important consideration in the analysis of West African popular fiction. The same writer may shift ideologically as she or he generates and reprocesses genres. Gyamfuaa-Fofie's literary production is not confined to 'romantic' or 'feminist utopian' texts. She has also written several detective novels, which are jam-packed with adventure, including gun-battles, conspiracies, secret societies and sensational discoveries. These detective novels, in which brave Ghanaian policemen slaughter fraternities of criminals, contrast starkly with her romantic fiction, in which isolated heroines make courageous life-choices in the most difficult circumstances. Unlike her romances, the overabundance of action in these novels leaves little space for the narrator's critical meta-narratives.

Popular genres exist in West Africa as dynamic fields of meaning rather than as textual templates in which distinct formulas can be found. Gyamfuaa-Fofie deliberately moves between a range of genres in order to present different themes and convey different messages to her readers. By sidelining her detective fiction from the above discussion and excluding her many Twi folktales and children's workbooks, it has been possible to focus on the way in which she creates fiction for the staging of polemical interventions in local Ghanaian gender debates.

The romance has provided Gyamfuaa-Fofie with a potentially radical form which gives her the opportunity to imagine utopian marriage models: these models can be viewed as idealised responses to women's experiences of marriage in the 'off-page' world. Locally published romances have been in widespread circulation in West Africa for at least two generations. Perhaps it is the central status of the heroine in the conventional romance which allows writers to find in the genre a tool to critique gender relations in their societies: the romance is employed to open up discussions of marriage-related issues, including the merits of wifely 'submission'. The romance is not a static genre in West Africa: it is put to different uses, employed within different types of text as women utilise and rewrite what has, in Western societies, long been labelled a stultifying, 'dead' form. Romantic publications in West Africa are not 'pure' genres modelled from or upon Western templates, but historically situated texts containing an array of preoccupations that relate in precise terms to contemporary religious and gender debates, as well as to family relationships and political events within their region of production.

To conclude, let us briefly return to Ama Ata Aidoo's ironic comments about the love story she published. In the process of writing *Changes* (and completing her 'exercise in words-eating'), Aidoo *does* in fact contribute to current debates about female autonomy and the status of women in relationships. During the narrative, she *does* have her heroine employ the concepts and language of romantic love in order to leave one unhappy, male-dominated marriage and to enter a new liaison which starts with passion, mutual respect and equality between the partners. Perhaps in the end, Aidoo has demonstrated to the sceptics among her readers that the romance is a far more politicised, capable, complex and 'uprising' genre than their previous bias had led them to imagine.

Conclusion

Popular Novels &
International African Fiction

Locally published West African novels are dissimilar in numerous ways to the African fiction produced by international publishing houses and marketed on a global scale. There is an uncompromising specificity about the novels published locally in Ghana and Nigeria: front cover illustrations often signal precisely which generic expectations are to be operationalised during the reading process; prefaces list the type of reader who will benefit most from the text; back covers describe the moral lessons contained within the narrative; and, within the first few pages, popular character types and plots are set in place, all of which presuppose interpretive conventions that are culturally specific and locally learnt.

Local West African novels are anchored within particular social formations in a far more explicit manner than internationally available African texts. Using 'paratextual' spaces such as book covers and prefaces, local novelists aim their fictions at specific constituencies of readers, promising to teach essential moral truths about marriage or gender. By contrast, the Western publishing houses responsible for disseminating the best-known African authors have tended to disavow precisely these aspects of creativity. For example, the promotional material on the back cover of Tsitsi Dangarembga's *Nervous Conditions* (1988) describes the novel as 'exploring human conditions that have a general echo for us all'; similarly, Ngugi wa Thiong'o's *Petals of Blood* (1977) is praised for the author's universal 'hatred of exploitation, cruelty and injustice'; one early reviewer of Flora Nwapa's *Efuru* (1966) insisted, in a comment included on the back cover, that, 'The persons in Miss Nwapa's story have an *objective* complexity and sophistication' (emphasis retained).

When promoting their material, Ghanaian novelists and publishers rarely hide behind such notions of 'objectivity'; nor do they support universalist conceptions of art. Rarely, if ever, are local novels marketed or appreciated in terms of their timeless, cross-cultural, 'complex' or experimental qualities. Indeed, when E. K. Mickson's first 'Lucy' pamphlet was published in Ghana in 1966, it contained a preface which disallowed the very 'objectivity' deemed necessary by Heinemann to confer upon Nwapa her international appeal. As was shown in Chapter 7, Mickson marks out particular target-groups of readers in the preface. The narrator declares, 'I am telling this story firstly because I feel it will be a great lesson, in fact, a fore-warning, to many a young man desperately in love, against heartbreaks' (1966: 5); a second reason is that the story 'will serve as a reprimand and perhaps a "purgative" to those our ladies who ... make not only a folly but also donkeys of themselves by remaining rolling stones in the hands of men – changing from man to man' (*ibid.*). Clearly, the publishers of *When the Heart Decides* have made no effort to suppress these references to local 'young men' and 'our ladies', nor have they sought to stem the preaching tone of the preface.

Book production and consumption patterns in West Africa differ greatly from late capitalist economies and the term 'popular' requires re-settling if it is to retain validity in modern West African contexts. A great deal of local Ghanaian literature is published in relatively small print-runs on private printing presses and is distributed to bookshops and market stalls within the immediate region of production. Also, novels are luxury items, perhaps purchased regularly by the salaried elite but regarded as scarce commodities by clerical and informal sector workers. At most, literate low-income workers might buy religious pamphlets, novelettes, or weekly popular magazines. These factors have to be taken into account in discussions of 'popular' publishing in Ghana.

In the West, popular genres are intimately connected with the development of large publishing conglomerates, which have an 'entrepreneurial vision of the book as an endlessly replicable commodity' (Radway, 1987: 23). Cultural commentators in the West tend to take for granted mass-production and mass-consumption when defining and analysing popular genres (p. 45). The vast majority of Ghanaian readers, on the other hand, are excluded from definitions of 'popular literature' that depend upon the idea of mass-consumption, for most literature in the country costs too much for the small reading public to buy regularly. While the profit motive is a vital consideration to author-entrepreneurs, book production in the country remains small-scale, regional and artisanal. Private jobbing printers are employed by many authors, without the intervention of a publishing house or an editorial team. Given these fundamental structural and economic differences, popular publications in the region cannot be seen to inherit and mimic the genres marketed by Western publishers. Frequently produced *outside* the genre-determining relationships that characterise Western popular fiction, West African texts are less rigid in their adherence to generic formulas and in consequence, as I hope to have shown in this book, they remain receptive to a wider variety of intertextual currents.

Considering the lack of mass-marketing and the dynamic nature of literary genres in the region, in what sense is the word 'popular' appropriate to describe locally published literatures in West Africa? 'Popular' is a troublesome and amorphous term, but it is also immensely useful in demarcating a field of African creativity which is non-elite, unofficial and urban (see Barber, 1987). Specifically 'popular' elements cannot, however, be quarried and quantified from local publications. The definitive feature of African popular art forms, as Karin Barber has argued for several years, is their lack of formal and stylistic regulation from without: any effort to define popular culture in Africa must therefore account for the manner in which local practitioners constantly absorb new cultural currents, adapt and innovate and operate outside of 'official' art forms (1987: 9–12).

In this book, the word 'popular' has been deployed to describe those types of narrative which never fail to generate debate amongst readers on moral and behavioural issues. In terms of their content, such texts are 'popular' in the sense of containing ubiquitous character types and plots, reworked with each re-usage by authors; in terms of their appeal, they are 'popular' in the sense of being in demand by African *readers*. As the latter part of this chapter will demonstrate, however, these 'popular' features permeate many types of literary discourse, not least the very novels which are labelled 'elite' and set apart for international audiences.

By positioning locally published texts in a 'proverbial' space, I have attempted to move beyond the dismissive labels which have, until recently, characterised studies of popular literature in Africa. Heroes and heroines need not be interpreted as signs of the author's conservatism, nor as static imitations of mass-produced Western art forms, and texts need not be viewed as imperfect mirrors held up to society, reflecting the 'real' world in an unmediated form. When the success or failure of a text is judged by how well it captures the 'real' society, critics erase the whole field of textuality and close down an area of African novels that deserves more detailed exploration. Locally published novels are *texts*, existing as dynamic fields of meaning in which an author's authority to write is asserted through a variety of textual strategies. The repetition of particular character types that one finds in popular narratives can be seen as one such textual strategy, signifying far more than an author's effort either to 'stereotype' or to 'reflect' the real world. The intertextual density of local publications prevents simplistic links from being made between literature and society, for each of the texts discussed in the preceding pages is an authored, mediated, historically situated *version* of the world.

Authors and audiences play important roles in the production and processing of popular narratives. Authors read and quote from local and international literary resources in order to establish their authority as creators of texts; in addition, writers seem to presuppose an interpretive process whereby readers participate actively in narratives. The comments of readers reveal that they recognise behaviours, interpret roles and morally judge the behaviour of characters.

The local publications studied here open up spaces in which narrators can comment on their changing societies and offer fictional solutions to relationship dilemmas. Protagonists in popular narratives are 'typed' by writers and interpreted with reference to a cast of residual characters. Renovated and reapplied by different authors across different genres, versions of these characters can be found in the earliest Anglophone literatures published in West Africa, as well as in African-language films, soap-operas, highlife songs and stage plays. Characters such as the good-time girl, the errant husband and the ideal wife hold the power of semantic grenades, containing within themselves the potential to explode into a multitude of moral meanings. New character types also are generated in local narratives, containing lessons within themselves about the consequences of moral and immoral behaviour in a changing society.

African popular literatures are heterogeneous and dynamic, often resisting critical efforts to locate influences and ideologies, or to fix specific art forms within distinct genealogies (Barber, 1987: 14–19). Ghanaian popular literatures are no exception, for each text is a dynamic, urban cultural transaction. Authors' emphases and preoccupations will shift and slide during the continual national and international exchange of ideas and genres. While emphasising this hetero-geneity, in several chapters of this book it has been suggested that many narratives contain moments of ideological fixation around particular issues. When urban social relations are narrativised and transposed into the symbolic space of popular novels, shared concerns surface, often clustering around issues of money, marriage and masculinity. In particular, male characters frequently are represented in the process of urgently reasserting their positions of power over supposedly deviant women.

The good-time girl is a recurrent character type in West African narratives, inscribed with masculine concerns that have persisted in a variety of forms since local publications first appeared in Ghana in the 1930s. It is the persistence and repetition of the good-time girl that marks her out as a figure of ideological fixation. Few male-authored narratives neglect this character type and in many plots she is punished severely or reformed according to a Christian model of feminine submission. The repetition of character types such as E. K. Mickson's 'Lucy' signals an ideological complex which far outweighs the presence of such women in society at large. Filled with compressed meanings, containing warnings, advice, judgements and guidance, these characters need to be *applied* by readers in order to fulfil their potential meanings.

Ghanaian women's writing seems to manifest a 'feminine positionality' which transforms, embellishes and amplifies the plots and character types to be found in popular, male-authored narratives. Women seem to read the same texts differently from men. Often, readers divide down a primary gender line and within texts male and female readers are often invited to position themselves in relation to the character type who shares their own gender identity and to learn different lessons from these separate reference points.

In Chapters 2, 9 and 10, I tested the validity of feminist paradigms which position women on the outskirts of 'masculine' ideologies. In planning how to organise this material, a paradoxical situation emerged: structurally, the book positions women's writing in separate chapters and thus in separate spheres from men's writing, from where it is argued that women writers are embedded *within* the same popular cultures and contexts as their male colleagues. My primary concern in these separate chapters on women's writing was to replace the 'exclusion from masculine discourse' model with dynamic, culturally located interpretations, for Ghanaian women writers seem to be far more involved in the production of popular plots and character types than allowed for by many feminist literary theorists.

The chapters focusing exclusively on women writers therefore tread a thin line, arguing on the one hand that as socially constructed and gendered subjects, Ghanaian women writers offer distinctive 'feminine' interpretations of local popular templates; on the other hand, in these chapters it is emphasised that women writers occupy positions within their own cultures, from where they are actively involved in the interpretation and generation of popular art forms. To this extent, their writing is seen to be thoroughly located within the same cultural configurations as male writers. By studying the similarities and differences between women's texts in the context of popular fiction by men, my intention has been to explore the extent to which women writers engage with or dislodge the 'masculine ideology' that was located in much male-authored literature.

Tensions and silences remain in much existing research into African popular literatures, particularly surrounding the role played by 'locals' in the production and reception of their own art forms. Contemporary theorists have tended to focus upon the migration of ideas and peoples through different locations and a consequence of this bias is that non-migratory locals tend to be presented as the simple receivers of Western popular culture. When local writers and performers include references to foreign sources in their own work, they are seen to be gesturing outward to the metropolitan culture rather than inward to their own communities; they are simply aspiring towards the 'modernity' of the country from which the quoted text originates. In Ghana and Nigeria, however, authors and readers seem to be bringing culturally specific quoting modes to bear upon their local and international literary resources. As was shown in Chapter 1, the manner in which they quote from popular models bears little relation to the met-ropolitan 'centres' from which some of their forms might once have originated. When images and texts are translocated, and when 'mimics' pick up and perform the narrative templates circulating around their societies, prior meanings might be transformed beyond the recognition of supposedly original audiences.

In the European realist tradition which continues to dominate the production of new fiction in the West, despite the challenges of postmodernism, readers tend to be informed of developments by omniscient or first-person narrators. Jane Eyre's synoptic, 'Reader, I married him', might be said to characterise the explanatory nature of Western realist narratives. By contrast, the central role of readers in the co-creation of textual meaning is acknowledged openly by local West African novelists. If we transplant Jane Eyre into a Ghanaian popular novel, undoubtedly the original statement would be replaced with the question, 'Reader, shall I marry him?' Book sales in West Africa are enhanced by the inclusion of space for precisely such active, productive readerly interventions in texts.

The didacticism and popular formulas in local novels have caused authors such as Asare Konadu and, more recently, Akosua Gyamfuaa-Fofie to struggle to find international publishers willing to accept their manuscripts. Fully aware of the selling-power of those narratives rejected in the West, both authors set about establishing their own publishing companies in Ghana and overcame the obstacles to become successful, best-selling book entrepreneurs. Their difficulties illustrate the fact that, despite the implicit references to Western literary genres within their narratives and despite the explicit quotations from great masters such as Shakespeare, many Ghanaian novels do not appear to possess sufficient cultural resonance to grip the attention of European and North American readerships. The most obvious reason for this 'lack' is that local narratives are replete with popular, locally generated plots, character types and themes which have been produced with reference to the expectations and interpretive conventions of situated local audiences. As will be suggested in the following pages, however, such apparently indubitable evidence of the divide between 'high' and 'low' literature, or elite and popular styles, cannot easily be upheld in discussions of West African fiction.

In an essay first published in 1965, the Nigerian novelist Chinua Achebe describes the passionate comments of a young Ghanaian teacher who 'took me to task for not making the hero of my *No Longer at Ease* [1960] marry the girl he is in love with' (1975: 43). In a manner reminiscent of J. Benibengor Blay's readers in the mid-1940s, who demanded that the happy marriage scene at the end of *Emelia's Promise* be supplemented and problematised through a follow-up text, Achebe's young respondent confronts him with his moral responsibilities as a writer: 'Did I know, she said, that there were many women in this kind of situation I had described and that I could have served them well if I had shown that it was possible to find one man with enough guts to go against custom?' (*ibid.*). While rejecting any degree of 'dictation' from readers, Achebe confesses to having 'squandered a rare opportunity for education' by disallowing this reader's preferred resolution. If the creative writer is a teacher, as Achebe and his African correspondents believe (*ibid.*), then each episode in a novel should describe a *moral trajectory*, through which readers can produce meanings to apply to their own lives: in the case of Achebe's female reader, perhaps unsurprisingly the desired moral trajectory involves *feminine* romantic fulfilment and the wish for fiction to provide the model of an ideal husband.

Achebe's anecdote reveals two important points about so-called 'elite' African fiction, the first of which relates to readers and the second to the content of texts. Firstly, while scholars might divide novels into 'literary' and 'popular' genres, West African *readers* seem unwilling to discriminate between high and low forms. As with the Ghanaian readers whose comments have appeared throughout this book, Achebe's young critic possesses a pre-determined array of expectations about the didactic function of literature which she brings to his novel, anticipating fulfilment. In expressing her romantic requirements, she projects on to 'high' literature a marriage model which would not be disappointed by any of J.

157

Benibengor Blay's popular romances. Given this reader-centred aesthetic, in which literary content and style are of secondary importance to the lessons that texts generate for readers, it becomes easier to understand how novels as different to Western eyes as *Emelia's Promise* and *No Longer at Ease* can be assessed using the same sets of tools by local readers.

When West African novels are viewed from a local, reader-centred perspective it becomes exceedingly difficult to differentiate 'elite' from 'popular' material. Despite the visible differences in terms of packaging, price, length and print quality, internationally available African novels are not necessarily read and discussed by locals using different interpretive conventions from those in operation for locally published fiction. Quite the reverse: as we saw in Chapter 3, when West African readers discuss the function of literature, the distinctions between 'high' and 'low' literature often melt away. Whether readers prefer Danielle Steel and Akosua Gyamfuaa-Fofie or Chinua Achebe and Ama Ata Aidoo, their reasons for reading remain remarkably consistent across genres. Whilst readers in Ghana have a clear sense of the genres they prefer – selecting thrillers above romantic fiction, for example, or African literature above European literature – their aesthetic criteria remain stable.

The second point arising from Achebe's encounter is that, rather than eclipsing local popular templates with new material, many internationally available African novelists are redeploying the narrative resources circulating around their cultures, in much the same way as their local counterparts inherit and rework popular plots and character types. Many of the best-known West African authors include themes and concerns in their narratives which spring from the same popular sources as those informing local novelists: in Ghana, Ama Ata Aidoo and Amma Darko immediately come to mind, with their images of unfaithful or abusive husbands and their sympathetic rewritings of the 'good-time girl' (see e.g., Aidoo, 1970, 1991; Darko, 1995).

In order to appreciate the complexity of African literary discourse, it is not enough simply to bypass the popular and read African literature for signs of 'oral traditions', for proverbs, or for African 'folk story' elements; nor is it necessary to define 'literary' texts over and against 'popular' novels. A striking example of the dissolution of 'high'–'low' literary boundaries can be found in Asare Konadu's *Ordained by the Oracle* (1969), a novel whose title and promotional blurb promise to develop the 'traditional', village-orientated themes which became the staple of international African fiction in the decade following Achebe's *Things Fall Apart* (1958). In fact, as was revealed in Chapter 2, the title of Konadu's novel was imposed by the editors at Heinemann: the original manuscript carried the 'popular' title, *Come Back, Dora!*, and as such would have been far more appealing to local readers. By renaming the text, Heinemann thus encouraged readers to adopt a particular reading-position based upon its rural, 'traditional', non-Christian elements rather than its potentially popular themes.

While there are plentiful village scenes and customary ceremonies in *Ordained by the Oracle*, the narrative in fact revolves around a different axis: the central

158

moral problem of the novel is that Dora, the protagonist's wife, has died from an illness precipitated by Boateng's shortcomings as a husband. At each hiatus in the funeral rites, which occur in the village and form the present-time of the narrative, the story returns to the desolate hero's confession of his marital sins, committed with good-time girls and loose women in the hotels and bars around Elmina.

In a short synopsis of the couple's married life, the author crams in numerous popular story-lines. As for the husband, Boateng, his first common failing is that, in the manner of Blay's 'Joe', he 'knew that Dora did not like the things that he did. She wanted him to stay at home but he roamed the nightclubs seeking pleasure which her delicate life did not allow her to join' (p. 52). Secondly, Boateng resembles the popular, theatrical baddies who brutalise their wives on the concert party stage, for readers are told that his 'temper raged over trivial things and he sometimes knocked her in many of the arguments that shaped their quarrels' (*ibid.*; see Bame, 1985). Thirdly, following convention and conforming to a persistent character type developed in devastating detail by many women writers, including Amma Darko (1995), this confirmed patriarch 'even starved her as he refused to give her the monthly housekeeping money because she had annoyed him' (*ibid.*). As with so many fictional husbands before him, Boateng's final sin is to attempt to assert his masculine authority over Dora by marrying a second wife – an attractive, educated young beauty – without obtaining the senior wife's permission (see also Darko, 1995). Konadu has quoted from numerous narratives and impressed them upon his hero.

Inheriting the mantle of the tolerant, typical 'good wife', Dora 'bore all patiently and despite his erratic behaviour she carried out her duties to the best of her ability in an effort not to give him cause for anger' (*ibid.*). But poor Dora 'fell sick most of the time' and spends many evenings 'crying in her bed because he had rushed to the garage and driven off while she wanted him to sit and talk to her' (*ibid.*). By the end of this page-long review of the marriage, Dora and Boateng have become saturated with popular marital templates. Indeed, they have accrued so many local themes by the conclusion of the novel that they have become *prototypical* characters and, as a result, their story can be viewed as both a rehearsal of and a comment upon an entire history of popular representations of marriage within Ghana.

By having Dora die in response to her husband's moral and marital failings, Konadu pulls one dominant Ghanaian plot-line to snapping point. In the popular literary archive explored in previous chapters, errant husbands such as Blay's 'Joe' (1945) and Amarteifio's 'Bediako' (1967) return to the warm embraces of their loving first wives after unhappy, often disastrous, affairs with good-time girls. In *Ordained by the Oracle*, Konadu appears less forgiving of the husband's infidelities, for Boateng is punished in absolute terms for his neglect of Dora. 'Oh, Dora come back', he sobs, feeling 'guilty and ashamed' about his role in her death (1969: 160). While the narrator holds out the possibility that Dora's ghost might put in an appearance, clearly there is no hope that the wife herself will be re-embodied; nor does Boateng's new young wife feature in the novel; nor, indeed, does the younger wife exploit and emasculate the hero in the manner of a conventional 'peacock' woman. By invoking but also transforming the 'quoted' characters, Konadu seems to be mounting a subtle critique of the gender politics in his predecessors' stories, for he uses the didactic character types to suggest that married men should change their attitudes *before* the marriage dissolves and they should work harder within marriage to obtain the trust and respect of their wives.

In order to fully appreciate the cultural significance of Boateng and Dora – the way their author 'speaks to' and also rewrites the moral meanings embedded in their character types – it is necessary for literary scholars to transcend the binary division between 'elite' and 'popular' that has prevailed until recently in discussions of African literature. Local and urban popular discourses about marriage, women, wealth and good fortune are, in many cases, precisely where the plots and characters of 'high' African literature are fertilised and raised. Where would Ama Ata Aidoo be without the Ghanaian 'good-time girl', a figure she appropriates from popular, male-authored narratives on numerous occasions and instils with new, politicised messages for readers? Where would Amma Darko be without the brutal husband and the victimised wife, character types which, as we have seen, have persisted in the Ghanaian popular imagination since the late 1930s, generating new social commentaries with each appearance in pamphlets, stage shows, videos and novels?

In the quest for 'original', realistic and non-didactic material, Western-trained literary critics have tended to neglect or deride those West African novels containing popular formulas (see e.g. Umelo, 1983; Ehling, 1990).[1] An important question not asked by critics who are dismissive of 'stereotypes' in African literature relates to the *function* of these 'quotations' from foreign and local resources. As was suggested in Chapter 1 and reiterated above, a far more productive and culturally entrenched process is underway than the parrot-like 'imitation' of admired texts (Umelo, 1983: 4). Just as many proverbs are incomprehensible to those without detailed contextual knowledge and experience of a culture, so too the 'deep' meanings that attach to popular plots and character types require contextualisation in order to be understood. It is necessary to remain sensitive towards the *embeddedness* of fictional characters in African cultural and social histories, for characters such as Dora and Boateng open up rare opportunities for latter-day readers to glimpse the kinds of didactic, historically specific commentaries that were being composed by Ghanaians in the past.

This book has illustrated the manner in which resourceful people – authors and also readers – continually produce popular narratives about themselves and

---

[1] It should be noted that internationally available African novels also contain their own distinctive set of endlessly repeated themes, characters and plots. For example, numerous novels published in Heinemann's *African Writers Series* chart the failure of anti-colonial nationalist movements: preoccupied with the plight of alienated, highly educated heroes who are stranded in corrupt nation-states, novelists such as Ayi Kwei Armah offer bleak, often despairing visions of postcolonial Africa. Another resilient strand of internationally available literature presents cultures on the point of transformation, as 'African traditional values' give way to an inevitable colonial or Western modernity.

their futures. The behavioural models and explanations that are generated by locally published novels reveal the existence of a robust 'civil society' in Ghana which has survived in spite of the corruption, economic collapse and political turbulence characterising recent West African history. Popular literature in Ghana does not function as a sop, or a 'coping mechanism', for downtrodden peoples. Rather, since its inception in the late 1930s, it has served as an expository force in individual readers' lives: popular narratives help readers to generate their own explanations of personal success and failure, and assist 'locals' to make sense of an ever-globalising world.

Bibliography

Primary Texts

'A Concert Enthusiast'. 1942. 'Review: *Twere Nyame*', *The Gold Coast Observer*, 20 February, 475–7.

Abbam, K. 1971. 'From the publisher', *Obaa Sima (Ideal Woman)* August, 4.

—— 1971. 'From the publisher', *Obaa Sima (Ideal Woman)* October, 4.

—— 1972. 'From the publisher', *Obaa Sima (Ideal Woman)* October, 4.

—— 1974. Interview with Richard Priebe, 4 June, Accra.

—— 1981. 'From the publisher', *Obaa Sima (Ideal Woman)* 10 (1), 9.

—— 1995. 'From the publisher', *Obaa Sima (Ideal Woman)* 22 (2), 3–4.

Abedi-Boafo, J. [1938] 1946. *And Only Mothers Know: a thrilling discovery in conjugal life*. Aburi: Mfantisiman Press.

Abiakam, J. (pseud. Anorue, J. C.). 1966? *How to Speak to Girls and Win their Love*. Onitsha: J. C. Brothers Bookshop.

—— [1961] 1995a. *Never Trust all that Love you*. Earlier editions by R. Okonkwo (pseud. Anorue, J. C.). Onitsha: J. C. Brothers Bookshop.

—— [1964?] 1995b. *How to Speak to a Girl about Marriage*. Onitsha: J. C. Brothers Bookshop.

—— [1971a] 1995c. *How to Make Friends with Girls*. Earlier editions by R. Okonkwo (pseud. Anorue, J. C.). Onitsha: J. C. Brothers Bookshop.

—— [1971b] 1995d. *The Game of Love (a classical drama from West Africa)*. Earlier editions by R. Okonkwo. Onitsha: J. C. Brothers Bookshop.

Achebe, C. 1960. *No Longer at Ease*. Oxford: Heinemann.

Addae, W. 1973. 'The deceitful one', *Obaa Sima (Ideal Woman)* July–August, 12–13.

African Morning Post. 1954. 'First women study group formed', 3 May, 3.

—— 1954. 'Ladies Union formed', 6 May, 4.

—— 1954. 'Our Readers' Forum', 30 July, 2.

Bibliography

—— 1954. Editorial, 4 October, 2.

Aidoo, A. A. 1970. *No Sweetness Here*. Harlow: Longman.

—— 1990. 'Interview with Adeola James: 13 July 1986, Harare', in A. James (interv. and ed.), *In their own Voices: African women writers talk*, pp. 9–27. London: James Currey.

—— 1991. *Changes: a love story*. London: The Women's Press.

Albert, M. O. (pseud.) 1960. *Rosemary and the Taxi Driver*. Onitsha: Chinyelu Printing Press.

Amarteifio, V. [1967] 1985. *Bediako the Adventurer*. Accra: Amaa Books Ltd.

Antwi-Boasiako, K. 1982. *Not This Time Mercy*. Accra: Anima Publications.

—— 1994. *My Run-away Daughter*. Accra: Anima Publications.

—— 1995. *The Hidden Agenda*. Accra: Anima Publications.

Aririguzo, C. 1963. *The Work of Love*. Onitsha: Aririguzo & Sons.

Badoe, A.-E. (pseud. Abbam, K.). 1973. *Beloved Twin*. Accra: Scorpio Books.

Bediako, K. A. (pseud. Konadu, A.). 1966. *Don't Leave me Mercy!!* Accra: Anowuo Educational Publishers.

Blay, J. B. 1944. *Emelia's Promise*. Accra: Benibengor Book Agency.

—— 1945. *After the Wedding*. Accra: Benibengor Book Agency.

—— 1957. *Love in a Clinic*. Accra: Benibengor Book Agency.

—— 1958. *Stubborn Girl*. Aboso: Benibengor Book Agency.

—— 1961. *Thoughts of Youth*. Aboso: Benibengor Book Agency.

—— 1967. *Emelia's Promise and Fulfilment*. Accra: Waterville Publishing House.

—— 1970. *Coconut Boy*. Accra: West African Publishing Co.

—— [1947] 1971. *Be Content with your Lot*. Aboso: Benibengor Book Agency.

—— [1953] 1972. *Dr Bengia wants a Wife*. Aboso: Benibengor Book Agency.

—— 1974. Interview with Richard Priebe, 13th June, Accra.

The Cape Times and Daily Advertiser (Cape Town), Jan–March 1932.

Clay, B. M. [1884] 1977. *Beyond Pardon*. Akure: Fagbamigbe.

Dangarembga, T. 1988. *Nervous Conditions*. London: The Women's Press.

Danquah, J. B. (ed. and intro.). 1928. *Cases in Akan Law*. London: Routledge.

—— 1943. *Self-help and Expansion: a review of the work and aims of the Youth Conference, with a statement of its policy for 1943, and the action consequent upon that policy*. Accra: Gold Coast Youth Conference.

Darko. A. 1995. *Beyond the Horizon*. Oxford: Heinemann.

Dartey, D. [1981] 1993. *Hints for a Happy Marriage*. Accra: CCMFL & Asempa Publishers.

Dove, Mabel. (Marjorie Mensah). 1933. *Us Women: Extracts from the Writings of Marjorie Mensah*. Ed. Kathleen Hewitt. London: Elkin Mathews and Marrot.

—— 1934. 'The Adventures of the Black Girl in her Search for Mr. Shaw.' *The Times of West Africa*. Sept. 25 1934–Oct. 16 1934.

Dwaase, R. M. 1990. *Falling in Love*. Accra: Asempa Publishers.

Eni, E. 1987. *Delivered from the Powers of Darkness*. Ibadan: Scripture Union.

Ephson, I. 1974. Interview with Richard Priebe, 4 June, Accra.

—— 1981. *Legends of the Lawless Lord*. Accra: Ilen Publications.

Gadzekpo, A. 1994. 'Sister to Sister: what two things would make you leave your man?', *AWO (African Woman's Option)* 2 (3), 13–14.

Gold Coast Observer. 1942. 'New Tafo Literary and Social Club', 22 May, 41–2.

—— 1942. Advertisement. 3 July, 141.

—— 1942. 'Some wise sayings for the student', 10 July, 150.

Gold Coast Times. 1929. 'Sekondi Literary and Social Club', 21 September, 4.

—— 1929. 'St. Augustine's Theological College; students' self-help club', 21 December, 6.

—— 1931. 'The Wesleyan Girls' High School, Cape Coast', 21 March, 8–9.

Gyamfuaa-Fofie, A. 1989. *The Tested Love.* Kumasi: Beginners Publishers.

—— 1990a. *The Forbidden Love.* Accra: Beginners Publishers.

—— 1990b. *Because she was a Woman.* Accra: Beginners Publishers.

—— 1991. *Only the Fittest can Survive.* Accra: Beginners Publishers.

—— 1995. Interview with Stephanie Newell, 10 July, Accra.

—— 1996a. *Suffered because of Love.* Kumasi: Beginners Publishers.

—— 1996b. *Agony of an African Woman.* Accra: Beginners Publishers.

—— 1997. Written interview with Stephanie Newell, 26 May.

—— 1998. Interview with Stephanie Newell, 14 January, Kumasi.

Gyawuh, T. B. 1988? *Life is a Stage.* Tamale: Except God Enterprise.

Kofie, P. 1973. 'My sordid past', *Obaa Sima (Ideal Woman)* August–September, 16–23.

Konadu, A. 1969. *Ordained by the Oracle.* London: Heinemann.

—— 1974. Interview with Richard Priebe, 29 May, Accra.

—— [1966] 1989. *Devils in Waiting.* Accra: Anowuo Paperback.

Koranteng, D. A. 1987. *Two Wives or One?* Accra: Presbyterian Church of Ghana.

Kwarteng, E. K. 1990. *The Premature Marriage.* Kumasi: Cita Printing Press.

Lawrence, L. S. 1929. 'Vice on the increase – the cause and remedy', *Gold Coast Times* 15 June, 7.

Maxwell, H. (pseuds. Obi, C. and Obi, T. A.). 1959. *Our Modern Ladies Characters towards Boys.* Onitsha: Students Own Bookshop.

Mensah, M. see Dove, Mabel.

Mickson, E. K. 1966. *When the Heart Decides.* Tema: Ghana Publishing Corporation.

—— 1967. *Who Killed Lucy?* Tema: Ghana Publishing Corporation.

Ngugi wa Thiong'o. 1977. *Petals of Blood.* Oxford: Heinemann.

Njoku, N. O. 1960. *Beware of Women.* Onitsha: Njoku & Sons Bookshop.

Nortey, K. 1964. *The Man with Two Wives.* Accra: Peacock Publication.

—— 1974. Interview with Richard Priebe, 10 June, Accra.

Nwapa, F. 1966. *Efuru.* Oxford: Heinemann.

Nwoye, M. I. 1993. *Endless Search.* Ibadan: Kraft Books Ltd.

—— 1994. *Tides of Life.* Lagos: Uto Publications.

Nyaku, F. K. 1984. *The Marriage Experiment and other Stories.* Accra: Sedco Publishing.

Obaa Sima (Ideal Woman). 1971. 'What every woman should know', October, 9.

—— 1971. 'What every woman should know', November, 9.

—— 1972. 'What every woman should know', January, 9.

—— 1972. 'Food for thought: no tears for a jealous wife', March, 26.

Bibliography

—— 1972. 'Food for thought: opinions', June, 24.

—— 1995. 'A woman's creed: declaration of the women's global strategies meeting', vol. 22, no. 3, 41.

Ogali, O. A. [1956] 1963? *Veronica my Daughter*. Onitsha: Appolos Brothers Press.

Olayinka, M. S. 1987. *Sex Education and Marital Guidance*. Lagos: Lantern Books.

Opong-Ofori, E. 1988. *The Wounds of Love*. Accra-North: Quick Service Books & Stationery Supply.

Osei-Poku, Kwame. 1989. *Blood for Money*. Accra: Accra Educational Press.

Owusu-Ansah, K. and Owusu-Ansah, B. 1995. *Receiving Your Breakthroughs Through Fasting*. Kumasi: Greatline Publications & Great Expectations Ministries.

Sam, G. A. 195? *The Disappointed Bestman*. Accra: Gilisam Publishing Syndicate.

—— 1950? *Who Killed Inspector Kwasi Minta? (or for the sake of a woman)*. Kumasi: Adom Press & Bookshop.

Shaw, George Bernard. [1st ed. 1932] 1934. 'The Adventures of the Black Girl in her Search for God', in G. B. Shaw, *The Black Girl in Search of God and Some Lesser Tales*. London: Constable and Co.

Uzorma, I. N. 1993. *Occult Grand Master Now in Christ*. Benin City: Uzorma Warfare Treatise.

Wilson, G. de. 1930. 'Abbontiakoon Literary and Social Club', *Gold Coast Times* 29 March, 4.

Wilson, T. B. 1942. 'Review: *Short Essays* by John Benibengor Blay', *Gold Coast Observer* 6 February, 454.

Secondary References

Abba, S. and Ibrahim, J. 1995. 'Creative writing, writers and publishing in northern Nigeria', Unpublished research paper, Ibadan: IFRAA.

Abu, K. 1983. 'The separateness of spouses: conjugal resources in an Ashanti town', in C. Oppong (ed.), *Female and Male in West Africa*, pp. 156-68. London: Allen & Unwin.

Achebe, C. 1975. *Morning Yet on Creation Day: essays*. London: Heinemann.

Adeleye-Fayemi, B. 1995. '*Shinamania*: gender, sexuality and popular culture', in S. Newell (ed.), *Images of African Women: the gender problematic*, pp. 45–56. Stirling: Centre of Commonwealth Studies.

Adepoju, A. 1994. 'The demographic profile: sustained high mortality and fertility and migration for employment', in A. Adepoju and C. Oppong (eds), *Gender, Work, and Population in sub-Saharan Africa*, pp. 17–34. London: ILO & James Currey.

Agovi, J. E. K. 1990. 'A Dual Sensibility: the short story in Ghana, 1944–80.' Ed. Ernest Emenyonu. *Literature and Black Aesthetics*, pp. 247–71. Ibadan: Heinemann Educational Books.

Akpabio, A. 196? *The Sayings of the Wise: Ibibio proverbs and idioms*. Uyo: Marshall Press.

Akyeampong, E. K. 1993. 'Alcohol, Social Conflict and the Struggle for Power in Ghana, 1919 to Recent Times', Unpublished PhD thesis, Charlottesville, VA: University of Virginia.

Bibliography

—— 1997. *Drink, Power and Cultural Change: A Social History of Alcohol in Ghana*. Oxford and Portsmouth, NH: James Currey and Heinemann.

Althusser, L. 1971. *Lenin and Philosophy and Other Essays*. trans. B. Brewster. London: New Left Books.

Amadiume, I. 1987. *Male Daughters, Female Husbands: gender and sex in an African society*. London: Zed Books.

Aminu, J. 1993. 'Books into peoples', in S. Bello and A. R. Augi (eds), *Culture and the Book Industry in Nigeria*, pp. i–xxxvi. Lagos: National Council for Arts and Culture.

Anderson, B. 1991. *Imagined Communities*. London: Verso.

Anderson, R. 1974. *The Purple Heart Throbs: the sub-literature of love*. London: Hodder and Stoughton.

Angmor, C. 1996. *Contemporary Literature in Ghana 1911–1978: a critical evaluation*. Accra: Woeli Publishing Services.

Appadurai, A. 1990. 'Disjuncture and difference in the global cultural economy', *Public Culture* 2 (2), 1–24.

—— 1991. 'Global ethnoscapes: notes and queries for a transnational anthropology', in R. G. Fox (ed.), *Recapturing Anthropology*, pp. 191–210. Santa Fe, New Mexico: School of American Research Press.

Arhin, K. 1995. 'Monetization and the Asante State', in J. Guyer (ed.), *Money Matters: instability, values and social payments in the modern history of West African communities*, pp. 97–110. Portsmouth, NH and London: Heinemann & James Currey.

Asante-Darko, N. and van der Geest, S. 1983. 'Male chauvinism: men and women in Ghanaian highlife songs', in C. Oppong (ed.), *Female and Male in West Africa*, pp. 242–55. London: George Allen & Unwin.

Assimeng, M. 1986. *Saints and Social Structures*. Accra: Ghana Publishing Corporation.

—— 1989. *Religion and Social Change in West Africa: an introduction to the sociology of religion*. Accra: Ghana Universities Press.

Bame, K. 1985. *Come To Laugh: African traditional theater in Ghana*. New York: Lillian Barber Press.

Barber, K. 1982. 'Popular reactions to the petro-naira', *Journal of Modern African Studies* 20 (3), 431–50.

—— 1986. 'Radical conservatism in Yoruba popular plays', in *Drama and Theatre in Africa*, pp. 5–32. Bayreuth African Studies Series 7, Bayreuth: University of Bayreuth.

—— 1987. 'Popular arts in Africa', *The African Studies Review* 30 (3), 1–78.

—— 1995a. 'Literacy, improvisation and the public in Yoruba popular theatre', in S. Brown (ed.), *The Pressures of the Text: orality, texts and the telling of tales*, pp. 6–27. Birmingham: Centre of West African Studies.

—— 1995b. 'Money, self-realization and the person in Yoruba texts', in J. Guyer (ed.), *Money Matters: instability, values and social payments in the modern history of West African communities*, pp. 205–24. Portsmouth, NH and London: Heinemann & James Currey.

Barthes, R. 1977. 'The death of the author', in *Image, Music, Text*, trans. S. Heath, pp. 142–8. London: Fontana.

Bastian, M. 1993. '"Bloodhounds who have no friends": witchcraft and locality in the Nigerian popular press', in J. Comaroff and J. Comaroff (eds), *Modernity and its Malcontents: ritual and power in postcolonial Africa*, pp. 129–66. Chicago: University of Chicago Press.

Bell, R. 1978. 'The absence of the African woman writer', in *CLA Journal* 21 (4), 491–8.

Bhabha, H. K. 1994. *The Location of Culture*. London: Routledge.

Boahen, A. 1975. *Ghana: evolution and change in the nineteenth and twentieth centuries*. London: Longman.

—— 1989. *The Ghanaian Sphinx: reflections on the contemporary history of Ghana, 1972–1987*. Accra: Academy of Arts & Sciences.

Boehmer, E. 1991. 'Stories of women and mothers: gender and nationalism in the early fiction of Flora Nwapa', in Susheila Nasta (ed.) *Motherlands: Black Women's Writing from Africa, the Caribbean and South Asia*, pp. 3–23. London: The Women's Press.

Boyce Davies, C. 1986. 'Introduction', in C. Boyce Davies and A. Adams Graves (eds), *Ngambika: studies of women in African literature*, pp. 1–23. Trenton, NJ: Africa World Press.

—— 1994. *Black Women, Writing and Identity: migrations of the subject*. London: Routledge.

Brown, A. K. 1987. 'State publishing in Ghana: has it benefitted Ghana?', in S. O. Unoh *et al.* (eds), *Literacy and Reading in Nigeria: vol. 3*, pp. 113–27. Zaria: Ahmadu Bello University.

Clark, G. 1994. *Onions are my Husband: survival and accumulation by West African market women*. Chicago: University of Chicago Press.

Cole, C. M. 1997. '"This is actually a good interpretation of modern civilisation": popular theatre and the social imaginary in Ghana', *Africa* 67 (3), 363–88.

Collins, J. and Richards, P. 1982. 'Popular music in West Africa – suggestions for an interpretative framework', in D. Horn and P. Tagg (eds), *Popular Music Perspectives: vol. I*. Exeter: International Association for the Study of Popular Music.

Collins, J. 1994. *Highlife Time*. Accra: Anansesem Publications.

Comaroff, J. and Comaroff, J. 1993. 'Introduction', in J. and J. Comaroff (eds), *Modernity and its Malcontents: ritual and power in postcolonial Africa*, pp. xi–xxx. Chicago: University of Chicago Press.

Connell, R. W. 1987. *Gender and Power: society, the person and sexual politics*. Cambridge: Polity Press.

Coulon, V. 1987. 'Onitsha goes national: Nigerian writing in Macmillan's *Pacesetter* series', *Research in African Literatures* 18 (3), 304–19.

Coward, R. 1984. *Female Desire: women's sexuality today*. London: Paladin Books.

Crowder, M. 1986. 'The book crisis: Africa's other famine', *African Research and Documentation*, 41, 1–6.

Davidson, B. 1973. *Black Star: a view of the life and times of Kwame Nkrumah*. London: Allen Lane.

Dekutsey, W. A. 1993. 'Ghana: a case study in publishing development', *Logos* 4 (2), 66–72.

Denzer, La Ray. 1992. 'Gender and Decolonization: a study of three women in West African public life', in J. F. Ade Ajayi and J. D. Y. Peel (eds), *People and Empires in African History: essays in memory of Michael Crowder*, pp.217–36. London: Longman.

Dinan, C. 1983. 'Sugar-daddies and gold diggers: the white-collar single women in Accra', in C. Oppong (ed.), *Female and Male in West Africa*, pp. 344–66. London: Allen & Unwin.

Djoleto, S. A. 1985. *Books and Reading in Ghana*. Paris: Unesco.

Dodson, D. 1973. 'The role of the publisher in Onitsha market literature', *Research in African Literatures* 4 (2), 172–88.

Eagleton, T. 1989. 'The ideology of the aesthetic', in P. Hernadi (ed.), *The Rhetoric of Interpretation and the Interpretation of Rhetoric*, pp. 75–86. Durham, NC: Duke University Press.

Ehling, H. 1990. 'The Biafran War and recent English-language "popular" writing in Nigeria: Kalu Okpi's *Crossfire!* and Kalu Uka's *Colonel Ben Brim*', in R. Granqvist (ed.), *Signs and Signals: popular culture in Africa*, pp. 151–71. Umea: Acta Universitatis Umensis.

Ekejiuba, F. 1995. 'Currency instability and social payments among the Igbo of eastern Nigeria, 1890–1990', in J. Guyer (ed.), *Money Matters: instability, values and social payments in the modern history of West African communities*, pp. 133–61. Portsmouth, NH and London: Heinemann & James Currey.

Fanon, F. [1963] 1990. *The Wretched of the Earth*. London: Penguin.

Fielding, H. [1751] 1983. M. C. Battestin (ed.), *Amelia*. Middletown, CT: Wesleyan University Press.

Fish, S. 1989. *Doing What Comes Naturally: change, rhetoric, and the practice of theory in literary and legal studies*. Oxford: Clarendon Press.

Frederiksen, B. F. 1991. '*Joe*, the sweetest reading in Africa: documentation and discussion of a popular magazine in Kenya', *African Languages and Cultures* 4 (2), 135–55.

Gedin, P. 1984. 'Publishing in Africa – autonomous and transnational: a view from the outside', *Development Dialogue* 1 (2), 98–112.

Griswold, W. and Bastian, M. 1987. 'Continuities and reconstructions in cross-cultural literary transmission: the case of the Nigerian romantic novel', *Poetics* 16, 327–51.

Guyer, J. (ed.). 1995. *Money Matters: instability, values and social payments in the modern history of West African communities*. Portsmouth, NH and London: Heinemann & James Currey.

—— 1995. 'Introduction: the currency interface and its dynamics', in J. Guyer (ed.), *Money Matters: instability, values and social payments in the modern history of West African communities*, pp. 1–33. Portsmouth, NH and London: Heinemann & James Currey.

Gyedu, T. 1976. 'Constraints on book development in Ghana', *Greenhill Journal of Administration* 2 (3), 68–78.

Hagan, K. 1968. 'The Growth of Adult Literacy and Adult Education in Ghana, 1901–1957'. Unpublished B.Litt. University of Oxford.

Bibliography

Hannerz, U. 1987. 'The world in creolisation', *Africa* 57 (4), 546–59.

—— 1990. 'Cosmopolitans and locals in world culture', in M. Featherstone (ed.), *Global Culture: nationalism, globalization and modernity*, pp. 237–51. London: Sage.

—— 1992. *Cultural Complexity: studies in the social organization of meaning*. New York: Columbia University Press.

Hill, A. 1992. 'British publishers' constructive contribution to African literature', *Logos* 3 (1), 45–52.

Hofmeyr, I. 'Texts, Travels, Transitions: making Bunyan English via Africa.' Paper presented at the ASA-UK Biennial Conference, SOAS, University of London, 14–16 Sept 1998.

Holmes, A. B. 1972. 'Economic and Political Organisations in the Gold Coast, 1920–1945'. Unpublished PhD. University of Chicago.

Holroyd, M. 1997. *Bernard Shaw: the one-volume definitive edition*. London: Chatto and Windus.

Hutcheon, L. 1985. *A Theory of Parody: the teachings of twentieth century art forms*. New York: Methuen.

Ike, V. C. 1993. 'Problems of book industry in Nigeria', in S. Bello and A. R. Augi (eds), *Culture and the Book Industry in Nigeria*, pp. 129–47. Lagos: National Council for Arts and Culture.

Ikiddeh, I. 1971. 'The character of popular fiction in Ghana', in C. Heywood (ed.), *Perspectives on African Literature*, pp. 106–16. London: Heinemann.

Iser, W. 1989. 'Towards a literary anthropology', in R. Cohen (ed.), *The Future of Literary Theory*, pp. 208–88. New York: Routledge.

—— 1993. *The Fictive and the Imaginary: charting literary anthropology*. Baltimore: Johns Hopkins University Press.

Jahoda, G. 1959. 'Love, marriage, and social change: letters to the advice column of a West African newspaper', *Africa* 29, 177–89.

—— 1961. *White Man: a study of the attitudes of Africans to Europeans in Ghana before Independence*. London: Oxford University Press.

Jauss, H. R. 1982. *Toward an Aesthetic of Reception*. Trans. T. Bahti. Brighton: Harvester.

—— 1990. 'The theory of reception: a retrospective of its unrecognised prehistory', in P. Collier and H. Geyer-Ryan (eds), *Literary Theory Today*, pp. 53–73. Cambridge: Cambridge University Press.

Kern, A. 1973. 'Woman is Poison', Unpublished seminar paper, African Literature Seminar, 14 Feb, Ibadan: University of Ibadan.

Kotei, S. I. A. 1981. *The Book Today in Africa*. Paris: Unesco.

—— 1987. 'Some cultural and social factors of book reading and publishing in Africa', in S. O. Unoh *et al.* (eds), *Literacy and Reading in Nigeria: vol. 3*, pp. 174–208. Zaria: Ahmadu Bello University.

Larkin, B. 1997. 'Indian films and Nigerian lovers: media and the creation of parallel modernities', *Africa* 67 (3), 406–40.

Manuh, T. 1995. 'Changes in marriage and funeral exchanges among the Asante: a case study from Kona, Afigya-Kwabre', in J. Guyer (ed.), *Money Matters: instability, values and social payments in the modern history of West African communities*, pp.

188–201. Portsmouth, NH and London: Heinemann & James Currey.

McCaskie, T. C. 1995. *State and Society in Pre-Colonial Asante*. Cambridge: Cambridge University Press.

Meyer, B. 1995a. 'Translating the Devil: an African appropriation of Pietist Protestantism (the case of the Peki Ewe in southeastern Ghana, 1947–1992'. Unpublished PhD thesis, Amsterdam: University of Amsterdam.

—— 1995b. 'Delivered from the powers of darkness': confessions of satanic riches in Christian Ghana', *Africa* 65 (2), 236–55.

Miescher, S. F. 1997. 'Becoming a Man in Kwawu: gender, law, personhood, and the construction of masculinities in colonial Ghana, 1875–1957'. Unpublished PhD thesis, Evanston, Illinois: Northwestern University.

Newell, S. 1996. 'From the brink of oblivion: the anxious masculinism in Nigerian market literature', *Research in African Literatures* 27 (3), 50–67.

Nugent, P. 1995. *Big Men, Small Boys and Politics in Ghana: power, ideology and the burden of history, 1982–1994*. London: Pinter.

Obiechina, E. 1973. *An African Popular Literature: a study of Onitsha market pamphlets*. Cambridge: Cambridge University Press.

Oduyoye, A. 1979. 'The Asante Woman: socialization through proverbs, part one', *African Notes* 8 (1), 5–11.

—— 1995. *Daughters of Anowa: African women and patriarchy*. New York: Orbis Books.

Ogundipe-Leslie, M. 1985. 'Women in Nigeria', in S. Bappa *et al.* (eds). *Women in Nigeria Today*, pp. 119–31. London: Zed Books.

—— 1987. 'The female writer and her commitment', in E. Durosimi Jones (ed.), *Women in African Literature Today*, pp. 5–13. London and Trenton, NJ: James Currey & Africa World Press.

Opoku-Agyemang, N. J. 1997. 'Recovering lost voices: the short stories of Mabel Dove Danquah', in S. Newell (ed.), *Writing African Women: gender, popular culture and literature in West Africa*, pp. 67–80. London: Zed Books.

Oquaye, M. 1980. *Politics in Ghana, 1972–1979*. Accra: Tornado.

Owusu, M. 1970. *Uses and Abuses of Political Power: a case study of continuity and change in the politics of Ghana*. Chicago and London: University of Chicago Press.

Parry, J. and Bloch, M. 1989. 'Introduction: money and the morality of exchange', in J. Parry and M. Bloch (eds), *Money and the Morality of Exchange*, pp. 1–32. Cambridge: Cambridge University Press.

Parry, J. 1989. 'On the moral perils of exchange', in J. Parry and M. Bloch (eds), *Money and the Morality of Exchange*, pp. 64–93. Cambridge: Cambridge University Press.

Penfield, J. 1983. *Communicating With Quotes*. Westport, CT: Greenwood Press.

Price, T. 1954. *African Marriage*. London: S.C.M. Press.

Priebe, R. 1978. 'Popular writing in Ghana: a sociology and rhetoric', *Research in African Literatures* 9 (3), 395–432.

Quayson, A. 1995. 'Orality – (theory) – textuality: Tutuola, Okri and the relationship of literary practice to oral traditions', in S. Brown (ed.), *The Pressures of the Text: orality, texts and the telling of tales*, pp. 96–117. Birmingham: Centre of West

Bibliography

African Studies.

Rabinowitz, P. J. 1987. *Before Reading: narrative conventions and the politics of interpretation*. Ithaca, NY: Cornell University Press.

Radway, J. [1984] 1987. *Reading the Romance: women, patriarchy and popular literature*. London: Verso.

Rimmer, D. 1992. *Staying Poor: Ghana's political economy, 1950–1990*. Oxford: Pergamon Press.

Robertson, C. 1984a. *Sharing the Same Bowl: a socioeconomic history of women and class in Accra, Ghana*. Bloomington, IN: Indiana University Press.

—— 1984b. 'Women in the urban economy', in J. Hay and S. Stichter (eds), *African Women South of the Sahara*, pp. 33–49. London: Longman.

Said, E. W. 1993. *Culture and Imperialism*. London: Vintage.

Sanneh, L. 1983. *West African Christianity: the religious impact*. London: Hurst.

—— 1995. *Translating the Message: the missionary impact on culture*. New York: Orbis Books.

Schild, U. 1980. 'Words of deception: popular literature in Kenya', in U. Schild (ed.), *The East African Experience: essays on English and Swahili literature*, pp. 25–34. Berlin: Dietrich Reimer Verlag.

Sheng-Pao, C. 1970. *The Gold Coast Delegation to Britain in 1934: the political background*. Taipei, Taiwan: National Chengchi University Studies in African Affairs.

Tauber, S. and Weidhaas, P. 1984. 'Ghana', in S. Tauber and P. Weidhaas (eds), *The Book Trade of the World: vol. 4, Africa*, pp. 125–38. New York: K. G. Saur Munchen.

Turner, T. 1985. 'Petroleum, recession and the internationalization of class struggle in Nigeria', *Labour, Capital and Society* 18 (1), 6–42.

Udoeyop, N. J. 1972. 'The Nigerian publisher and his chief', in A. Irele (ed.), *Publishing in Nigeria*. pp. 26–33. Bendel State: Ethiope Publishing Corporation.

Umelo, R. 1983. 'Applying the Formula: a preliminary survey of recurring plots, situations and characters in unsolicited fiction manuscripts.' Paper presented at the Third International Conference on African Literature, 2–6 May. University of Calabar, Nigeria.

Unoh, S. 1993. 'The promotion of good reading habits in Nigeria for leisure and lifelong education: problems and prospects', in S. Bello and A. R. Augi (eds), *Culture and the Book Industry in Nigeria*, pp. 97–116. Lagos: National Council for Arts and Culture.

Vail, L. and White, L. 1991. *Power and the Praise Poem: southern African voices in history*. Charlottesville, VA and London: University Press of Virginia & James Currey.

Vellenga, D. D. 1983. 'Who is a wife? Legal expression of heterosexual conflicts in Ghana', in C. Oppong (ed.), *Female and Male in West Africa*, pp. 144–55. London: Allen & Unwin.

Walsh, G. 1991. *Publishing in Africa: a neglected component of development*. African Studies Center working papers no. 156, Boston, MA: Boston University.

Waterman, C. A. 1990. *Jùjú: a social history and ethnography of an African popular music*. Chicago: University of Chicago Press.

Bibliography

Watts, M. 1994. 'Oil as money: the Devil's excrement and the spectacle of black gold', in S. Corbridge, N. Thrift and R. Martin (eds), *Money, Power and Space*, pp. 406–45. Oxford: Blackwell.

Wilentz, G. 1992. *Binding Cultures: black women writers in Africa and the diaspora*. Bloomington, IN: Indiana University Press.

Yankah, K. 1989. *The Proverb in the Context of Akan Rhetoric: a theory of proverb praxis*. Bern: Peter Lang.

Index

175

Index

Index

Index